THE UNITED STATES, BRITAIN AND
APPEASEMENT, 1936–1939

St Antony's/Macmillan Series

General editor: Archie Brown, Fellow of St Antony's College, Oxford

This new series contains academic books written or edited by members of St Antony's College, Oxford, or by authors with a special association with the College. The titles are selected by an editorial board on which both the College and the publishers are represented.

Titles already published or in the press are listed below, and there are numerous further titles in preparation.

S. B. Burman CHIEFDOM POLITICS AND ALIEN LAW

Wilhelm Deist THE *WEHRMACHT* AND GERMAN REARMAMENT

Ricardo Ffrench-Davis and Ernesto Tironi (*editors*) LATIN AMERICA AND THE NEW INTERNATIONAL ECONOMIC ORDER

Richard Holt SPORT AND SOCIETY IN MODERN FRANCE

Albert Hourani EUROPE AND THE MIDDLE EAST

THE EMERGENCE OF THE MODERN MIDDLE EAST

Paul Kennedy and Anthony Nicholls (*editors*) NATIONALIST AND RACIALIST MOVEMENTS IN BRITAIN AND GERMANY BEFORE 1914

Richard Kindersley (*editor*) IN SEARCH OF EUROCOMMUNISM

Gisela C. Lebzelter POLITICAL ANTI-SEMITISM IN ENGLAND, 1918–1939

C. A. MacDonald THE UNITED STATES, BRITAIN AND APPEASEMENT, 1936–1939

Marilyn Rueschemeyer PROFESSIONAL WORK AND MARRIAGE

David Stafford BRITAIN AND EUROPEAN RESISTANCE, 1940–1945

Rosemary Thorp and Laurence Whitehead (*editors*) INFLATION AND STABILISATION IN LATIN AMERICA

Rudolf L. Tőkés (*editor*) OPPOSITION IN EASTERN EUROPE

Further titles in preparation

THE UNITED STATES, BRITAIN AND APPEASEMENT, 1936–1939

C. A. MacDonald
Joint School of Comparative American Studies
University of Warwick

in association with
St Antony's College, Oxford

© C. A. MacDonald 1981

All rights reserved. No part of this publication may be
reproduced or transmitted, in any form or by any means,
without permission

First published 1981 by
THE MACMILLAN PRESS LTD
London and Basingstoke
Companies and representatives
throughout the world

ISBN 0 333 26169 0

Printed in Hong Kong

To AKS and KLM

Contents

Acknowledgements		viii
Introduction		ix
1	American Appeasement: Origins and Objectives	1
2	American Appeasement and British Policy	16
3	The 'Quarantine' Speech and the Welles Plan	34
4	The *Panay* Crisis	50
5	The American Peace Initiative	63
6	The United States and the Sudeten Crisis	76
7	Munich	92
8	The Failure of Appeasement	106
9	The January Crisis	124
10	The United States and the Guarantee System	140
11	The Approach of War	155
12	The Last Days of Peace	168
	Conclusions	179
	Notes	183
	General Bibliography	205
	Index	215

Acknowledgements

I am indebted to Esmonde Robertson of the London School of Economics who first encouraged me to take up the subject of American appeasement, and to Professor A. E. Campbell of the University of Birmingham who provided constructive criticism whilst supervising the topic as an Oxford D.Phil. thesis. Grants from the Scottish Education Department and the American Council of Learned Societies financed research in Britain and the United States. A research fellowship at New College, Oxford, allowed time for reflection and writing. I am grateful to the following individuals and institutions for access to papers and for permission to quote: the University of Birmingham Library; the Library of Congress; the University of Delaware Library; the ·University of Columbia Library; the Houghton Library, Harvard; the National Archives of the United States; the Public Record Office; the US Navy Yard, Washington, D.C.; the Franklin D. Roosevelt Library; the National Library of Scotland; the Scottish Record Office; and Mr Kenneth John Young who generously allowed access to the Arthur P. Young Papers. Finally, I would like to thank the staff of Rhodes House Library, Oxford, for bearing with me during my periodic raids on their stack in search of bound copies of the *New York Times*.

C. A. MacDonald

University of Warwick
September 1979

Introduction

Previous work on the origins of the Second World War has largely avoided broad consideration of Anglo-American relations in the critical period 1936–9. British historians of European appeasement, such as Taylor and Gilbert,[1] have devoted their efforts to a critique of Anglo-German relations which ignores the role of the United States in British policy. America, when considered at all, is merely dismissed as an isolationist power with no real influence on European affairs.[2] Writers on Far Eastern developments during the period, such as Louis,[3] have naturally devoted greater attention to the American role, but any attempt at a synthesis of the American impact on British policy in both Europe and Asia remains lacking. American historians have failed to redress the balance. The standard work on Roosevelt's foreign policy, Langer and Gleason's *The Challenge to Isolation*,[4] devotes minimal attention to the pre-war period and is mainly concerned with events after 1939. When Anglo-American relations before 1939 are considered, it is generally in works devoted exclusively to the situation in the Far East such as Borg's *The United States and the Far Eastern Crisis*.[5] Offner's book, *American Appeasement*,[6] fails to remedy this situation. Offner discusses American policy towards Nazi Germany between 1933 and 1938, but his book is unsatisfactory, partly because it is marred by the author's strong personal bias against appeasement, and partly because the narrative is not taken beyond Munich, when crucial changes in American policy occurred. Offner does not discuss the shift from appeasement to containment which took place in October 1938, a change which predated Chamberlain's decision to abandon conciliation and which led to friction between Washington and London. By 1939 American policymakers had come to believe that Chamberlain was the agent of selfish City interests, which were not above handing over Europe to Hitler in return for a guaranteed share of its trade. Nor does Offner emphasise the central part played by the German 'moderates' – bankers, industrialists and army officers – in American appeasement before 1938. This group stood not only for an Open Door economic order in Europe, but also for cooperation with other industrial powers against Japan in the Far East. Leading advocates of appeasement, such as Sumner Welles, were well aware that cooperation with the 'moderates' was the key to an Open Door system in Europe and Asia and hence to the American goal of a stable world and an export-led recovery from the Depression. By appeasement Welles hoped to avoid the alternative, an expanding totalitarian system led by German and Japanese 'extremists', which would exclude the United States from world markets and undermine its position in Latin America. American policy was thus based on a world view which Offner ignores.

After the 'moderates' were purged in 1938 and Hitler had embarked upon an obviously expansionist course, American policy moved from appeasement to containment. Langer and Gleason discuss the origins of the change but do not consider its domestic implications. The American role in containment was to supply Britain and France with arms, but they were to be paid for by the liquidation of Allied assets in the United States. Hopkins, for one, believed that such foreign orders would relieve unemployment and help the Democrats win the presidential election in 1940. Moreover, the United States, although a non-belligerent, was to have a substantial voice in any peace settlement in return for its material assistance. This meant that the demand for an Open Door world could again be brought forward, as indeed it was in the Atlantic Charter of 1941. Prior to December 1941, American policy can be viewed as an attempt to secure a stable world, open to American trade, without the actual deployment of military strength. This was the aim of appeasement, as it was of containment after Munich.

This book, therefore, attempts to fill a gap in the historiography of the thirties, first with a detailed study of American policy between 1936 and 1939, and secondly with an examination of the American impact on British foreign relations in the classic era of appeasement. Several important questions are considered in the course of the study. What was the American conception of the German problem and its relationship to the crisis in the Far East? How did Roosevelt's solutions differ from Chamberlain's ideas? Why did the United States abandon appeasement before Britain and how successful were American efforts to persuade Chamberlain to adopt a stiffer line with Hitler? What impression did the Americans form of British policy in Europe and the Far East, and were their suspicions in any way justified? The answers to such questions explain the considerable degree of mistrust which marked the attitude of the Roosevelt administration towards the Chamberlain government.

1 American Appeasement: Origins and Objectives

At the end of 1936 the United States began to use its influence to stimulate appeasement in Europe. The object of American intervention was to secure peace, stability and the expansion of international trade in the interests of world order and domestic recovery. It was hoped in Washington that a final settlement of European problems outstanding since the peace of Versailles would establish the rule of law in international affairs. A just settlement in Europe would be guaranteed by the liberalisation of world trade which would give every power an interest in the new system and eliminate the grievances of 'have-not' nations such as Germany and Italy. Since mutual suspicion prevented the European powers from reaching a final settlement, it was believed that the United States must intervene and lend its moral leadership to the cause of peace. As a disinterested outsider, uninvolved in European power struggles, the United States might perhaps establish a basis for settlement upon which Britain, France, Germany and Italy could agree. These objectives were first collected into a definite peace plan by Sumner Welles in November 1937, but they had been under consideration in administration circles since the summer of 1936.

In 1936 a settlement seemed a matter of urgency. It was felt that Europe was drifting towards war. Hitler abandoned the negotiated solution of Versailles in March when German troops reoccupied the Rhineland. The outbreak of the Spanish Civil War in July, which was followed by German, Italian and Russian intervention, saw the first outbreak of large-scale fighting in Europe since 1918. The resurgence of Germany and Italy, and the intensification of great power rivalries, led to American fears that the outcome would be a catastrophe like that of 1914. John Cudahy, the American ambassador in Warsaw, wrote to Roosevelt in March 1936 predicting that 'only a miracle can preclude a war in Europe . . . the catastrophe may be averted but if the Hitler Government is not overthrown a war in Europe is as certain as the rising sun'.[1] In November 1936 William E. Dodd, the ambassador in Berlin, noted in his diary 'How far can this go without actual conflict. Am I to be caught here in another European war?'[2] In December 1936 Sumner Welles, the Assistant Secretary of State, was discussing the 'possibility of war starting in Europe' and its likely effect on American interests.[3] The President himself was 'deeply concerned' about the situation and 'shuddered' at the thought of another European war.[4]

The initial reaction to threatening events abroad was to emphasise American isolation from Europe. In February 1936 Congress extended for a further year the Neutrality Act of 1935 which imposed a mandatory ban on the export of arms to belligerents, and empowered the President to prohibit travel by American citizens on belligerent vessels. Based on the findings of the Nye Committee, which concluded that arms sales to the Allies had involved America in the First World War, the Neutrality Act was intended to prevent a similar situation arising in any future European struggle.[5] Although the act enjoyed widespread public support, Roosevelt did not himself believe that the United States could remain unaffected in the event of war. In a speech at Chautauqua on 14 August 1936 the President emphasised that while he wished to isolate America 'completely from war . . . so long as war exists on earth there will be some danger even to the nation that most ardently desires peace, danger that it also may be drawn into war'.[6] Roosevelt hoped to avert this danger by using American influence to prevent war. Two weeks after the Chautauqua speech, Arthur Krock of the *New York Times* revealed that the President had a plan to alleviate international tension and encourage disarmament and free trade. According to Krock, Roosevelt, if re-elected in November, planned to summon a conference of world leaders which would consider peace and disarmament. It would also discuss the elimination of trade barriers and the general lowering of tariff walls. The President hoped to mobilise world opinion behind such ambitious goals. He believed that once re-elected he would be in a powerful position to 'serve the cause of peace'. Unlike Woodrow Wilson at Versailles he would be'freshly certified' by the electorate which would minimise potential opposition at home and increase his stature as a world leader. Moreover Roosevelt's conference would be a discussion among equals, whereas at Versailles the victors had imposed their terms on the vanquished. Krock emphasised that the President had not made a definite decision to launch his scheme. 'Much will depend . . . on the responses which will come to the diplomatic "feelers" that will precede the actual despatch of notes of invitation.'[7]

The State Department received Krock's report with 'utter surprise' and apparently Roosevelt had not discussed his plans with the Secretary of State, Cordell Hull.[8] There had, however, already been much consideration of European problems by American diplomats. It was recognised that German claims for 'justice' were the main danger to European peace. The Americans were particularly worried about the possibility of war resulting from distortion of the German economy. Hitler had introduced exchange control and autarky to stimulate recovery and hasten rearmament. In the United States these expedients were viewed with alarm and considered particularly dangerous and short-sighted. The State Department held that trade barriers and armaments led to war 'or war conditions of rising prices and stimulus of industrial effort in machinery that is essentially unproductive'.[9] Rearmament diverted national resources from normal trade, curtailing exports and thus leading to a falling level of foreign exchange with which to purchase imports. This situation necessitated the introduction of autarky. Autarky, however, could itself be only a temporary expedient which would fail in the long run, leaving the country concerned with the choice of massive unemployment or war to capture new sources of raw materials. The working out of this process in Germany was believed to be behind Nazi radicalism in foreign affairs.

Concern with economic conditions in Germany was evident as early as April 1935, when Robert Bingham, the American ambassador in London, pointed out the dangers inherent in the German situation. The economic equilibrium attained under Hitler was

> purely temporary. . . . About one third of the German people normally depend upon world trade for their livelihood and the degree of the standard of living of another third is determined by world trade. Naziism will be forced to seek economic as well as political gains. If they cannot be obtained in the normal way of trade, other expansionist methods will doubtless be tried.[10]

Dodd in Berlin also feared that economic pressure might push Hitler into war. On 10 October 1936 he remarked in his diary that he was unable to see 'how universal war activities with enormous debts and certain unemployment a year or two hence can have any other result than war'.[11] Dodd saw a direct connection between economic difficulties and radicalism in foreign policy. On 28 November 1936 Dodd reported that Ribbentrop had been responsible for the recent conclusion of the German–Japanese Anti-Comintern Pact and that he was now urging Hitler to adopt a more adventurous foreign policy. This coincided with

> the economic difficulties inherent in the internal situation to which . . . Hitler must and does give primary attention . . . our feeling is that the difficulties of the internal situation are now reaching a point where it is increasingly demanding Hitler's attention and thereby exacting a greater influence in foreign policy in the direction of a more adventurous course.[12]

Other observers shared Dodd's apprehension. Cudahy, the American ambassador in Warsaw, visited Berlin in autumn 1936 and reported to Roosevelt on 26 December that Germany was 'in a bad way economically'. The standard of living was falling due to

> the failure to find markets for German exports and the limitation of imports to those materials requisite for war preparation. As suffering becomes more acute there will be evidence of social unrest unless they [*sic*] are offered some compensation. The future looks dismal unless something can be done to relieve the economic condition of Germany in return for its assurance to stop or diminish its great rearmament program.[13]

Roosevelt agreed that the situation was serious. On 15 January 1937 he replied to Cudahy noting that 'the fundamental economic evils of the situation grow worse and that means greater difficulty each time a new crisis arises'. The President feared that economic strains would make it difficult for future crises to be 'tided over' as they had been in the past.[14] The State Department shared this view and felt that Europe stood 'at the crossroads' between peace and war. On 16 February 1937 a memorandum was drawn up defining the essence of the European problem. 'Can a compromise be found or a price paid which will satisfy the economic necessities of the German people without war or without making Germany paramount on the continent'?[15]

A compromise of this nature seemed to depend on the outcome of a struggle within Germany itself about the future course of foreign and domestic policy. In 1936 Hitler had yet to embark upon a policy of war-like expansion and two groups could be identified within the Reich competing for influence with the Führer. The first was a group of party 'extremists' or 'war men' such as Goebbels, Hess, Ribbentrop and Rosenberg. They stood for an uncompromising policy both at home and abroad: harsh measures against dissenters within Germany and the use of force to achieve foreign policy aims while France was disunited and British rearmament incomplete. In broad terms the 'extremists' stood for a policy of autarky and external adventure. German economic problems would be solved by seizing *Lebensraum* rather than by reintegration into the world economy.[16] The 'extremists' were opposed by a coalition of 'moderates' consisting of three main elements: the industrialists, the army general staff and the higher civil servants. The civil servants, particularly in the Foreign Office, were known to object to the policies of Goebbels and Ribbentrop. Men such as Neurath, Dieckhoff and Bülow disliked measures against the Churches and the Jews, and the German intervention in the Spanish Civil War. The industrialists were unhappy about the stringent economic controls imposed under autarky. Dodd noted in February 1936 that Fritz Thyssen, 'the greatest manufacturer of arms after the Krupps . . . was troubled about the present situation. . . . He was fearful that the radical wing of the Nazi Party was becoming almost Communist.' Generals such as von Fritsch were known to object to the anti-Christian policies of Rosenberg and Goebbels and to military intervention in Spain, which threatened to involve Germany in a European war for which it was unprepared.[17]

The spokesman of the 'moderate' group was Schacht, Reichsminister of Economics and President of the Reichsbank. On 27 August 1936 Dodd reported that Schacht was seeking a way out of German economic difficulties other than war. The Reichsminister had visited Paris to sound out the possibility of a European settlement based upon the return of German colonies lost in 1919. The French had been 'surprisingly receptive to the idea of Germany acquiring rather extensive colonial areas in the Cameroons section of Africa. . . . Large French capitalists . . . are at present well disposed towards Germany in view of a Communist menace to their property at home.'[18] It was rumoured that

Schacht's search for a settlement was conditioned by 'the desperate desire of German manufacturers for some relief from the cramped position in which they find themselves due to the narrow lines in which German trade has become crystallised'.[19] Schacht's search for peace was supported by the Foreign Office and the army which, like the industrialists, desired a European settlement and restoration of a normal economic system.[20]

American policymakers had to consider what attitude the United States should adopt towards this power struggle in Germany. As in Britain a division emerged between 'appeasers' and 'anti-appeasers'. The 'anti-appeasers' tended to be those who had experienced the Nazi regime at first hand through service in Germany. George Messersmith, the leading 'anti-appeaser' at the State Department, was a former Consul-General in Berlin and ambassador to Austria. He had been a bitter anti-Nazi from the first, warning as early as 1933 that Hitler wanted war and that many of his associates were 'psychopathic cases'.[21] The 'moderates', although vocal, did not have 'a controlling voice' in the German government. Messersmith suspected that the regime was displaying 'a restrained attitude' in 1936 only in the hope that Britain, France and the United States would be thus persuaded to help it out of its economic difficulties. Once the German economy had been strengthened, however, the true nature of the Nazi movement would become evident and Hitler would unleash his war machine. Messersmith argued, therefore, that negotiations with Schacht would be 'dangerous and destructive of the best interests of the United States'. Instead of promoting appeasement, America should withhold economic aid from Hitler and encourage Britain and France to form a united front against aggression. The Nazi regime, deterred from military expansion and weakened by a deteriorating economy, would eventually be overthrown by the army which would install a 'moderate' government with which the United States could 'do business'.[22] Dodd, in Berlin, shared Messersmith's personal aversion towards the 'gangsters' who led the Nazi party and avoided personal contact with them as much as possible. While he cultivated the friendship of 'moderates' such as Schacht, he doubted whether they had much influence on a criminal regime dedicated to war. Dodd believed that the influence of Ribbentrop and Rosenberg was uppermost with Hitler and based this deduction on the Anti-Comintern Pact and the anti-Church campaign.[23] On 5 August 1936 Roosevelt asked Dodd for his opinion as to what would happen if Hitler were personally and secretly asked by me to outline the limit of German foreign policy objectives during . . . a ten year period and to state whether or not he would have any sympathy with a general limitation of armaments proposal.[24]

Dodd was unable to ascertain Hitler's views but he was able to approach Schacht. On 18 August he reported that Schacht wanted the United States to call a conference which would discuss German colonial claims.[25] This response may have tempted Roosevelt to toy with the scheme outlined in the *New York Times* by Arthur Krock, but it did not convince Dodd. He feared that the Nazi regime aimed at total domination of Europe and would reject any proposed settlement which did not guarantee such a result. On 19 October 1936 Dodd warned Roosevelt that 'events in Europe since last December all point the same way: Hitler and Mussolini intend to dominate all Europe. If that be agreed to beforehand a peace conference is quite possible, but what sort of peace?'[26] Dodd, like Messersmith, believed that the United States should encourage resistance of Nazi expansion, perhaps by amending the Neutrality Act to allow the President to discriminate against the aggressor in the event of European war. This would act as a deterrent by placing American economic strength squarely behind Britain and France.[27]

Others, however, were more optimistic than Messersmith and Dodd about the prospects of a successful American peace initiative. Bullitt, the American ambassador in Paris, believed that Hitler was behind Schacht's peace moves which should be supported by the United States. On 8 November 1936 he reported that the French were delighted with Roosevelt's election victory and hoped that the President would soon take an initiative in Europe. Bullitt cautioned Roosevelt against summoning a conference without adequate preparation, but believed that the United States should promote Franco-German détente. Schacht's visit to Paris had encouraged Bullitt to 'believe that it may be possible to get together the French and the Germans on the basis of an economic agreement'. This would be accompanied by an arms limitation treaty. Bullitt recommended that 'if we can assist diplomatically in laying the basis for a reconciliation between France and Germany I think we should help. If we get anywhere . . . and see a fair chance of success you could then come forward with some tremendous public announce-

ment.' It was suggested that the ground might be prepared for 'some
great gesture' by sending an ambassador to Berlin who could
establish a 'confidential relationship' with the German 'bosses'
similar to that enjoyed by Bullitt with the French.[28] Bullitt's
support for appeasement was prompted by his fear of world
communism. A leading advocate of American recognition of the
Soviet Union in 1933, he had been transformed by his experiences
as ambassador in Moscow into a vocal anti-Bolshevik. According to
Bullitt only the Russians had a vested interest in another war which
would end with a 'general revolution' and the final victory of 'Stalin
and Company'. The only way to preserve European civilisation and
to contain communism was to avert a clash between France and
Germany. For this reason Bullitt opposed collective security which
he felt could only lead to war and made it clear to the French
government that the United States would not support a united front
against Hitler.[29]

   Voices urging American intervention in the cause of peace were
also heard from Eastern Europe. The Poles had a strong interest in
averting another European war which might tempt either Russia or
Germany to make good their outstanding claims to Polish territory
lost after 1918. On 29 December 1936 Lipski informed the
American ambassador in Warsaw that 'the only solution' to
European problems was 'leadership for peace on the part of your
President'.[30] Cudahy was not unsympathetic to an American
initiative but, like Bullitt, warned Roosevelt to make no move
before carefully sounding out the ground. He informed the
President that unless he acted 'under certain conditions
precedent . . . a Wilsonian pronouncement in favor of
peace . . . would be forgotten in two weeks time'. If an American
initiative were to succeed it must be accompanied by 'a definite
program for the improvement of conditions in Germany'.[31]

   Despite the arguments of the 'anti-appeasers', Roosevelt was
unwilling to abandon his scheme for a conference. Faced with
Dodd's pessimism about the prospects of appeasing Germany, the
President decided to use a second source to check on conditions
within the Reich. On 28 August 1936 he interviewed Joseph E.
Davies at the White House and asked him to go to Moscow as
American ambassador on the understanding that Davies would
ultimately replace Dodd at Berlin. Davies noted that Roosevelt
wanted him to

go to Germany as ambassador to see whether the situation could not be composed by providing living room for the German people and stop Hitler from making war. He thought I could find out whether Hitler wanted war or whether he really wanted peace. He sympathised with Germany's need for access to raw materials.

Davies felt that Roosevelt wanted him to draw up 'a general survey of the situation as between Germany in relation to France and England and the peace of Europe'.[32] It was clear that Davies' investigation of German conditions was to begin while he was en route to Moscow. In his talk with Davies, Roosevelt suggested no method of meeting the German demand for equal access to raw materials. He seems to have hoped, however, that Germany would be satisfied with an international agreement on the lines of the Congo basin scheme, under which it could join a consortium of European powers to exploit colonial resources. American financial support would be forthcoming for such a scheme. On 4 January 1937, the President spoke about a vague plan along such lines to Henry Morgenthau, the Secretary of the Treasury. He envisaged the establishment of an international cartel which would supply the raw materials desired by Germany. The colonial commodities thus secured would be used to employ workers currently engaged in arms production. This would allow arms limitation without unemployment.[33] It is clear from this conversation and from Roosevelt's expressed sympathy with Germany's needs for access to raw materials that he believed an appeal to Schacht and the 'moderates' would prove successful and that they would influence Hitler in favour of a settlement.

At this stage the State Department was also giving consideration to German claims. On 18 January 1937 Cordell Hull completed a paper setting out the possible American contribution to a European settlement. It took into account Schacht's demands for economic justice and was obviously intended to appeal to the 'moderate' group in Germany. Hull envisaged a general settlement of European problems which would include arms limitation, political guarantees and colonial readjustments. The United States would take no part in the political aspects of détente but would be prepared to make a large contribution in the economic field. The Export–Import Bank could extend commercial credits to Berlin and grant loans to rebuild the economy. The United States would also be prepared to conclude a trade treaty with the Reich and discuss the problem of equal access to raw materials. In return, Germany would be asked to abandon autarky and armaments. Hull went on to define the object of a general settlement. It was intended to promote peace and lay 'the foundation for the expansion of international trade and orderly development within nations'.[34]

American interest in 'the expansion of international trade' conditioned American interest in appeasement. Hull had always believed that the restoration of prosperity and full employment within the United States depended upon trade expansion. As early as 1935 a State Department memorandum argued that 'full employment is possible only when trade of all kinds is being carried on to the greatest extent compatible with material interest'.[35] As long as Hitler maintained autarky, however, world trade, deprived of the German internal market, would not revive. In the interests of escaping its own depression therefore, the United States had a vested interest in encouraging the German 'moderates' who wished to replace autarky with a more traditional economic system. In an article in *Foreign Affairs* published in January 1937, Schacht appealed to this American self-interest and argued that the United States should encourage appeasement to stimulate recovery. Schacht argued that European prosperity was impossible while Germany pursued a policy of self-sufficiency.

> European prosperity cannot be conceived of without German prosperity. And however much America may wish to stand aloof there is not the slightest doubt that the ebb and flow of European prosperity is important to her . . . if Germany could expand economically by acquiring her own sources of raw materials this could only contribute to the stimulation of world trade in general. It would help to increase consumption, promote prosperity and raise the standard of life not only of the German people but of the entire industrial world.

Germany, however, would not abandon autarky until other powers met its demands for economic justice.[36] Both Roosevelt and Hull were obviously aware of this argument about the value of a flourishing German economy to American recovery.

There were several problems connected with the American scheme for a European settlement. Some of these problems received consideration in Washington but others were ignored or pushed to one side. Roosevelt envisaged summoning a conference which would discuss all European problems, political as well as economic, yet the United States itself was not prepared to assume any responsibility for the political aspects of appeasement. This meant, for example, that America would not join a new Locarno or give any undertaking to support Britain and France if Hitler failed to live up to his word. Yet the Americans hoped to dictate the timing of a settlement to the powers most directly involved and which had most to lose if appeasement failed.[37] This was one of the major weaknesses in American attempts to give a lead to Europe. Washington perhaps placed too much emphasis on moral leadership and not enough on the hard political bargaining upon which a successful settlement depended. There were, therefore, grave problems about trying to lead the European powers while emphasising political isolation, but difficulties also existed about American participation in the economic aspects of appeasement. American plans assumed that public opinion would make a distinction between political and economic involvement in Europe. This was a large assumption which probably underestimated the strength of isolationist opinion. The defeat of the attempt to join the World Court had shown how easy it was to stir up the public with accusations of 'entanglement'. It may further be doubted whether American investors would have been prepared to lend freely to Germany following their experiences with the Dawes and Young loans. Curiously enough Mussolini appears to have been the only person to raise this basic question concerning American economic aid to Europe. In May 1937, during a conversation with an American journalist in Rome, the Duce remarked that he saw 'grave difficulties both political and psychological' about American aid 'and in this connection he mentioned specifically the Johnson Act and the aversion in America to loans to Europe'.[38] Lastly, even had Hitler supported Schacht's terms, the American plans did not meet the German demand for colonies. In his talks with Dodd and his article in *Foreign Affairs* Schacht had never implied that Germany would be satisfied with an international cartel or some other scheme guaranteeing equal access to raw materials rather than restitution to Germany in full sovereignty of colonies lost in 1919. Either Washington assumed that this was an extreme negotiating position on which compromise was possible or it was hoped that, should the Germans prove obdurate, Britain and France would solve the problem by returning some of the German possessions lost at Versailles.

Davies went to Europe at the beginning of January to pursue enquiries on behalf of the President. On 20 January he met Schacht unofficially in Berlin and sent Roosevelt an optimistic report of his meeting with the Reichsminister. Schacht stated that he had been asked by Hitler to seek a European settlement based on arms limitation and colonial restitution. Roosevelt could assist his efforts by summoning a peace conference in Washington. When Davies enquired about the disturbing aspects of German policy, such as militarism and racial persecution, Schacht explained that these were merely 'the manifestations of the desperation and terrible plight of a people bottled up and being economically starved in a world of plenty'. Once Germany enjoyed justice and prosperity they would simply disappear.[39] Dodd was sceptical about Schacht's claims when he learned about Davies' activities. He noted in his diary on 27 January 1937 'I have had so many similar assurances from officials in the Foreign Office that I am a bit sceptical of the sincerity of these professions'.[40] The ambassador's doubts, however, were ignored in Washington, where an American intervention in the cause of peace remained under consideration. At the end of January 1937 Roosevelt decided to take soundings in London to ascertain the British attitude towards an American initiative. It was realised that without British cooperation German claims could not be met and a lasting settlement would be impossible. British participation was the necessary precondition for any scheme to grant Germany access to raw materials. Britain would also be a leading participant in the political aspects of a settlement such as a new security pact to replace Locarno. Hull was aware of these facts and noted on 18 January 1937 that 'the logic of events' seemed 'to point to the possibility that Britain would assume the principal initiative in bringing about European negotiations'.[41]

The United States had a further reason for wishing to secure British commitment to appeasement which stemmed from its desire to stimulate world trade. Hull detested the system of imperial preference set up by Britain during the Depression with the introduction of the Ottawa agreements. During their first year in operation American exports to the Empire fell by $10.5 million. Hull hoped to win British support for his trade agreements programme and break open the Ottawa system by means of an Anglo-American trade treaty. He believed that such an agreement might 'stampede' the world towards economic liberalism by displaying the advantages of an unrestricted trading system.[42] The abolition of restrictions such as tariff walls played a major role in American appeasement schemes. The State Department argued that it would be pointless asking Germany to abandon its closed economic system unless other countries did likewise. British support for appeasement would imply support for a freer world economic system since Britain would have to grant Germany access to raw materials and generous trade concessions if Schacht's terms were to be met. It could hardly, therefore, refuse to make similar concessions to American trade or reject an Anglo-American trade treaty. An Anglo-American trade agreement would be a fundamental element of economic appeasement. In terms of American self-interest, therefore, Britain and Germany were parts of the same problem, the problem of closed economic systems which excluded American trade. The United States believed that political stability was dependent on prosperity and that prosperity meant persuading Britain and Germany, the largest European trading powers with the greatest internal markets, to abandon trade restrictions. The increase in trade which would follow would banish the depression not only in Europe, but also in the United States which would gain access to flourishing new markets.

At the end of 1936 the British attitude towards appeasement was unclear. The French accused Britain of blocking their attempts to negotiate with Schacht. Blum informed Bullitt on 1 November 1936 that 'the one concrete proposal which had been made by the Germans had been during Schacht's visit' [to Paris]. Schacht had demanded the return of German colonies but this request had run against an 'absolutely adamantine refusal on the part of the British'.[43] Schacht made similar complaints about British obstruction to American diplomats in Berlin. He informed the commercial attaché on 15 January 1937 that Hitler sincerely desired peace and disarmament but that German offers were being ignored in London. Schacht hinted that unless other powers were prepared to negotiate, German claims might be pursued by other means. The United States should indicate to the British that Hitler was 'interested in a final and happy liquidation of the problems facing Germany'.[44] Roosevelt was determined to ascertain for himself the British attitude towards appeasement. He hoped to secure reliable information by sending a special observer to London. In February 1937 the President interviewed Norman Davis, the American delegate to an international sugar conference due to be held in London in April. He asked Davis to investigate the British attitude towards arms limitation and a comprehensive settlement of European problems. He also talked about the possibility of the League of Nations shedding its political functions and turning into an economic council in which case 'the United States ought to be able to go along'.[45] Significantly this possibility was first mentioned by Schacht. On 16 February 1937 the State Department drew up a memorandum for Davis on the European situation which also revealed the influence of Schacht's arguments on American policymakers. It remarked that war might be averted by granting Germany access to raw materials and attributed support for militarism and Nazi radicalism to the economic insecurity of the German people. For this reason 'German claims to colonies are not dismissed as wholly unreasonable and thought is being given to the possibility of underwriting German recovery, the United States to have a share'. The object of American intervention in European affairs

> Would be to precipitate a movement for a general political and economic settlement which would obviate the necessity for Germany to strike out to obtain sources of raw materials in markets deemed by the German leaders necessary to maintain the living standard of the German people.

As a preliminary, 'agreement, at least along broad lines, with the United Kingdom, would be essential'. The British who were 'most directly concerned' with the German problem should be 'persuaded to become sponsors of an initiative'. It was hoped that Britain and the United States, as satisfied powers with an equal interest in peace and disarmament, would be able to cooperate in meeting German claims.[46]

It is evident therefore, that Roosevelt and the State Department were anxious to encourage the German 'moderates' and accepted Schacht's claims as the basis for a settlement. It was feared that to ignore Schacht, as Messersmith recommended, would merely consolidate the German masses behind the 'extremists' and force Germany into a campaign of conquest to seize vital sources of raw materials. It appears likely that Norman Davis was sent to London to discover if British concessions were liable to match Schacht's demands. Both Norman Davis and Joseph E. Davies, therefore, were engaged in sounding out the possible reaction to an American initiative, a precaution which Krock had predicted in August 1936 would be taken before Roosevelt launched a peace plan. Having been reelected with a massive majority in November 1936, the President was clearly determined to find some method of solving European problems more permanently than Wilson had done at Versailles. By February 1937 what Cudahy had termed 'conditions precedent' for American action had been defined. American action depended upon prior agreement with Britain and the existence of a 'moderate' group in Germany influential enough to persuade Hitler to accept a negotiated solution of German grievances.

2 American Appeasement and British Policy

By the beginning of 1937 Roosevelt had defined the 'conditions precedent' for an American initiative in European affairs. In the course of the spring and summer, however, it proved difficult to fulfil these conditions. Britain was the main obstacle to American plans. It was one thing for the State Department to assume that Britain and the United States, as 'satisfied' powers with a vested interest in world stability, had an equal interest in appeasing Germany. It proved quite another matter, however, for the two countries to agree on a mutually acceptable method of solving the German problem. Britain neither rejected appeasement nor wished to exclude the United States from any part in a European settlement. Chamberlain, like Roosevelt, was anxious to cultivate Schacht and the 'moderates'. It was recognised in London, as in Washington, that domestic recovery could not take place without the revival of trade and that the revival of trade in turn depended upon the reintegration of Germany into the world economy. The government had recognised the importance of Germany to British and imperial prosperity as early as 1933, when a bilateral Anglo-German payments agreement was concluded committing Germany to use a proportion of the sterling earned by its exports to the United Kingdom to purchase British and colonial goods.[1] Britain was prepared to encourage participation by the United States in the economic aspects of appeasement since American funds could play a vital role in rebuilding German finances. Moreover any indication of American interest in Europe might of itself restrain the German 'extremists' and make Hitler more amenable to compromise. Despite this desire to involve the United States, however, obstacles rapidly emerged to cooperation on American terms.

In early 1937 Britain was itself considering the possibility of a European settlement on the basis of Schacht's demands. In February 1937 Neville Chamberlain, Chancellor of the Exchequer in Baldwin's Cabinet and heir apparent to the Prime Minister, arranged a meeting between Schacht and Sir Frederick Leith-Ross, Chief Economic Adviser to the government, at which the colonial question was raised. According to Schacht, if Britain was prepared to discuss colonial concessions. Hitler would be prepared to consider arms limitation and the termination of autarky. British credits would be necessary to ease the transition to a normal economic system. Chamberlain was anxious to follow up this opening and concede in principle Germany's right to acquire colonies. On 2 April 1937 he drew up a memorandum for the Cabinet committee on foreign policy which argued that there was a group in Germany which wished 'to restore international good relations and thereby alleviate the economic difficulties' facing the Reich. Hitler apparently supported their approach and Britain should not be responsible for the breakdown in negotiations which would follow rejection of any form of colonial concession. Chamberlain, on the one hand, believed that British rearmament was exercising a moderating influence on Germany and making Hitler readier to listen to those who advocated a peaceful settlement. On the other hand, he clearly feared that Germany might be driven to a war of desperation if nothing was done to avert an economic collapse or meet Hitler's claims for 'justice'. At a meeting of the Cabinet committee on foreign policy on 6 April 1937, Chamberlain won a decision in favour of considering the German demand for colonies. France was to be asked to consider handing over Togoland and French Cameroon. Britain would consider ceding its own West African mandates and some additional guarantee of access to raw materials was not excluded.[2] This was the origin of the plan finally presented to Hitler in February 1938 which envisaged the merging of British, French, Belgian and Portuguese possessions in 'the middle zone of Africa' into a new Congo Basin Scheme in which Germany could participate, a settlement which the United States was asked to underwrite financially.[3] In its final form it was not dissimilar to the solution to German claims sketched out by Roosevelt to Morgenthau in January 1937. At this stage, however, the terms were by no means settled. Schacht was merely to be informed that Britain accepted colonial concessions in principle and was to be kept talking in order to draw him out as to the full extent of German claims. Moreover Britain wanted something definite in return for a settlement of German colonial claims – guarantees of European security. This meant that a colonial offer would not be made to Hitler until Germany had agreed to join a new Locarno and given firm undertakings of good behaviour in Central Europe. As Chamberlain emphasised on 10 May 1937: 'It would be . . . wiser not to attempt at the present stage to be too definite [about colonies]. We ought to find out exactly how far Germany was prepared to meet our political desiderata'.[4] One of his first acts as Prime Minister was to invite Neurath, the German Foreign Minister, to London, for talks on outstanding political issues.[5] For Britain, therefore, political discussions were to precede any consideration of economic appeasement or arms limitation. Any other course would throw away valuable bargaining counters and risk encouraging a dangerous German belief in British weakness. It was this emphasis on a piecemeal approach which was to conflict with Roosevelt's desire for an early general settlement.

At this stage Britain was considering not only appeasement but also the American role in British policy. The Foreign Secretary, Anthony Eden, was anxious to encourage the United States to play a more active part in European affairs, not least because this might deter the 'wild men' in Hitler's entourage. As he informed Bingham, the American ambassador, if peace were to be preserved, knowledge in Berlin of Roosevelt's sympathy with Britain and France was 'all important'.[6] This could be best expressed in a concrete form by an amendment to the Neutrality Act discriminating against aggressors in the event of war, which would make it clear that American economic resources were behind the democracies. In default of action by Congress along such lines, however, Eden was prepared to welcome any other tangible evidence of Anglo-American solidarity. He believed that Britain should cooperate with the United States if Roosevelt launched his rumoured peace initiative. At best Hitler would be forced to cooperate in the knowledge that if he refused American public opinion would react against Germany. At worst, if Roosevelt's plans were rejected by Berlin, the American public might be prepared to support a larger American role in collective security. As Eden remarked in November 1936, a conference might

> not succeed, but if the attempt were made and failure the fault of the dictator powers, the process of education on world opinion (and particularly U.S. opinion) would be salutary. In any event it would clearly be a great error for us to discourage the President in his idea.[7]

This did not mean, however, unqualified approval of Roosevelt's approach to European problems. Rearmament played a major role in British policy since it discouraged German 'extremists' from believing that their aims could be easily attained by force. As Eden later noted 'I was convinced that in dealing with nations who thought so much in terms of armies, we must be prepared to make our contribution on land, while building large numbers of long range bombers to give us maximum striking power in the air'.[8] This meant the commitment of a British field force of five divisions to France and the construction of an air deterrent, including nearly 1000 bombers, which would guarantee parity with Germany, as set out in the Defence White Paper of 1936.[9] An American peace initiative which emphasised disarmament might encourage Hitler to believe that the democracies were hopelessly weak and easily blackmailed. British support for such a scheme would call into question Britain's determination to fulfil the White Paper commitments. Eden, therefore, was anxious to emphasise in conversations with Bingham that a lasting settlement would be impossible until British rearmament convinced Hitler that aggression would be resisted. In March 1937, Bingham noted Eden's fear that rearmament had 'not yet advanced far enough for Britain to risk participation in a disarmament conference because he felt the dictators would look upon it as indicating weakness . . . and inability to carry through [the British] program'. The Foreign Secretary believed that an American initiative should be launched only at an appropriate time and 'in consultation' with Britain.[10] While Eden would have supported an American sponsored conference had Roosevelt chosen to call one, he clearly had reservations about arms limitation which prompted him to advise indefinite delay pending completion of British rearmament.

If Eden was anxious to cultivate the United States, others in London placed less emphasis on Anglo-American cooperation. The British political elite tended to write off the United States as 'incurably isolationist'.[11] There was a strain of scepticism about American policy which was evident not only amongst cabinet ministers but also amongst high civil servants such as Warren Fisher. In such circles it was argued on the basis of bitter experience that Britain could expect little real assistance from across the Atlantic. The history of the post-war period showed the influence of an isolationist public opinion on American policy and the difficulty of securing any real commitment from Washington. As Hoare later noted, 'Rightly or wrongly, we were deeply suspicious, not indeed of American good intentions, but of American readiness to follow up inspiring words with any practical action.'[12] At its worst American policy threatened to drag Britain into dangerous situations without adequate guarantees of support. This seemed particularly true in the Far East after 1931 where first during the Manchurian crisis and later during the naval talks of 1934, the Americans seemed determined to push Britain into a confrontation with Japan which the government was anxious to avoid. Baldwin complained during the Manchurian crisis, 'You will get nothing out of the Americans but words. Big words, but only words', and later confessed that he had 'got to loathe the Americans so much' he hated meeting them.[13] Simon, the Foreign Secretary in 1932, noted 'We have to remember that though America expresses great surprise if we do not act with them . . . if we do they will leave us with the brunt of work and the blame.' Washington always left London to 'do the difficult work vis-à-vis Japan'.[14] Even Lindsay, the pro-American ambassador in Washington, remarked:

> the Americans are dreadful people to deal with – they cannot make firm promises, but they jolly you along with fair prospects and then when you are committed they let you down. Taking the short view it is hard to remember a bargain with them that has been really satisfactory to us in itself.

He could only advise perseverance coupled with caution in negotiations with Washington.[15] The difficulty of securing a form of Anglo-American cooperation which would adequately protect British interests in the Far East led one group, headed by Neville Chamberlain and Warren Fisher, to argue in favour of a non-aggression pact with Japan during the naval talks of 1934. Chamberlain believed that Britain should not allow itself to be 'browbeaten' by the United States into antagonising Japan. America always seemed to demand sacrifices from London while offering nothing in return. 'She will never repay us for sacrificing our interests in order to conciliate her and if we maintain at once a bold and frank attitude toward her I am not afraid of the result.' A non-aggression pact with Tokyo would protect British interests and free London to concentrate on the German problem in Europe.[16] This abrasive approach proved too much for Baldwin and Simon who hesitated to take a step which might alienate the United States, but an undercurrent of dissatisfaction remained with American policy in the Far East. Washington continued to veto any Anglo-Japanese rapprochement, while refusing to guarantee the safety of British possessions.[17] Asia was not the only area of frustration. Many in London blamed the United States for worsening the European situation, first by torpedoing the World Economic Conference of 1933 and subsequently by passing the Neutrality Act. As Hoare observed, these actions 'not only confirmed the doubts of many Europeans who disbelieved in any effective American help, but inevitably, by exposing the differences in the democratic front, strengthened the growing power of the dictators'.[18] Chamberlain felt that as long as the Neutrality Act existed, the United States could make little contribution to the stabilisation of Europe.[19]

Political relations were not the only cause of friction. American economic policy often aroused suspicion and resentment in London, particularly in circles closely identified with imperial preference, where Hull's insistence on lower tariffs was regarded as a device for American economic domination.[20] Chamberlain, who had favoured protection throughout his career, was unwilling to sacrifice the Empire to American friendship. While an Anglo-American trade treaty might be concluded, it must not be at the expense of the Ottawa system which he believed was a major force binding the Empire together.[21] Sir Frederick Leith-Ross, Chief Economic Adviser to the government, while not unsympathetic to closer economic relations with the United States, feared American domination if Britain were forced to cooperate on American terms.[22] Runciman, President of the Board of Trade, was pledged to maintain imperial preference 'as long as I am where I am', and his successor, Stanley, was no more prepared to undertake a fundamental revision of the Ottawa system.[23] Outside the government, protection enjoyed the wholehearted support of Tory right-wingers such as Amery and powerful economic groups like the Federation of British Industries and the National Association of Manufacturers.[24] As Cadogan argued in September 1937, it was difficult to persuade such interests that 'it would be wise to adopt . . . some other system'.[25] In economic, as in political relations, the major criticism of the United States was that it demanded too much while offering too little. Washington seemed determined to increase its foreign trade by attacking imperial preference without making sufficient reciprocal concessions which would assist British exports by reducing the high American tariff wall. As Ashton-Gwatkin of the Foreign Office noted:

> American commercial, financial and shipping policy has, since the war, been one of the major causes – possibly the principal cause – of economic strain . . . if the United States would contemplate a change of commercial policy comparable to our own repeal of the corn laws, then 'the removal of trade barriers' might really mean something; as it is it means very little, and her most liberal tariffs do not even meet our most severe protection.[26]

When he visited Washington in January 1937, Runciman pointed out these facts to Roosevelt and Hull emphasising that while the United States maintained high tariffs, it must accept the existence of imperial preference.[27] Hull's criticisms of British trade policy were dismissed out of hand. As Troutbeck, of the American department, remarked in March 1937, Hull seemed 'to think that by a combination of preaching and badgering he can force us to give way to any pretensions he may put forward . . . Negotiation with a fanatic is no easy thing . . . [and] the most urgent task before us is to bring Mr Hull out of the clouds . . . One cannot feel confident.'[28] It was this legacy of suspicion and frustration in both political and economic relations which was to hinder Eden's attempts at rapprochement with the United States.

When Chamberlain replaced Baldwin as Prime Minister in May 1937, therefore, he was more doubtful than Eden about the prospects of close collaboration with the United States. While he recognised the theoretical benefits of Anglo-American cooperation, he realised the difficulties of translating such a policy into practice. His experiences during the World Economic Conference and the later naval talks had left him with a profound distrust of American policy. As he remarked in September 1934:

> American representatives lay stress in private upon the immense advantages which would accrue to the world if only we worked together. In pursuance of this admirable sentiment they invite us to disclose our hand without disclosing their own. When we have laid all our cards on the table they shake their heads sadly and express their regretful conviction that Congress will have nothing to do with us unless we can make an offer that will suit them

better. Congress (and in particular the Senate) are the Mr Jorkins of American representatives.[29]

Chamberlain felt that an American peace initiative would be of doubtful value. At worst Roosevelt might summon a conference only to be forced to withdraw under isolationist pressure, wrecking Britain's approach to appeasement and leaving it to face Germany alone. As he informed the American chargé, 'If it was a matter of [the Americans] coming in an then going out, he would rather [they] never come in.'[30] At best Britain might be rushed by the United States into unilateral concessions in order to make the conference a success. Britain, therefore, must exercise caution in dealing with Roosevelt and must not allow its policy to be dictated by Washington. Appeasement was best conducted piecemeal, solving political questions in advance of economic issues or arms limitation. Any other approach risked giving away valuable bargaining counters in advance. The President should let Britain make the running and only participate, when he was asked, in the final stages of a European settlement when his intervention would be less potentially damaging.

The Prime Minister was clearly less sympathetic than Eden to an American peace initiative but at this stage differences over Roosevelt's scheme were neither evident nor acute. Partly this was because both men shared reservations about the detail of the American plan which concealed deeper differences of principle. Chamberlain, like Eden, was concerned about the American emphasis on arms limitation as the solution to European problems. Arms limitation could only be considered after German concessions on other subjects, since Hitler would only negotiate if Britain seemed serious about resisting expansion by force. He was, however, more concerned about the financial strain of rearmament than the Foreign Secretary as a result of his experience as Chancellor of the Exchequer, and placed a different interpretation on deterrence. Chamberlain 'wished to steer rearmament away from a massive commitment to overwhelming force, towards a programme aimed only at defending Britain and her vital interests against direct attack'.[31] Rearamamament must be strictly tailored to what Britain could afford and must not be allowed to interfere with normal trade. Ultimately this meant the construction of fighters rather than bombers and the switching of resources away from a continental expeditionary force towards imperial and home defence, changes in emphasis which were later to cause friction with Eden.[32] At this stage, however, both agreed that arms limitation talks must not precede German concessions on other issues.

If there was broad agreement between Chamberlain and Eden about the American emphasis on arms limitation, there was also unity on the question of American demands for a trade treaty and the coordination of economic policies. Eden hoped to conclude an economic agreement because this would give American farmers, particularly in the Mid-West, a 'bread and butter' interest in the survival of the British Empire and thus would be conducive to a decline in isolationist strength. As Lindsay remarked in March 1937

> In the event of a major crisis in Europe, the factor which will most impede any measure which the American Government might take in favour of Great Britain will be the Middle West which will be directly and favourably affected by the conclusion of a commercial treaty with the United Kingdom . . . It might even be a deciding factor in the attitude America might take.[33]

A trade treaty, moreover, would provide an expression of solidarity in an area where the restraints on American political action did not apply. As the Economic Department of the Foreign Office noted in April 1937;

> An agreement with the United States is becoming not merely desirable but necessary; there is an appearance of solidarity between British and American policy which is having its effect in curbing the dictators and keeping up the spirits of Central Europe.[34]

Chamberlain shared the desire of the Foreign Office to conclude a trade treaty. He was not, as some Americans suspected, an inflexible protectionist and had welcomed economic cooperation with the United States while still Chancellor of the Exchequer. Chamberlain saw the value of a reduction in American tariffs for British exports and the balance of payments. As he remarked in April 1937, 'world economic stability' largely depended on Anglo-American economic cooperation.[35] Neither Eden nor Chamberlain, however, was prepared to dismantle the Empire in the interests of Anglo-American Solidarity. This was too high a price for Britain to pay. When Runciman, President of the Board of Trade, visited

Washington in January 1937, he warned Hull and Roosevelt not to make excessive demands. The United States maintained a high tariff wall and must reconcile itself to the continued existence of imperial preference.[36] As the American Department remarked on 1 April 1937: 'however great the importance of having a friendly America, a friendly Empire is of greater importance still. We cannot destroy the Commonwealth for the beaux yeux of the Middle West'.[37] For this reason the initial list of American demands for economic concessions was rejected as too extreme.[38]

When Norman Davis arrived in London in April 1937 to take soundings on behalf of Roosevelt, the problems of trade policy and armaments immediately intruded themselves as obstacles to close Anglo-American cooperation in appeasement. Davis saw Eden on 10 April and pointed out the economic, political and financial instability caused by the arms race. He indicated that while the United States was:

> vitally interested in economic rehabilitation and disarmament and desirous of collaborating to that end, it would be futile to attempt anything . . . until the British, who are an essential factor in any effective steps for recovery and peace are prepared to get behind any efforts that may be made by anyone to achieve such a result.

'Anyone' in this context obviously referred to Roosevelt. Davis went on to remark that it was particularly 'absurd' to expect progress towards peace and stability while the two major trading powers, Britain and the United States, pursued 'diametrically opposite' economic policies. Eden, however, replied that the time was not yet ripe for 'an effective move towards international agreement' especially 'with regard to armaments'. As for the trade treaty, Britain was eager to strike a bargain 'but in view of the Ottawa agreements there were considerable difficulties and limitations as to what could be done'.[39] Chamberlain adopted a similar approach when interviewed by Davis on 29 April. He emphasised his enthusiasm for a trade agreement but explained that any modification of imperial preference 'necessitated negotiation and some delay'. He was even less hopeful than Eden about the prospects of a conference to settle outstanding European problems. He pointed out that Britain did not reject appeasement and had recently held 'semi-official exploratory talks with Schacht'. It would, however, be

Impossible to undertake simultaneously a comprehensive settlement of political, economic and disarmament questions. It was necessary to proceed by stages . . . political discussions and tentative agreements must precede any substantial steps towards economic rehabilitation, including the . . . removal of exchange controls and reduction in trade restrictions . . . He thought that disarmament must come last and implied that British rearmament must reach a more advanced stage before it would be practicable to call a halt.

Chamberlain was clearly unwilling to abandon the lever of British rearmament in advance of substantial political concessions by Hitler. Davis could only reply that the 'economic and financial situation . . . of Germany' was becoming 'precarious' and warn that events might not 'wait for the British time schedule'. His talks with British statesmen in April 1937 did not encourage Davis to feel optimistic about the prospects of a conference. In a gloomy report to Roosevelt on his soundings he remarked 'The British do not want to take any initiative to halt rearmament or to have anyone else take an initiative unless or until they are convinced it will succeed in establishing real peace.'[40]

The development of American relations with Germany in the opening months of 1937 ultimately proved to be no more rewarding. At the beginning of January 1937 there were some signs of readiness to respond to an American call for a conference. Schacht informed Cochran, the American commercial attaché, on 15 January that Hitler sincerely desired disarmament and that Roosevelt should summon a conference in Washington.[41] There were indications that Hitler might indeed share Schacht's views. The Führer's speech on 30 January was moderate in tone, raising only German colonial claims.[42] The French interpreted this to mean that 'Schacht and the businessmen' had more influence in Berlin 'than the Nazi Party'.[43] The United States seized the opportunity to sound out Germany once again about the possibility of disarmament and economic collaboration. On 4 March 1937, Dodd asked Schacht about 'the possibility of a world peace conference'. Schacht replied that Hitler would approve of such a scheme and requested an invitation to Washington for preliminary discussions about a European settlement. Dodd agreed to report the conversation to Roosevelt, but as usual he was unconvinced by Schacht's assurances of Hitler's essential moderation and his ability to influence the

Führer.[44] The ambassador's scepticism about Schacht's claims was well founded. At this point he was losing ground to Göring in economic affairs and perhaps hoped to recover his position by some dramatic coup such as an invitation to the White House. Roosevelt, however, seems to have been encouraged enough by developments in Germany to put forward unofficially his own personal solution to the problem of armaments. At the Gridiron dinner the President 'outlined to Luther, the German ambassador who was returning to Germany, the idea of a disarmament plan which provided simply that no nation should manufacture armaments heavier than that which a man could carry on his shoulders'. Roosevelt believed that 'this would in itself prevent aggression by land forces and would go a long way to preserve the peace'.[45]

The mood of hope with regard to developments in Germany, however, was not long sustained and events rapidly justified Dodd's pessimism. There was no positive response to the American soundings on disarmament and economic collaboration. On 15 April, in a conversation with Joe E. Davies, Schacht argued that German rearmament was necessary because other powers denied his country justice. They would not discuss German economic grievances unless the Reich were strong.[46] This was a repetition of the British response to soundings on arms limitation. Both Schacht and Eden believed that any advance commitment to limitation would be viewed as a weakness and would inhibit negotiations on political and economic issues. Even had Schacht introduced no reservations about discussing arms limitation in advance of economic appeasement, his declining power in the government at this stage raised doubts about official commitment to a 'moderate' policy. Dodd noted on 30 March 1937 that at a recent cabinet meeting on the economy 'Schacht is reported to have challenged Hitler's Four Year Plan in some of its items. But nothing has happened and cabinet decisions are reported all in favor of Hitler and Goering'. Schacht himself admitted that his position in the government was 'very critical'. He increasingly abandoned his previous criticism of autarky in order to survive. On 20 May 1937 Dodd reported that Schacht now appeared to be reconciled to the system and talked as if it were 'permanent'. Consequently there seemed to be 'no prospect of improving German-American relations, no chance at all'.[47] The French reported a similar failure in their efforts to appease Germany. According to Bullitt, François-Poncet, the ambassador in Berlin, had 'never been so pessimistic with regard to Germany's intentions ... He believed that Schacht's conversations would be in reality a smokescreen behind which Hitler would await the propitious moment to lay hands on Austria and Czechoslovakia.'[48]

Roosevelt was despondent about the British and German attitudes towards appeasement which denied him the opportunity to act. The conditions necessary for American action, prior British and German commitments to cooperate, had not been fulfilled. His soundings in London and Berlin had ended in frustration. Both countries seemed caught in a vicious circle of mistrust. Roosevelt described his predicament to Phillips, the ambassador in Rome, on 19 May 1937:

> The more I study the situation, the more I am convinced that an economic approach to peace is a pretty weak reed to lean on. . . . It may postpone war but how can it ever prevent war if the armament process continues at its present pace. . . . How do we make progress if England and France say we cannot help Germany and Italy achieve economic security if they continue to arm and threaten, while simultaneously Germany and Italy say we must arm and threaten because they will not give us economic security?[49]

Despite this apparent impasse, however, the President had not abandoned his hopes of launching an American peace initiative. Indeed the entrenched hostility and mutual suspicion of the European states revealed by his soundings seem merely to have reinforced his initial conviction that the United States must act as a disinterested mediator. Without American intervention lack of mutual trust would drag the European powers into war. His response to rejection, therefore, was not to abandon his plans but to restate them. This time the President concentrated his efforts on winning British cooperation. Unless Britain quickly agreed to make sweeping concessions, Germany would remain unappeased and the deteriorating economy would push Hitler towards the 'extremists' and a war of desperation.

On 10 June 1937 Roosevelt sent a letter to Chamberlain, via Norman Davis, inviting the Prime Minister to visit Washington in the autumn. The object of the visit would be to coordinate the British and the American approaches to appeasement. According to Roosevelt, it might 'become possible and advisable within a few months to make a concerted and comprehensive effort to achieve economic rehabilitation, financial stability, a limitation of armaments and peace'. It would, therefore, be 'most desirable' for Britain and the United States to 'do what they can to . . . prepare the way for a broader move to establish more healthy . . . conditions in the world'.[50] The message totally ignored Chamberlain's warning in April that it would be 'impracticable to undertake simultaneously a comprehensive settlement of political, economic and disarmament questions'.

Roosevelt did not even address himself to this British objection, he simply ignored it. Always a strong believer in personal diplomacy, the President obviously believed he could win Chamberlain round to his own views by extended direct contact in the White House. The invitation caused some irritation in London. Chamberlain remarked that Davis 'had misunderstood if he derived from my conversation any assurance that I should be able in any event to accept an invitation to go to the United States if the President were to extend one'.[51] The Prime Minister was still trying to open negotiations with Germany and felt that Roosevelt's remarks about a general settlement were premature. The German Foreign Minister, von Neurath, was due to visit London on 16 June for political talks which would augment the discussions with Schacht. Chamberlain hoped to ascertain German views on the security aspects of a European settlement, including Neurath's attitude towards non-aggression pacts in Central and South Eastern Europe. He was reluctant to become involved in arms limitation and economic appeasement schemes in advance of substantial German concessions in this area. The Foreign Office shared his reluctance. Vansittart felt that it was 'most important that we should not be drawn into any discussion with the USA on the limitation of armaments'. It was also feared that a visit while problems were in a 'fluid state' would only produce disappointment and might be 'disastrous for present cordial relations'. The American Department was worried about the effects on American public opinion if a visit ended fruitlessly.[52] This was a major consideration since it was believed that things were 'moving our way nicely in the United States'. The new neutrality law, while denying the President the degree of discretion hoped for in London, still favoured the power with 'command of the sea and the longest purse', a fact which had not been lost on Germany.[53] The Foreign Office was reluctant to risk the British position and the possibility of further favourable developments by reckless action. The greatest obstacle in the way of a visit was the trade treaty, since neither side had yet been able to agree on an acceptable basis of discussion. In his letter, Roosevelt was confident that 'a substantial trade agreement' would emerge by September which would open the way to a coordination of policy in other fields. The Foreign Office was less optimistic. The main obstacle, apart from Hull's excessive demands, was the impending December election in Australia. It was felt that trade negotiations could not be announced until after this date lest they affect the outcome. Troutbeck, the head of the American Department, noted that a visit would be pointless 'if the trade agreement made no progress and this is impossible until after the Australian elections'.[54]

The Foreign Office put forward an alternative proposal for Eden to visit Washington instead of the Prime Minister. It was felt that such a visit might lead to a valuable exchange of views and exercise a calming effect on Europe.[55] Chamberlain, however, vetoed this proposal. In a letter of 2 July he informed Eden that 'the disadvantages of undertaking a visit to America, unless the conditions and the timing are right, apply with very nearly equal force to a visit from the Foreign Secretary'.[56] The Foreign Office abandoned the proposal in the light of this opposition and on 28 June Roosevelt's invitation was rejected as premature. Chamberlain's reply made it clear that he did not share the American belief that a comprehensive settlement would soon be possible. He pointed out that Britain had as yet been unable to arrange even preliminary meetings with official German representatives to ascertain the true extent of German claims and the concessions which Hitler would be prepared to make in return for economic assistance. If such meetings materialised, they might provide 'a valuable indication of the direction in which the lines of advance might run and in this way provide a useful preliminary to any conversation between the President and myself'.[57] Chamberlain was simply repeating in this statement the old British argument that political discussions must precede any moves towards a wider settlement. Lest the warning in his letter was ignored in Washington, the Prime Minister called in Bingham and informed him that while Britain was anxious to grant Germany economic assistance it would do so only under strict guarantees which would ensure European security.[58] Chamberlain was not to be caught by personal diplomacy and had once again advised Roosevelt to remain on the sidelines.

The United States remained committed to its own version of appeasement despite this unencouraging response. On 7 July, in a speech at Charlottesville, Sumner Welles reiterated American ideas on the subject. He equated political extremism of both left and right with economic and political injustice and warned that such extremism must lead to war. If war came the United States could not 'stay clear of its consequences'. Welles, therefore, promised that his country would cooperate with any moves towards arms limitation and economic appeasement. At the same time he urged the European nations to undertake the 'political adjustments' which had to accompany 'military and economic disarmament', perhaps registering in this statement American concern at Chamberlain's slow and cautious approach to the problem of security. Welles went so far as to hint that the United States itself would welcome revision of Versailles. He remarked that the League of Nations had failed because of its association with a treaty which loaded the losers with intolerable 'moral and material burdens' and made clear his own support for a more equitable international system. In effect this was an implicit statement of American support for German revisionist demands.[59] Welles remained concerned about the extremism encouraged by the deteriorating German economy and privately warned Britain that a peaceful settlement must not be delayed much longer. Roosevelt also continued to press London to take further steps. On 28 July 1937 he wrote again to Chamberlain agreeing that any official British visit to Washington must be 'properly prepared' and asking if the Prime Minister could suggest any measures which might be taken in advance of an actual meeting.[60] If this message was designed to elicit more information about Anglo-German relations or to keep open the possibility of a joint approach to European problems, it proved a failure. Chamberlain did not even reply until September and when he did it was only to state yet again that the time was not ripe for a meeting because no progress had been made towards ascertaining Hitler's real demands.[61] Roosevelt could only complain that the British 'rearmament complex' was delaying a lasting settlement and remark that it might take some time to 'wipe the slate clean' in Anglo-American relations.[62] The President was being rather unfair to Chamberlain. As the Prime Minister himself pointed out, it had proved impossible to learn the real extent of German claims in the summer of 1937. Neurath's visit to London, during which political discussions were to have begun, had been cancelled, apparently because of Ribbentrop's interference. Moreover an Anglo-Italian crisis had broken out in the Mediterranean which gave the government additional cause for concern.[63] Whatever Roosevelt might have thought, it seemed hardly the time for British statemen to discuss arms limitation and economic appeasement with the Americans.

The first half of 1937 had gone badly for Roosevelt. He had failed, despite a sustained effort, to win British support for his appeasement schemes, or even to make progress towards the more limited goal of an Anglo-American trade treaty. In default of a general settlement, the deterioration of the German economy was undermining the power of the 'moderates' and seemed to be pushing Hitler towards an 'extremist' solution to German problems. By September 1937, moreover, two additional factors were beginning to complicate an already difficult situation – the outbreak of a new international crisis in the Far East and the first indications of an economic recession within the United States. For the first time the spectre was raised in Washington of an alliance between German and Japanese 'extremists', promoting the Closed Door on a world scale and menacing American security and prosperity. Simultaneously the new recession made the United States even more anxious to reintegrate Germany into the world economy in the interests of recovery. Both factors, therefore, acted to increase the pressures towards cooperating with the German 'moderates', who seemed to share American ideals of an Open Door order in which trade could flourish and the prosperity of the major industrial nations would be guaranteed. Impelled by the recession, but conscious of his previous difficulties in securing advance consent to American action, particularly from London, Roosevelt began to consider the possibility of a unilateral peace initiative, appealing to the European peoples over the heads of their governments, a tactic which his predecessor Wilson had used in 1917. By the beginning of autumn 1937, the President was clearly abandoning the 'conditions precedent' to American action laid down in January.

If the recession and the crisis in the Far East had an effect on American policy, they also had a powerful effect on Chamberlain. Under the pressure of Britain's own deteriorating economic position and the necessity of averting an alignment between Germany and

Japan, the Prime Minister began a more active search for a European settlement in which economic and political discussions were kept less rigidly separate, a development which was to cause the first friction with Eden. Despite the apparent convergence of the British and American positions in the second half of the year, however, it was to prove as difficult to coordinate policy between London and Washington as it had done between January and September 1937.

3 The 'Quarantine' Speech and the Welles Plan

On 17 July 1937 Japanese troops in the vicinity of Peking were involved in an incident with Chinese forces which, in the following weeks, escalated into a full-scale war. The 'China Incident' broadened the European crisis of 1933–6 into a world crisis in 1937, creating additional problems for both Britain and the United States. The fighting in China brought Japan into conflict with the Western powers and created an apparent identity of interest between Tokyo, Berlin and Rome. A world axis conspiracy appeared to be emerging.[1] Links between the 'dissatisfied' powers became closer with Mussolini's visit to Berlin in September and the tripartite Anti-Comintern Pact in November 1937. This development created strategic problems for Britain and America. It became vital to dispel the threat to the 'satisfied' powers of a world triangle of 'dissatisfied' powers. The British chiefs of staff warned that it was impossible to fight three antagonists simultaneously and asked the government to reduce by diplomacy the number of possible enemies.[2] The Americans were also affected by the new tripartite grouping, since their basic war plan 'Orange' took no account of possible outside assistance for Japan in the event of a war in the Pacific.[3] The United States also, therefore, tried to dissolve the axis by judicious diplomacy. The situation was complicated for Washington and London by the outbreak of a new recession in the autumn of 1937. On the one hand it inhibited any action against Japan along the lines of sanctions. On the other hand it strengthened the impulse to seek a settlement with Germany which would not only leave Japan isolated, but restore business confidence and stimulate trade.

The initial reaction of Britain and the United States to the new crisis was to attempt to prevent the outbreak of full-scale war between Japan and China. Britain in particular, wished to avert hostilities in the Far East because of the unsettled state of Europe and lack of sufficient military strength to protect its interests in both areas of the world. It was hoped that the United States would support British peace efforts. Chamberlain felt that Anglo-American cooperation might prove more possible in the Far East than in Europe, despite previous British disappointments with US policy in the area, since American interests were directly involved. [4] Eden believed that 'counsels of moderation' were unlikely to be heeded in Tokyo unless concerted between Washington and London. [5] It was suggested to the Americans, therefore, that Britain and the United States make joint approaches to Japan and China, calling for the suspension of troop movements and offering assistance in settling the dispute. The United States, however, refused to cooperate. London was informed that while America wished to avert a crisis in China, the administration preferred 'parallel' and 'independent' action to joint representations at Tokyo and Nanking. [6] It was feared in Washington that any appearance of a united front would endanger peace by mobilising Japanese opinion behind the army 'extremists' and complicate the task of re-establishing civilian control. Grew, the influential American ambassador in Tokyo, encouraged such thinking at the State Department. [7] Moreover joint action with Britain would offer the isolationists an issue around which to mobilise American public opinion. Roosevelt, having just suffered a major political defeat over his attempt to reform the Supreme Court, was reluctant to arouse a new controversy with Congress over foreign affairs. It could easily be claimed that by cooperating with London in the Far East, the United States was acting as the mere tool of selfish British imperialism in the area. A combination of diplomatic and domestic factors, therefore, dictated American caution. Independent representations from London and Washington failed to contain the crisis, however, and by the beginning of August it was clear that Japan and China had embarked upon an undeclared war. There was considerable disappointment in Britain at this development and Chamberlain blamed American caution for the spread of hostilities. His suspicions about the effect of public opinion on American diplomacy were confirmed by events in the Far East. On 29 August 1937 he remarked

> The Americans have a long way to go before they become helpful partners in world affairs. I have tried to get them to come in in Japan and China but they were too frightened of their own

people – though I believe that if they had been willing to play
there was enough chance of stopping hostilities.[8]

The United States, however, could not ignore indefinitely the
marked deterioration of the international situation in the autumn of
1937. By the beginning of October, developments in both Europe
and Asia seemed to demand a more active policy. In the Far East,
the Japanese government had been unable to reassert control over
the military 'extremists'. It was plain that the army aimed at
nothing less than the conquest of China. On 17 September Hull
remarked that the Japanese planned 'to dominate all of China and
all of Asia as far east as Lake Baikal'.[9] There were signs that in
Germany too, the 'extremists' were gaining control. It was
rumoured that Göring was about to replace Schacht as Minister of
Economics. This would be followed by the intensification of autarky
and rearmament.[10] In foreign affairs, Germany and Italy drew
closer together. Mussolini visited Berlin in September 1937 amid
speculation about a new alliance and Hitler delivered a speech
pledging the unity of the two regimes.[11] This strengthening of the
Rome-Berlin axis, complemented the already existing ties between
Germany and Japan, symbolised by the Anti-Comintern Pact of
1936. A united front of 'dissatisfied' powers appeared to be
emerging, threatening the 'satisfied' powers on a global scale. It was
feared in Washington that Germany might be tempted to emulate
Japan and solve its economic and social problems by force. A
Treasury report of September 1937 argued that in the long run a
Japanese victory in China would encourage other 'dissatisfied'
powers to attempt aggression against their neighbours. Germany,
for example, might seize Czechoslovakia or attack the Soviet Union
with Japanese assistance.[12] The only hopeful sign was that
opposition to 'extremist' policies continued to exist in Germany.
The intensification of autarky was causing resentment despite Party
appeals for sacrifice. The masses were believed to oppose a policy of
armed expansion.[13] Such trends encouraged Joseph E. Davies to
hope that while Hitler might want war, the country was not yet
ready to follow him.[14] The army, in particular, resented the new
links with Italy and Japan and the intensification of the anti-
Church campaign. The State Department was informed by a
German source that von Fritsch, the Commander-in-Chief, had
joined with Schacht and Göring in an opportunist alliance, aimed
at a Hohenzollern restoration. The plotters calculated that 'the

Germans are monarchists at heart and are pretty tired of the present conditions under which they are living'.[15] While the 'extremists' were increasingly influential, therefore, powerful sentiment in favour of a peaceful settlement continued to exist in Germany.

There was a debate in Washington about the proper course for the United States to follow in this complicated situation. It was recognised that the Japanese problem could not be viewed in isolation but must be considered in relation to the emerging grouping of 'dissatisfied' powers on a world basis. As Moffat noted on 28 August, 'The Far East is only one part, even if a vital part, of our foreign relations and policies must be determined with respect to analogous situations elsewhere'.[16] In some quarters sentiment developed for exerting pressure against Japan, as a symbol to 'extremists' everywhere that armed expansion would be resisted. Hull favoured invoking the moral sanction of world opinion against Tokyo. He believed that public opinion in all countries desired peace and hoped to mobilise this sentiment against aggressive governments. By issuing public appeals for peace in the Far East, which other powers were asked to support, he hoped to rally the masses against war, isolating not only the Japanese army in its own country, but also 'extremist' elements in Germany and Italy which would not dare ignore an aroused populace. The war in China would be thus transformed by sheer moral force into a means of bringing peace on earth.[17] Hull's approach incorporated old Jeffersonian notions about the natural 'goodness' of the people which could be mobilised against a 'corrupt' government. The problem about his naive ideas, as Hornbeck stated 'quite bluntly' at the time, was that 'no European Power believed in words and . . . unless [the United States] was prepared to talk deeds, they would not take anything from Washington too seriously'.[18] The same held true for Japan. By September 1937, there were signs that Hull himself was beginning to grasp this fact, given the failure of his moral lectures to move the world. In a discussion about the threatening international situation he remarked that:

> the United States had been stormcellar pacifists with the net result that . . . [the] 'desperado nations' had been encouraged to go on indefinitely. . . . There came a point at which failure to be willing to fight led literally to more fighting. The impression he wanted to convey was that America could not be counted out as a military force under all circumstances.

While Hull rejected economic sanctions against Japan, which he felt would be ineffective, he did not rule out a naval demonstration in the Pacific to prove that the United States was prepared to defend its interests.[19] Others, such as Norman Davis, felt that too great an emphasis on moral condemnation or physical threats would only tighten the emerging links between Berlin, Tokyo and Rome. As he remarked on 15 September 1937, simple condemnation of Germany, Italy and Japan as 'the dictators' would only drive them into 'a closer alliance than is at present the case'. A more subtle approach was necessary. A formula had to be found 'which would enable some of them to come back to a cooperative move'. Such a formula would balance threats with conciliation. The solution might be a peace initiative linked with the announcement of higher defence spending, or perhaps 'a preliminary education of public opinion to the effect that American security does not begin with the defense of the frontiers but in maintaining the supremacy of the law observing powers'.[20] If Davis wished to balance the stick with the carrot in American diplomacy, Sumner Welles wished to place the main emphasis on the carrot, in the hope of winning Germany away from Japan by appeasement. He remained anxious to work with the German 'moderates' towards a negotiated solution of European problems. This would not only break up the emerging axis threat, but revive world trade and hence allow the United States to escape from its own deepening recession. In July 1937, before the new slump began, Welles had emphasised the economic advantages of appeasement and subsequent events reinforced his desire to reach a settlement with Germany. On 28 September, Moffat noted that the Under Secretary was 'optimistic' about the European situation, perhaps because of reports that the German army remained a powerful force for peace and the masses did not want war.[21] At the beginning of October 1937, Roosevelt accepted the appeasement plan on which Welles had been working as the basis of American policy towards the axis.

By September 1937, the President himself seems to have become convinced that a more active foreign policy was necessary, although there were few signs of the exact course he meant to take.[22] In October he embarked on a speaking tour of the Mid-West where he intended, at the urging of Hull and Davis, to make some pronouncement on foreign affairs which would educate public opinion and raise doubts abroad about continued American inaction in the face of aggression.[23] On 5 October 1937, speaking at

Chicago, the President made a statement about the international situation which in some ways went beyond the recommendations of Hull and Davis. Roosevelt claimed that a 'reign of terror had broken out in the world' from which there was 'no escape through mere isolation or neutrality'. The peace-loving nations, therefore

> should make a concerted effort in opposition to those violations of treaties and those ignorings of human instincts which today are creating a state of international anarchy. . . . When an epidemic of physical disease starts to spread, the community approves and joins in a quarantine of the patients in order to protect the community against the spread of the disease.[24]

The 'quarantine' speech was partly intended, as Roosevelt later claimed, 'to educate American opinion and show the world in which direction that opinion is running'.[25] It is probably no coincidence that the President chose the Mid-West, the centre of isolationist influence, to deliver a warning that security could not be found in 'mere isolation or neutrality'. His statements were also clearly meant to deter 'extremists' in Germany and Japan. The President implied that something would be done by the 'peace-loving' nations if aggression continued to spread, although the threat was kept vague and imprecise. Roosevelt may even have envisaged his speech, which hinted at a democratic front against dictators, as a reply to Hitler's statement of 28 September, pledging the unity of Fascism and National Socialism. The precise meaning of the word 'quarantine' never became clear, however, since Roosevelt refused to supply a narrow definition. It has been argued that he wished the 'peace-loving' states to form a league of neutrals which would somehow exert an influence on world affairs without resort to force. This was an extension of the Pan-American doctrine of collective isolation from war enunciated at the Buenos Aires conference of December 1936. Under such a system the 'peace-loving' nations would 'draw away' from the totalitarian powers, adopting a common policy towards aggression. How such a grouping was to influence aggressors without resort to sanctions, which would mean a breach of neutrality, Roosevelt never made clear, a fact which perhaps reveals the President's own confused thinking on this point. He simply denied that 'quarantine' implied sanctions and claimed that the concept was perfectly compatible with the provisions of the Neutrality Act.[26]

In this confused situation it was left up to Sumner Welles to give a positive direction to American policy. Perhaps fearing, as did others, that the 'quarantine' speech led the United States too far towards sanctions,[27] Welles put forward his own scheme for the appeasement of Germany on 6 October 1937. It reflected ideas about the German problem and its solution first articulated in his speech at Charlottesville of July 1937. Welles envisaged holding a world conference under American auspices which would re-establish the rule of law in international affairs and guarantee justice by granting all powers equal access to raw materials. It was hoped that the lure of treaty revision would secure German support for appeasement. In its final version the Welles plan, while carefully emphasising American non-involvement in political questions in order to avert isolationist attacks, cleverly hinted at revision of Versailles.[28] The whole scheme was intended to appeal to the German 'moderates' and German public opinion. It was also designed to break up the emerging grouping of 'dissatisfied' powers by offering Germany justice without war. Hull stated this explicitly in a conversation with Tweedsmuir, Governor-General of Canada, after the Welles plan had been adopted by the administration. According to Hull, a policy of economic appeasement which the Americans had 'worked out in considerable detail' was the key to peace. Germany had 'no immediate bellicose aims' and everything looked 'well for her except the solemn fact that she is on an economic slide'. If 'the great democracies, led by Britain and America, would offer her their help in getting her economic situation stable she could be detached from her . . . alliance with Italy and Japan'. According to Hull there was a 'solid and rational element in Germany' with which the United States could work.[29] It was assumed in Washington, therefore, that appeasement in Europe would leave Japan morally and politically isolated, thus forcing Tokyo to conclude a just peace with China. Certainly a successful settlement with Berlin would have removed German support for Japanese expansion. The groups which stood for a negotiated settlement of European problems were also the groups which opposed Nazi support of Japanese policy in the Far East. The army, the Foreign Office and big business all disliked close association with Tokyo and Hitler's rejection of the traditional policy of friendship with China. In such quarters it was felt that German interests were being sacrificed to ideology.[30] Germany, therefore, seemed to hold the key to world peace and the revival of trade.

Appeasement would not only establish an Open Door order in Europe but would also prevent the construction of a Closed Door system in the Far East. As Welles later remarked his plan looked towards 'an ultimate international economy based upon reduced armaments, a greater common use of world resources, and the improvement and simplification of economic relationships between all peoples'. In this new world order American trade could expand and flourish.[31]

Roosevelt adopted the Welles plan as the solution to the problem of 'dissatisfied' powers which refused to accept the existing international system. It satisfied his desire to take some dramatic initiative in world affairs while remaining firmly rooted in a policy of peace and neutrality which, it was assumed, the American public would support.[32] The President was to launch the American initiative by calling a meeting of foreign diplomats at the White House on 11 November 1937. Armistice day was an evocative date on which to put forward a peace plan designed to remove the injustices of Versailles, and was obviously chosen for the effect it would have on world opinion. There was more to the choice of date than this, however. After the 'quarantine' speech, the United States had agreed to attend a conference of signatories of the Nine Power treaty to be held in Brussels, which would discuss the dangerous situation in the Far East. Welles predicted:

> By the time November 11 is reached, the Brussels conference will have been in session for . . . eight days. A proposal of the character noted will, I think, definitely strengthen the hands of those powers that are seeking to avoid world anarchy.

Japan would feel unable to ignore sentiment for a settlement at Brussels and would be persuaded to end the dispute with China.[33] There was to be no advance consultation about the Welles plan with powers which might share the American desire to establish a more stable world system. The initiative was to be sprung upon 'satisfied' and 'dissatisfied' countries alike on 11 November. Chamberlain was not to be granted the privilege of prior warning, perhaps because Roosevelt suspected that the Prime Minister would request him to postpone the scheme. Previous soundings in London gave the President little ground for hope that American meddling would be spontaneously welcomed in Britain. Chamberlain would be made to accept American plans by presenting him with fait accompli. The force of public opinion would compel the British government to cooperate with the United States. Roosevelt, therefore, was pinning his faith on the moral effects of an appeal to the peoples of Europe, which would force their rulers to collaborate in the creation of a new world order.

The 'quarantine' speech came as a complete surprise to London and caused both confusion and concern. It increased Chamberlain's irritation with the United States which had been growing since the outbreak of the China incident. Britain's deteriorating economic position and the emerging threat to the Empire of Germany, Japan and Italy had confirmed the Prime Minister in his desire to conclude a European settlement. He hoped to divide the axis, appeasing Germany and perhaps Italy, while doing nothing in the meanwhile likely to lead to a clash with Japan. As he later remarked, he had 'far reaching plans . . . for the appeasement of Europe and Asia and for the ultimate check to the mad armament race which, if allowed to continue, must involve us all in ruin'.[34] His aims, therefore, did not differ fundamentally from those of Sumner Welles. Roosevelt's speech, however, 'embarrassed the situation' and endangered Chamberlain's own schemes. On 6 October the Prime Minister complained that whether or not 'quarantine' meant sanctions, Roosevelt's use of the term was likely to promote public pressure in Britain for a stronger line against Japan. It would be made use of 'for political purposes by the Opposition Parties' which would claim that the 'USA would put economic sanctions on Japan if we would do the same'. Chamberlain himself believed that

> in the present state of European affairs, with the two dictators in a thoroughly nasty temper, we simply cannot afford to quarrel with Japan and I very much fear that after a lot of ballyhoo the Americans will somehow fade out and leave us to carry all the blame and the odium.

Even in the short term Roosevelt had disturbed British policy in the Far East by effectively destroying 'some quiet conversations with the Japs which might or might not have led to something'. American interference was particularly galling because when Britain had 'asked USA to make a joint demarche at the very beginning of the dispute they refused. At that time, before the Japs were involved, it might have stopped the whole thing. Now they jump in, without saying a word beforehand and without knowing what they mean to do.' The damaging effects of Roosevelt's speech, however, were not confined merely to relations with Japan. In addition it might 'cause the Germans and Italians to draw closer to the Japs'. Roosevelt, by condemning aggressors, threatened to lock the democracies into confrontation with all three 'dissatisfied' powers, while Chamberlain's aim was to divide them. The only consolation which the Prime Minister could see was that at least Roosevelt had warned the dictators that 'there was a point beyond which the United States of America would not permit them to go'. It is clear that he felt the disadvantages of the President's statement far outweighed this solitary advantage.[35] Had Chamberlain known about the existence of the Welles plan, it is unlikely that he would have been any less critical of American policy. He had always emphasised that appeasement could not be tackled on a comprehensive basis and, as in January 1938, would have viewed an American initiative as dangerous to his own schemes.

Eden's reaction to the 'quarantine' speech was much more enthusiastic and pointed to an emerging difference between Foreign Secretary and Prime Minister over the American role in British policy. Eden was worried by the tightening links between the axis powers as symbolised by Mussolini's visit to Berlin and wished to reply with a show of Anglo-American cooperation in the Far East. At Cabinet on 6 October, he welcomed the 'quarantine' speech because, whatever Roosevelt had meant, it would make it impossible for the Americans to avoid participation in the Brussels conference, called by the League of Nations to discuss the China incident. Eden remarked that the conference would offer the 'fullest scope' for Anglo-American cooperation. Neither then nor later did he rule out the possibility of sanctions against Japan if the United States wished to impose them, a fact which divided him from the rest of the Cabinet.[36] Eden interpreted the 'quarantine' speech as evidence that the United States was abandoning its 'psychological withdrawal' from the world stage and wished to encourage the process in the interests of British security. He responded enthusiastically to Roosevelt's hints about the necessity for a democratic front against aggression in a speech at Llandudno on 15 October 1937 in which he welcomed the words 'of the President of the most powerful republic in the world' and promised to cooperate with the United States at Brussels 'in the spirit of President Roosevelt's declaration'.[37] Events before the conference confirmed Eden in his ideas, particularly the news at the end of October that Italy was about to join the German-Japanese Anti-Comintern Pact. Although it was denied that the extended pact would be anti-British, this was undoubtedly the intention.[38] The Foreign Secretary suspected that the dictators planned to blackmail Britain into extensive concessions by a display of axis solidarity. He wished to reply to this threat by stepping up rearmament and by eliciting some evidence of Anglo-American cooperation in the Far East. On 1 November 1937, just before setting out for the Brussels conference, Eden stated frankly in the Commons that Britain would accept 'dictation from none'. He went on to emphasise that 'In order to get the full cooperation of the United States at an international conference, I would travel, not only from Geneva to Brussels, but from Melbourne to Alaska, more particularly in the present state of the international situation.'[39] On 2 November he sent a letter to Chamberlain demanding an expansion of British rearmament programmes. Eden admitted that the British financial position might be affected but argued that 'we have got to meet the challenges of the dictators and . . . to do so we have to be strong in armaments, even at some cost in other spheres'.[40]

This theme of accelerated rearmament and democratic solidarity divided Eden from Chamberlain. The Prime Minister did not believe that Britain could afford more arms, particularly in a recession, and feared that by pursuing the chimera of a democratic bloc, the Foreign Secretary was merely threatening to solidify the axis. The way out of Britain's deteriorating strategic and economic situation lay in appeasement. In a speech at the Guildhall on 3 November 1937, the Prime Minister publicly dissociated himself from Eden in the interest of improving relations with the dictators. He played down democratic solidarity and remarked that he wished to see relations with the axis 'established on a basis of mutual friendship and understanding which should not . . . be affected by differences in methods of internal administration'.[41] Chamberlain, moreover, did not restrict such sentiments to mere rhetoric. At the end of October he arranged for Lord Halifax to visit Berlin in the following month to sound out Hitler on his terms for a settlement. The Foreign Office opposed the visit and Eden was himself unhappy about it, fearing it would be interpreted by the Germans as a sign of weakness. He appears to have agreed to the initiative at least partly in the hope that Halifax would warn Hitler against the use of force in Central Europe.[42] Chamberlain, however, saw the

Halifax mission as the first stage in his 'far reaching plans' for a European settlement which would end the arms race and revive British trade.[43] At this point, therefore, Chamberlain, like Welles and Roosevelt, was seeking escape from the threatening international situation and the recession through the appeasement of Germany. It is ironic that Eden's alternative policy was based upon a misreading of American intentions which did not look towards any form of joint action in the Far East. Indeed Norman Davis, the chief American delegate to the Nine Power conference, was instructed by Roosevelt to warn Eden not to 'push the United States out in front at Brussels'.[44]

There was some confusion at the Brussels conference because both Eden and Davis were prepared to discuss courses of action not previously approved by their respective governments. Japan's refusal to attend, which ruined hopes of successful mediation, encouraged the tendency of both men to seek a more forceful solution to the problems of the Far East. Davis, a firm believer in Anglo-American cooperation, surrendered to this sentiment and made statements which horrified the rest of his delegation. As Moffat complained, 'Mr. Davis starts on the premise that the existence of the British Empire is essential for the national security of the United States'.[45] Davis was a victim of the confusion which surrounded Roosevelt's precise meaning in the 'quarantine' speech. He was convinced that the President planned joint action with Britain against Japan if a diplomatic solution did not emerge from the conference.[46] He had not been informed about the Welles plan and as a result based his actions on a totally false impression of thinking in Washington. While Davis imagined that the United States was moving towards greater involvement in the Far East, his country was in fact moving away from such a course and towards European appeasement. Eden was equally misled by the 'quarantine' speech which he imagined presaged a more active American role in Asia. As a consequence he made extravagant promises of support for American policy which he had not been empowered to give and discussed possible courses of action which were quite unacceptable to Chamberlain. By the end of the conference both men had embarrassed their governments.

Eden and Davis first met on 2 November 1937. Eden remarked that the more Britain examined the international situation 'the more she came to the conclusion that only by Great Britain and the United States standing shoulder to shoulder could the present threats be dispelled'. He assured Davis that Britain would be prepared to go as far as the United States in the Far East. This statement reflected Eden's speech of 1 November rather than cabinet opinion which had displayed a marked reluctance to become involved in the area even with American support. At this stage Davis resisted the temptation to exceed his instructions and replied that while Roosevelt was 'sincerely anxious to cooperate in an attempt to stop the rot' in the international situation, everything would depend on the reaction of American public opinion if mediation failed.[47] By 5 November, however, Davis was suggesting a joint boycott of Japanese goods as a means of bringing pressure to bear on Tokyo. Eden replied that

> This had been done in the case of Italy without success. There were two kinds of sanctions, effective and ineffective: to apply the latter was provocative and useless. . . . To apply the former meant some risk of war; we were prepared to examine this, but if so we must share the risks.

A mutual guarantee of possessions in the Pacific would be necessary if effective sanctions were to be imposed.[48] Eden must have realised that such an American guarantee of the Empire was impossible. One of his aims was to dissuade the Americans from pursuing the dangerous course of partial sanctions without guarantees which Britain would feel compelled to reject, thus damaging cordial relations. He probably hoped, however, by opening a broad discussion of the situation in the Far East, to steer the United States into some form of joint action short of sanctions, such as a naval demonstration in the Pacific. This would repeat the success of the Nyon patrol in curbing Italian action in the Mediterranean. The Americans had long suspected that this was Eden's aim in the Far East and indeed he later suggested it to Davis as the best form of pressure against Japan.[49]

When Eden returned to London on 8 November to report on progress at Brussels, he found Chamberlain intensely annoyed to learn that the subject of sanctions had been raised with the United States. The two men quarrelled over Eden's whole approach to foreign policy. Chamberlain rejected Eden's renewed demand for increased rearmament and accused the Foreign Office of never making a genuine effort to 'get together' with the dictators. He remarked that on 'no account' would he consider sanctions against

Japan and emphasised the restrictions placed on foreign policy by the economic situation.[50] Eden returned to Brussels the next day expressing doubts about Chamberlain's capacity as Prime Minister.[51] The quarrel seems to have brought home to him, for the first time, the emerging differences with Chamberlain over foreign policy. Despite the Prime Minister's marked distaste for any form of forceful action in the Far East, however, Eden continued to press for some tangible evidence of Anglo-American cooperation. At this next meeting with Davis he offered to send British warships to the Pacific as a show of force if the Americans thought sanctions impracticable.[52] The Foreign Secretary was thinking as much of Europe as of the Far East when he made this suggestion. Italy joined the Anti-Comintern Pact on 6 November 1937. The Germans then demanded a public acknowledgement that the initiative for the Halifax mission had come from London. Eden felt this would look 'almost like a Canossa'. The Germans would think that Britain was 'running after' them as a result of the extension of the Anti-Comintern Pact.[53] A strong Anglo-American stand against Japan in the form of a naval demonstration would balance the apparent weakness of the Halifax mission and show that Britain could not be blackmailed by the extended axis. At this stage, therefore, Prime Minister and Foreign Secretary were pursuing diverging policies.

In the event, however, no dramatic action was initiated before the conference broke up on 15 November. The Welles plan was not launched on armistice day as previously planned. One reason appears to have been that the United States was awaiting the results of the Halifax mission. Welles had originally conceived his scheme, at least partly, as a means of pressing Britain into action rather than allowing Europe to drift into war,[54] but now Chamberlain had taken the initiative. As Berle noted, the aims of the plan had changed. Welles' goal 'now was to try to put . . . a seal on the political solutions . . . worked out in Paris, London and Berlin'.[55] Britain would assume the main burden of dividing the strengthened axis, while Welles held his scheme in reserve to ensure that the United States had a voice in the economic aspects of any European settlement which emerged. Welles may also have felt that public opinion was not at this stage in favour of an American initiative, particularly an initiative which appeared to involve cooperation with Britain. Eden's actions at Brussels had allowed the Hearst press to claim that Britain was manoeuvring the United States into the defence of the Empire, a view shared by some members of the

American delegation.[56] If Welles had his own reasons for postponing his plan, others, such as Hull, had definitely turned against it in the light of the extended Anti-Comintern Pact and German and Italian support for Japan's position in China. According to Welles, by November 1937, certain of Roosevelt's 'closest advisers' were 'hysterically opposed' to his project.[57] In this situation, with his administration divided and public opinion opposed to any form of American action, the President decided to await events. The United States would neither launch an initiative nor respond to British pressure at Brussels. The Welles plan was shelved and Davis' controversial conduct at the conference curbed. On 13 November, to his disappointment and disgust, Davis was instructed to initiate 'nothing more than platitudes' since the administration did not 'wish this conference at least to take any positive steps'.[58] Simultaneously the British ambassador in Washington was informed that Davis' speculations about future policy 'could in no sense be construed as implying that this Government was prepared to take the action which was discussed'. The United States did not believe that questions of economic sanctions or fleet movements should 'be considered at this time'.[59] The Brussels conference, therefore, ended with the inoffensive resolution desired by all the powers except China and did not lead to firmer action against Japan.

The 'quarantine' speech and the Brussels conference had an important effect on future Anglo-American relations. Chamberlain was irritated by the speech which seemed to threaten his own policy of appeasement. He was appalled by the behaviour of the Americans at the conference and drew the conclusion that events had displayed 'the difficulty of securing effective cooperation from the United States of America'.[60] The Prime Minister's attitude had undergone a change since the outbreak of the China incident when he had appeared to hope that cooperation might prove possible in the Far East where American interests were directly involved. Chamberlain's disappointment with American policy in China helps explain why he rejected Roosevelt's peace initiative when it was eventually launched in January 1938: If the United States would not cooperate in an area where its interests were directly involved, were the Americans capable of sustained intervention in Europe? Chamberlain concluded that they were not and that Roosevelt was unreliable. It was 'always best and safest to count on *nothing* from the Americans except words'.[61] By contrast, Eden had not abandoned hope of close cooperation. He believed that although the conference had produced 'inglorious' results, there had been encouraging features. 'Cordial relations and complete cooperation' had been maintained with the American delegation. 'The door had been kept open for some possible future initiative by the United States and ourselves with a view to securing peace'.[62] The differing reactions of the two men to events in October and November 1937 displayed the first signs of the breach which was to result in Eden's resignation two months later. Indeed only the American decision to postpone the Welles plan and to avoid any action in the Far East averted a rupture at an earlier stage.

4 The *Panay* Crisis

After the Brussels conference a new element entered American diplomacy. The President increasingly abandoned a policy of appeasement in favour of a show of strength and placed more emphasis on deterring 'extremists' than on encouraging 'moderates'. The reason for this change was the tripartite Anti-Comintern Pact of November 1937 which Roosevelt believed was an instrument of world conquest, threatening American interests in Europe and Asia. In response he announced the formal opening of Anglo-American trade negotiations as the 'democratic answer' to the new axis while simultaneously rejecting Italian demands for an economic agreement. He also supported increased naval rearmament as the only means of securing respect from the 'bandit' nations. American public opinion, however, would not allow Roosevelt to go beyond these relatively innocuous moves until the sinking of the *USS Panay* on the Yangtse river by Japanese warplanes in December 1937. This incident offered the President an opportunity to implement the warning contained in the 'quarantine' speech and to show the axis powers that there was a point beyond which the 'democracies' would not allow them to go. Roosevelt hoped to make an example of Japan and deter Germany and Italy from pursuing similar courses of expansion. While this new policy did not preclude the Welles approach, with which it could be combined, the President was clearly placing more emphasis on deterrence rather than conciliation after November 1937.

The tripartite Anti-Comintern Pact of November 1937 aroused considerable anxiety in the United States, since it was assumed to be more than a simple expression of anti-communism. Ciano's 'frank' denial that it contained any secret clauses was received sceptically by the American ambassador in Rome who noted: 'This was one of his pet remarks which always roused my suspicions.'[1] The French believed that the treaty delimited axis spheres of influence and 'almost guaranteed Germany control of Austria and Czechoslovakia'.[2] Roosevelt shared this view. He suspected that the pact constituted 'a secret offensive and defensive alliance between Japan, Germany and Italy'. It contained clauses granting Germany domination in Central Europe, Italy domination in the Mediterranean and Japan domination in the Far East.[3] The President, therefore, saw the pact as the formal expression of a totalitarian conspiracy aimed at world conquest. For this reason the axis was as much a danger to American as to British security. Since both were 'satisfied' powers, any grouping of 'have-nots' was bound to be viewed as a threat. In fact the pact never amounted to more than a vague expression of anti-communism, despite Ribbentrop's later attempts to convert it into a firm alliance. It was not the instrument of world domination feared by Roosevelt.[4] At the time, however, it appeared a menace, if only because the axis powers had in the past used a wide interpretation of 'anti-communism' to excuse acts of aggression. Anti-communism was the excuse for Italo-German intervention in Spain and for Japanese expansion in Asia.[5] The previous record of the 'bandit' nations, therefore, gave Roosevelt every reason for suspicion about the nature of the Anti-Comintern Pact.

Roosevelt chose to reply to the pact with an expression of democratic solidarity in an area where the inhibitions caused by public opinion did not apply: economic cooperation. In response to a British initiative it was announced that trade negotiations had begun. Eden, like Roosevelt, was disturbed by the failure of the Brussels conference and the signature of the pact. He therefore desired the announcement of trade negotiations as a matter of urgency. Chamberlain also favoured such action since it would have 'a steadying effect' on the international situation, replying to the 'Berlin-Rome-Tokyo axis' without leading to a confrontation with the dictators.[6] On 16 November Lindsay, the British ambassador in Washington, informed Hull that the announcement of trade talks would balance the definite setback to the orderly conduct of international affairs experienced at Brussels 'and hold out the prospect of further, stronger and more fruitful Anglo-American cooperation in the future'. Britain, therefore, was anxious to 'join Brussels failure to trade agreement success and . . . frankly to lend political importance to the latter'.[7] This appeal found a ready response and talks were announced on 20 November. In contrast to Anglo-American economic cooperation, negotiations for an Italo-American trade treaty were suspended as an expression of disapproval of recent Italian policy. Phillips had been anxious to secure an agreement. On 19 November, however, Sayre of the

Trade Division wrote to him expressing Hull's views on the subject. Sayre remarked that the international situation had recently 'been the cause of grave concern to the Secretary. A few days ago . . . he told me that in view of the existing international situation . . . it would be unwise to bind our hand by entering into a treaty with Italy.' The administration understood Phillips' desire 'not to drive Italy into the camp of Germany and Japan. Yet we believe that these three countries are even now tied together as closely as possible.'[8]

Outside the economic sphere, which offered America the opportunity to reward friends and punish enemies, Roosevelt looked to increased naval building to deter the axis from expansionist designs. The idea was first put forward at a cabinet meeting in early December. According to Ickes, both Hull and Roosevelt believed that a strong navy was 'the only way to hold proper respect from the bandit nations'. The President planned to ask Congress for two battleships in his annual message and then 'for the psychological effect, later to send in a special message asking for a third one'.[9] The President perhaps believed that increased rearmament would have a 'psychological effect' on public opinion as well as on the 'bandit' nations, awakening it to the dangers of axis expansion. Roosevelt certainly acted on his statements to the cabinet. On 28 December 1937 he sent a letter to the House Appropriations Committee warning it that because of the threatening world situation he might demand an increased naval budget.[10]

There were also moves to establish secret naval contacts with Britain. On 28 November Admiral Leahy, the Chief of Naval operations, discussed the international situation with Hull. Leahy noted: 'A decision was reached that I should have a completely informal unofficial talk with the British naval attaché about the possibility of a naval demonstration in Asiatic waters by European Powers.'[11] Leahy was interested in cooperation with other powers because the Anti-Comintern Pact challenged the basis of American naval strategy, which assumed that Japan would be without allies in the event of a war in the Pacific.[12] Hull had believed that a demonstration of naval power might be the best way to curb Japan and to deter its allies as early as September 1937. He obviously wished to follow up Eden's hints at the Brussels conference and to ascertain if the British were seriously considering a redeployment of their fleet to the Far East. It appears likely that the success of the

Nyon patrol, which had apparently curbed Italy without war, had as great an effect on Hull as on Eden.

The American decision to initiate naval contacts coincided with a British approach on the same subject. In the period after the Brussels conference relations between Eden and Chamberlain became more cordial, because the Prime Minister seemed to take into account the arguments put forward in the Llandudno speech about the necessity of cultivating friends as well as possible enemies. Eden was not hindered in his attempts to secure Anglo-American cooperation in the Far East. On 24 November the Cabinet discussed an Anglo-Japanese dispute about the customs at Tientsin and Eden pressed for naval staff talks with the Americans. He remarked that there might come a time when Britain would 'have to approach the United States and ask if they would send ships to the Far East if we would do the same'. Chamberlain consented to an enquiry in Washington but he did not believe that the Americans would agree to talks.[13] While staff contacts with the United States would be a useful precaution lest Japan go too far in attacking British interests, the Prime Minister remained anxious to avoid a confrontation with Tokyo. On 8 December 1937, he expressed the hope that the possibility of negotiations with Japan could be 'kept open'.[14] Chamberlain believed that it was better to divide the axis than to put pressure on Tokyo, a dangerous policy which might involve Britain in a war with Japan. He continued to place the main emphasis on Europe and still believed that Britain's economic and strategic problems could best be solved by appeasement of Germany. The results of Halifax's talk with Hitler convinced him that a settlement based on colonial concessions and qualitative limitation of armaments was possible. The Prime Minister planned to discuss the question with both his colleagues and the French in the near future.[15] Chamberlain was convinced that the British economic situation demanded such a solution in the light of the new recession. On 22 December the Cabinet 'took note' that the financial limitations on rearmament demanded a fresh approach to Germany and Italy.[16] Simultaneously British defence policy was remodelled to keep expenditure within acceptable limits. The army was relieved of its continental role and the expensive commitment of five divisions to France. Priority in air production was to be given to fighters rather than bombers.[17] Eden had clearly lost the battle to remove financial restrictions from the rearmament programme which followed the creation of the tripartite axis and the Llandudno speech. Foreign and defence policy were to be strictly tailored to economic necessity. The Foreign Secretary was unhappy about the reduction of the military commitment to France and concentration on the defensive in the air, but he deferred to the arguments of his colleagues.[18] In the absence of a greater rearmament programme, Eden was left with the empty form of the Llandudno speech, consultation with France and the United States, which was regarded by Chamberlain as harmless since it was unlikely to produce concrete results and which reduced Eden's obstruction of his own policy.

As Chamberlain had predicted, the approaches on naval cooperation ended inconclusively. Hull was evasive when Lindsay raised the possibility of staff talks on 30 November. Although personally in favour of military contacts with Britain, he emphasised the grave dangers of an adverse public reaction if news of staff talks leaked out and refused to make any definite commitment.[19] On the same day Leahy reported the results of his talk with the British naval attaché. The attaché had informed Leahy that he knew nothing about any plans for a demonstration of British naval power in the Far East. He would, however, always be available for talks with the American Navy about the strategic situation.[20] On 3 December 1937, Leahy learned about Lindsay's conversation with Hull. Perhaps in deference to the Secretary's fear of public opinion, the Admiral concluded that nothing more could be done about naval contacts until 'further developments' occurred 'in the Orient'.[21]

The trade treaty negotiations, the decision on rearmament and the unofficial naval talks with Britain, all reflected Roosevelt's growing pessimism about the prospects of successful appeasement following the tripartite Anti-Comintern Pact. This feeling, however, was not universal and the administration was divided between 'pessimists' and 'optimists'. Among the former were Roosevelt, Hull and Leahy, among the latter Welles and Bullitt. Both Welles and Bullitt continued to believe that a European settlement was possible. On 23 November 1937, Bullitt recommended that Roosevelt use his influence with Germany to promote peace.[22] Welles continued to work on his project for a new 'Congress of Berlin' which would transform the existing international economic and legal system. He appears to have been encouraged by Hitler's remarks to Halifax about the necessity for arms limitation and statements by Dieckhoff that Germany desired to conclude a liberal trade agreement with the United States.[23] The pessimism of Hull and Roosevelt, however, ensured that the Welles plan remained shelved. The President was convinced that it was impossible to negotiate with Hitler. On 8 December 1937, he informed Joseph E. Davies that 'It was perfectly clear there was no possibility of doing anything to divert the forces in Germany which, under Hitler's concepts of world domination and conquest, were driving inevitably to war.' In these circumstances there was no point in sending Davies to Berlin as Roosevelt's personal representative when Dodd retired. The Berlin post should be 'distinctly formal for conventional representation only' and Davies should go instead to Brussels, the best 'listening post' in Europe.[24] At this point the President, unlike Welles, obviously believed that the 'extremists' were in complete control of Germany. Although Roosevelt feared axis plans for world domination, public opinion would not allow him to take strong action against the 'bandit' nations until they struck directly at the United States. Such an incident occurred on 12 December 1937 when Japanese aircraft sank the American gunboat *Panay* on the Yangtse river. Simultaneously the British warship *Ladybird* was shelled by Japanese artillery. This attack seemed to give Roosevelt an opportunity to implement the warning implicit in the 'quarantine' speech and to take strong action against Japan. He was careful, however, not to outrun public opinion and was anxious to let Britain set the pace. This rapidly became evident in the first Anglo-American exchanges about the incidents on the Yangtse.

Eden immediately seized upon the attacks as an opportunity for Anglo-American cooperation in the Far East which might halt the Japanese advance and impress the European axis with a display of democratic strength. He interviewed the American chargé on 13 December and pointed out that some action would have to be taken against the Japanese. He suggested that Britain and the United States should send similar notes to Tokyo and promised that if America mobilised the fleet, Britain would do likewise.[25] Lindsay repeated this offer directly to Welles the same day. Welles welcomed Britain's readiness to associate itself with a stiff note, but made no direct response on the naval question.[26] That afternoon the American chargé informed Cadogan that Grew already had a note for the Japanese government. The British ambassador in Tokyo would be shown the text, but Grew had been instructed to deliver his protest without waiting for the British note.[27] In the evening

Welles explained to Lindsay that this had been done to forestall a Japanese apology.[28]

Eden did not stop pressing for action despite this initial rebuff. On 14 December, Lindsay informed Hull about Eden's disappointment with the American attitude. The Foreign Secretary felt that there should be 'joint action in such a serious and critical situation'. A display of the 'possibilities of force on a large scale' was necessary to curb the Japanese. Lindsay was obviously referring to some form of naval mobilisation. Hull agreed that the situation was dangerous, but claimed that the difficulty was to bring public opinion to a point 'where the fleet could be moved without panic'. Roosevelt also realised the dangers of the situation and might deliver 'another address on foreign affairs' in the course of the month.[29] The President felt inhibited by public opinion. Roosevelt feared that if he made any move which seemed belligerent the isolationists might whip up a campaign against him. At this stage the Americans did not know for certain whether the sinking had been deliberate or accidental because the report of the *Panay* survivors was not received until 16 December.[30]

Public opinion might react to any action, such as a joint protest with Britain, which appeared to prejudge the issue. The administration had no intention of being pushed into hasty action by Eden. The American note was, therefore, milder than the British and reflected uncertainty about the incident by failing to demand the punishment of the officers involved.[31] Roosevelt nevertheless suspected that the attack had been deliberate and made some preliminary moves lest public opinion developed in favour of strong action. On 14 December, he informed Morgenthau that there were 'lots of ways of declaring war. In the old days the sinking itself would have been a cause for war.' Roosevelt asked Morgenthau to find out what authority was required to confiscate Japanese assets in the United States as compensation for the outrage.[32] The President, however, would go no further and rejected Leahy's requests for naval mobilisation. He informed the Admiral on 13 December that he was 'not prepared to take that action at the present time'.[33]

The British Cabinet discussed the American attitude on 15 December. A telegram to Washington had been prepared the previous day requesting staff conversations and raising the possibility of despatching part of the British fleet to the Far East. Chamberlain, however, was clearly reluctant to become involved in possible hostilities with Japan and suggested that joint naval mobilisation should be put forward to the Americans as a possible alternative. This would give weight to diplomatic protests about Japanese actions. In the light of the American attitude both Eden and Chamberlain were 'very dubious' whether Roosevelt would even agree to mobilise the fleet. Eden informed his colleagues that the administration did not want to be pressed into action because of public opinion. It was finally agreed to consult Lindsay about the form of an approach to Washington.[34] After the Cabinet meeting a telegram was sent to Lindsay which reflected British uncertainty about the American position. The ambassador was informed that he could suggest joint naval mobilisation or offer a British naval contribution to the Far East if he felt it advisable.[35] The situation became more hopeful that evening when Lindsay reported that Roosevelt wished to interview him on 17 December about initiating secret naval talks. The ambassador informed Eden that in the absence of instructions to the contrary he would use his discretion and offer a British naval contribution to the Far East.[36] The Foreign Secretary immediately asked Lindsay to press for firm action when he saw the President. He should

> talk along the line that the democracies have to meet strong criticism of inaction and helplessness and that it seems to us the time to restore our damaged prestige. Firm action would have its effect not only in the Far East but in Europe and would give notice to the Dictators that Democratic governments are as jealous of their authority as they are and as willing to defend it.

Close Anglo-American cooperation was the best way to ensure peace 'without a shot being fired'.[37]

At this point Roosevelt appeared to be contemplating strong action along the lines advocated by Eden. On 16 December, the report of the *Panay* survivors arrived in Washington. It stated that the Japanese attack had been deliberate and that the lifeboats had been attacked after the sinking.[38] The American attitude immediately hardened. The administration now felt that public opinion would support a stronger line. A second note was sent to Tokyo, this time demanding punishment of the officers responsible for the sinking and asking what Japan intended to do in future to safeguard American interests in China. Grew presented this note to Hirota on 17 December.[39] The same day Lindsay reported that the American attitude was 'much stiffened' as a result of publication of the facts of the sinking. He suspected, however, that any swing away from isolationism would be purely temporary.[40] Roosevelt was much more confident than Lindsay that public opinion would support strong action. He hoped to make an example of Japan if Tokyo made no satisfactory apology for the *Panay* sinking. He informed the Cabinet on 17 December that he was considering economic retaliation against Japan. He envisaged a joint naval blockade with Britain, France and Holland.[41] On 18 December, Roosevelt informed Morgenthau that he desired to ascertain the real purpose of the Japanese. Morgenthau noted 'He wants to see how sharp their teeth are and what's their real feeling towards us. He feels that this is the time to do it . . . and the way to do it is to be extremely stiff at this time.'[42] The President meant that by demanding compensation and punishment of the officers who bombed the *Panay* he was challenging Japan to risk confrontation with the United States. If Tokyo was not prepared to make suitable amends, Roosevelt would take action against Japan before its axis partners were materially prepared to support their ally.[43] At this stage the President suspected that even if Japan met American demands there would soon be another incident, necessitating strong measures on the part of the United States.[44]

After Cabinet on 17 December, Morgenthau, on Roosevelt's instructions, telephoned Simon, the British Chancellor of the Exchequer, to sound out the British attitude towards sanctions. Simon was too cautious to commit himself on the telephone. He remembered the misunderstandings caused by a similar telephone conversation with Stimson during the Manchurian crisis. Morgenthau then sent Simon a telegram informing him that Roosevelt was sending a naval officer to London for staff talks who would have full power to discuss sanctions.[45] These staff talks were arranged at a meeting between Roosevelt and Lindsay on 17 December. Roosevelt stated that he wanted a secret exchange of naval information, as between 1915 and 1917. Talks should take place in London rather than in Washington, where a secret was impossible to keep. The President remarked that the first object of staff talks should be to arrange a blockade of Japan. This would be imposed at the next Japanese outrage and would bring Tokyo to terms without war. Lindsay was 'horrified' at this remark and suggested joint mobilisation instead. The President argued that would have no effect on the Japanese military 'extremists' but agreed as an interim measure to advance the date of American naval manoeuvres and to send a cruiser squadron to visit Singapore. He terminated the interview by claiming that eighty per cent of his mail was anti-Japanese. Even the Mid-West favoured firm measures. Lindsay urged Eden to give close consideration to Roosevelt's remarks, even though they might sound like 'the utterances of an amateur strategist'.[46]

The British Cabinet discussed Lindsay's message on 22 December. Eden was obviously pleased by developments in Washington. He informed his colleagues that Roosevelt favoured Anglo-American cooperation in the Far East. The idea of joint naval mobilisation had not appealed to the President, but he had talked about blockading Japan at the next incident. For the moment he was prepared to open staff talks and to advance the date of the American fleet manoeuvres, perhaps sending some cruisers to visit the British naval base at Singapore. Eden welcomed Roosevelt's proposals, although he would have preferred immediate action to deter another incident. Chamberlain welcomed the idea of an American naval visit to Singapore because he felt that this might deter the Japanese, but he was seriously alarmed by Roosevelt's vague remarks about military and economic sanctions at the next anti-Western outrage. He remarked that 'Our difficulty was not in President Roosevelt's goodwill but in his failure to appreciate the needs of the situations.' The President seemed to be under the illusion that sanctions could be imposed without the risk of war. Chamberlain did not share this view and hoped that staff talks would bring home to the Americans 'the realities of the strategical situation'. Although he recognised that Western prestige was suffering in China, he felt that 'except in the event of a serious aggression by the Japanese . . . it would be a mistake for us to send ships to the Far East'.[47] The Prime Minister clearly continued to feel that any weakening of British forces in Europe would encourage the dictators to achieve their aims by force. Moreover he remained suspicious that Roosevelt might force him into a joint Anglo-American confrontation with Japan only to back down under isolationist pressure, leaving Britain to face the unpleasant consequences alone. He did not share the President's optimism about the development of American opinion against the axis.[48]

Washington was informed about Chamberlain's attitude towards sanctions before staff talks had even begun. On 21 December 1937, Simon sent a message to Morgenthau emphasising that long range economic pressure on Japan would not produce immediate results and that short-term pressure was 'indistinguishable from other forceful devices'. The message implied that Britain did not feel 'forceful devices' would be in order. Morgenthau concluded that Chamberlain had 'tactfully said no'.[49] Roosevelt at first talked about going ahead alone 'with exchange control etc. against Japan' if he did not receive a satisfactory answer to his demand for an apology and compensation.[50] Japan, however, met these terms on 23 December, thus ruling out sanctions or a naval demonstration in the near future. Public opinion was satisfied with the apology. The isolationists in any case, far from being converted as Roosevelt had hoped, used the *Panay* crisis to press for a complete American withdrawal from China and public control of foreign policy. The 'Ludlow Amendment' was introduced in Congress, which called for a plebiscite before the President could declare war. It was defeated in January 1938 by the narrow margin of twenty votes.[51] Any form of cooperation with Britain in the Far East, or apparently belligerent move would only have increased support for the isolationists and harmed the President.

Roosevelt nevertheless continued to toy with the idea of putting pressure on Japan in the future. He was convinced that the Japanese might soon commit another outrage which would make public opinion demand retaliation. This feeling was shared by his ambassadors in Japan and China. Grew noted that the future of American-Japanese relations was not 'by any means serene . . . the danger of further incidents is very great and . . . the patience of the American people cannot be expected to last permanently'. He kept his private papers packed 'in case we have to leave Japan suddenly' and remarked, 'I do not think that such a contingency is by any means unlikely'.[52] Johnson, in Nanking, noted that the Japanese were still attacking ships which contained Western refugees. 'Unless the Japs can be made to realise that these ships are the only refuge available to Americans and other foreigners, a terrible disaster is liable to happen.'[53] Despite the Japanese apology in the *Panay* case, therefore, Roosevelt sent a naval officer to London to initiate staff contacts. The 'anti-appeasers' saw in this move the beginnings of coordinated Anglo-American action against the axis. Hull believed that Japan was growing increasingly 'desperate and dangerous' and that Tokyo was working in close association with Berlin and Rome. Britain and the United States, therefore, should cooperate against Japan in the Far East while coordinating their economic and monetary policies in Europe to face Germany and Italy with their combined strength. Hull was obviously thinking of some form of naval demonstration in the Pacific, coupled with a policy of leaving the European axis to 'stew in its own juice'.[54] He had moved a long way from his previous position under the impact of the China incident and the tripartite Anti-Comintern Pact. Messersmith, now less isolated than in the earlier part of 1937, renewed his arguments for a firm line against the axis powers. He emphasised that Japan had invaded China 'as a result of understandings with Germany'. The United States must reply by cooperating with Britain in both the Far East and Europe, bringing economic and financial pressure to bear on the 'bandit' nations.[55] The 'anti-appeasers', therefore, hoped for the emergence of an Anglo-American power bloc as a counterweight to the Anti-Comintern Pact. Indeed Messersmith went further and argued for the establishment of closer relations with the Soviet Union which he believed, was a power factor in both Europe and the Far East that the United States could not afford to ignore.[56] The 'anti-appeasers' based their hopes of a more active American role in international affairs on the possibility of the development of public opinion against the axis, perhaps as the result of further Japanese outrages in China.[57]

An American naval representative, Captain Ingersoll, visited London secretly in January 1938 to hold staff talks with the Admiralty. The conversations produced an informal agreement on joint action in the event of a war with Japan. Britain would base its main fleet at Singapore, while America would station its warships at Pearl Harbor. Each navy could operate freely in the territorial waters of the other. The conference 'took note' of the problem which would be posed by a hostile Germany. The only immediate results of the conference were an exchange of information on naval building programmes and a visit by some American cruisers to Singapore when the new naval base opened there in March 1938.[58] Roosevelt made a parallel move to establish contact with the Soviet Union. In January 1938, Davies was instructed:

> to explore the possibility of securing a liaison between the military and naval authorities of the United States and the Soviet Union with a view to the inter-change of information as to . . . the military and naval situations of the United States and the Soviet Union vis-à-vis Japan and the general Far Eastern and Pacific problem.[59]

This approach was clearly provoked by the increasing tension with Japan and the knowledge that the USSR planned to strengthen its Pacific fleet based at Vladivostock. At the beginning of 1938, the Soviet government had announced its intention of building a fleet 'second to none'.[60] Stalin and Molotov displayed considerable interest in the American initiative but it was never followed up by Roosevelt.[61] On 10 January 1938, the President swung away from the idea of curbing the axis by pressure against Japan and readopted the idea of isolating Japan and dissolving the Anti-Comintern Pact by appeasing Germany and Italy. His adoption of this course aroused the opposition of the 'anti-appeasers' within the administration who felt that the plans laid during the *Panay* crisis were being undermined. It also caused a crisis in Anglo-American relations and brought to a head the differences between Eden and Chamberlain which had been building up since the outbreak of the China incident.

5 The American Peace Initiative

On 10 January 1938 Sumner Welles again presented his appeasement plan to Roosevelt. It was a more elaborate version of the scheme proposed in October 1937. The President was to consult the other powers about their attitude towards a world conference which would establish new rules of international conduct, discuss arms limitation and consider the questions of tariff reduction and equal access to raw materials. If the answers were favourable, Roosevelt would call representatives of the American republics and the smaller European nations to Washington, where they would draw up international agreements on these subjects. The agreements would then be sent to the other powers for ratification. Welles hoped that the American initiative would give an impetus to British negotiations with Germany and Italy. The United States would act as a 'channel of information' between both sets of discussions.[1] Welles was leaving political negotiations in the hands of Britain, while guaranteeing the United States a major role in remodelling the world economy. As the greatest power in a group of 'disinterested' nations meeting in Washington, America would inevitably enjoy the predominant influence over any agreements which emerged. The Welles plan took account of 'economic realities'[2] by reducing barriers to American trade, thus offering the administration an escape from the continuing recession. It would encourage Germany to abandon autarky and to withdraw its support of Japan, forcing Tokyo to conclude a 'just' peace with China. Moreover it would ensure that Anglo-German negotiations did not produce an economic settlement which benefited Britain to the exclusion of the United States. As in October 1937, therefore, the ultimate aim was to prevent the establishment of a Closed Door system in both Europe and Asia, replacing it with a world economic order favourable to American interests.

Welles believed that his appeasement scheme would prove more acceptable to public opinion than the formation of an Anglo-American front against the axis, involving the use of economic pressure and perhaps a naval demonstration in the Far East to curb the 'bandit' nations.[3] He complained that the 'anti-appeasers' did not take account of the 'political realities' of the situation. Moreover they ignored the 'economic realities' produced by the Depression[4] which set definite limits on American policy and dictated a world settlement. Unlike the 'anti-appeasers' Welles did not accept that the 'extremists' were in complete control of Germany and that nothing could, therefore, be done to meet German grievances. He felt that the army in particular remained a powerful force for peace and that Hitler would not dare to ignore his generals.[5] If he did so he would risk a coup which might topple his regime. This estimate was supported by information from both the American embassy in Berlin and from neutral sources. Smith, the military attaché in Germany, reported on 30 December 1937 that the 'Prussian Army . . . is the only force in modern Germany which has not been sufficiently absorbed by the Nazi Party' to guarantee Hitler complete control. It supported the policies of the regime only because it believed that Germany was threatened and besieged.[6] Moffat noted on 5 January 1938 that, according to the Hungarian minister, the German army

> had more power today than ever before and that it had about reached the point where it no longer needed the Party. If at any time the Party should try to force the hands of the Army, he believed it not impossible that the Army would 'have matters out'.[7]

It was hoped that the masses and the business community would support the army if it brought pressure to bear in favour of a settlement because of the widespread discontent caused by intensification of the Four Year Plan under Göring.[8] There were those in the administration who were prepared to follow Welles and gamble on forcing Hitler's hand. Berle, an Assistant Secretary involved in drafting the appeasement plan, remarked on 7 February 1938 that he supported the Welles scheme rather than the alternative put forward by Hull and the 'anti-appeasers':

> There are dangers either way, but I think less by following Sumner's plan than by taking the Secretary's view . . . There

might be implied out of the latter policy some kind of an alliance which might lead to our participation in a new war.[9]

Others, however, backed Hull in his opposition to a 'general negotiation' with the European axis.[10] Messersmith argued that appeasement could only strengthen the Nazi regime and weaken the forces of opposition. Hitler would give 'assurances' in return for assistance, but would not alter the basic structure of the totalitarian state or abandon his expansionist designs. Only by maintaining a firm stand would the United States encourage those 'good Germans' who desired peace, stability and the restoration of international trade.[11]

Roosevelt accepted Welles' recommendations. It might seem strange that the President should have supported the scheme in view of his earlier statements to Joseph E. Davies about the possibilities of a settlement. Roosevelt perhaps believed that the Anglo-American trade negotiations and the firm line adopted towards Japan during the *Panay* crisis had displayed democratic strength and deterred the dictators. Appeasement would, therefore, seem to be a concession from strength rather than an admission of weakness which would only encourage Hitler to increase his demands. The Welles plan was accompanied by a campaign for American rearmament designed to further this impression. The President's message to Congress on 3 January 1938 contained a condemnation of totalitarian governments and a demand for increased defence spending.[12] Acting on this speech, Roosevelt requested a large increase in the naval budget on 28 January.[13] He may reasonably have assumed that since everything had been done to deter the German 'extremists', a final attempt might be made to build up the 'moderates' and to tap the discontent of the German masses. Moreover the President was as well aware of the political and economic realities as Welles. By the beginning of January 1938 he must have realised that the policy of the 'anti-appeasers' would be at best unpopular and could do nothing towards alleviating the economic recession. By contrast the Welles plan was rooted in a policy of peace and neutrality which would appeal to the public and might succeed in reviving the world economy. Roosevelt, therefore, retreated from the position adopted during the *Panay* crisis, which had favoured Hull's ideas, and encouraged Welles and the appeasers in the administration.

Roosevelt adopted the Welles plan with the proviso that Chamberlain should be informed in advance. This may have been due to Hull's insistence that it would be 'unwise and unfair' to spring the plan on Britain.[14] Yet the President had been prepared to act without consultation in November 1937 despite such advice. He may have believed that the British were less likely to object to an American initiative in January 1938 than in November 1937. Chamberlain had always insisted that the grounds for a settlement with Germany must be sounded out before any wider appeasemnt scheme was discussed. When the Welles plan was first under consideration there had been no Anglo-German exchange of views on the subject of a European settlement. The Halifax mission, however, had explored issues such as colonial compensation and Roosevelt may have hoped that Chamberlain would no longer object strongly to American intervention because progress had been made towards ascertaining German demands. By informing the Prime Minister in advance, the President hoped to avoid the confusion which might follow unilateral action and to coordinate American and British appeasement plans.

On 11 January 1938 Welles interviewed Lindsay and informed him of American intentions. He emphasised that his plan would constitute 'valuable parallel action' to Anglo-German negotiations. Disarmament would not be emphasised in order to spare Britain any embarrassment on this subject. Public opinion would support American action provided it was limited to economic appeasement and arms limitation. If Chamberlain did not express 'cordial and wholehearted support' for the scheme within five days, Roosevelt would abandon it.[15] Lindsay was enthusiastic about the plan and on 12 January urged London to welcome American action.[16] The Foreign Office agreed with his recommendations. Eden was absent in France but Cadogan, the leading permanent official, forwarded the ambassador's message to Chamberlain with a covering note advising close cooperation with the United States. Cadogan believed that Roosevelt's 'readiness to enter the arena' was a 'fact of the first importance'. Britain should not risk alienating the President by rejecting the American plan.[17] Chamberlain, however, did not agree. He was about to begin his own negotiations with Germany and Italy, bargaining colonial concessions and *de jure* recognition of the Italian position in Abyssinia, against arms limitation and a political settlement in Europe. The Prime Minister was being forced towards appeasement by a combination of economic and strategic factors. By the end of 1937 the worsening recession had created a balance of payments deficit of £56 million.

Armaments were a 'grievous burden' and on 22 December 1937 the Cabinet 'took note' that financial limitations on rearmament necessitated following up the Halifax mission as soon as possible.[18] Chamberlain believed that a European settlement would ease the strain on the British economy by ending the arms race and reintegrating Germany into the world trading system. As his Chancellor of the Exchequer, Simon, remarked, an indefinite arms race would have 'appalling' financial consequences and was 'no substitute for political appeasement which is the only real basis of peace'.[19] Moreover appeasing Germany and Italy would avert the threat to the Empire posed by a world triangle of 'dissatisfied' powers. As Chamberlain argued, a European settlement was imperative with 'the Japs . . . getting more and more insolent and brutal'.[20] The Prime Minister feared that Roosevelt's 'preposterous' scheme would ruin his own approach to European problems. The dictators would only be 'frozen off' by the 'vague propositions' in the American plan.[21] Hitler and Mussolini would either be repelled by the idea of accepting recommendations drawn up by the smaller powers meeting Washington, or would inflate their claims and attempt to play off the United States against Britain. Moreover there was no guarantee that American public opinion would support Roosevelt if Britain encouraged the President to launch his initiative. The isolationists might force him to abandon the whole idea once it was made official. The experience of American policy in the Far East had encouraged the Prime Minister to expect such erratic conduct.[22] At worst, therefore, the dictators would be alienated, Chamberlain's own approach ruined and Britain left facing three enemies simultaneously without American support. The Prime Minister was not prepared to gamble British security against the uncertain reaction of the dictators and the American public to Roosevelt's 'ill prepared' proposal.[23]

Chamberlain rejected Roosevelt's scheme without consulting Eden who was visiting France. The British reply, despatched on 13 January, stated that the American plan would 'cut across' Chamberlain's own efforts to reach a settlement. Britain planned to reach an early agreement with Italy involving recognition of the Italian position in Abyssinia. It was also hoped to open the colonial question with Germany. Chamberlain was optimistic about the prospects of success in both sets of negotiations.[24] Cadogan tried to soften the blow of this rejection by stating that if Roosevelt wished to continue with his plan despite this explanation of the British position, London would support the American initiative. Chamberlain struck this passage from the final copy of the telegram.[25] In his own defence the Prime Minister argued that it was impossible to consult Eden about the American scheme. He excused his conduct on the grounds that to telephone Eden in France would be to jeopardise the secrecy requested by Roosevelt.[26] Eden was to have talks with Delbos on 16 January and could not be recalled without arousing speculation. Yet Chamberlain might have requested Roosevelt to accept a short postponement until Eden returned to London and could be consulted. The truth seems to be that the Prime Minister wanted the American initiative killed off as quickly as possible before it came to Eden's knowledge. Chamberlain suspected that the Foreign Office was not really behind his policy of seeking a settlement with the dictators and feared that Eden might drag in the American scheme to sidetrack his own approach. This was precisely what occurred when Eden returned.

On 14 January 1938, the day the British rejection was delivered in Washington, Eden was recalled from France. The excuse that this would cause speculation was no longer valid because the Delbos government had fallen and Anglo-French talks were postponed. Cadogan and Harvey, Eden's Private Secretary, hoped that the Foreign Secretary could persuade Chamberlain to revise his attitude towards the American scheme. Harvey drew up a memorandum for Eden which seems to confirm Chamberlain's worst suspicions about the Foreign Office. He argued that Roosevelt's plan contained

> dangerous possibilities (e.g. danger of British public wishing to slack off Re-armament – danger of Great Britain being called upon to pay lion's share of sacrifices in respect of Colonies and Economic Concessions).

On the other hand it offered the opportunity which Britain had long been seeking for close cooperation with the United States:

> No real progress is expected by us in the Foreign Office from our own attempts at general settlements with Italy and Germany. . . . We only hope to gain time thereby pending our own rearmament. . . . The only fatal risk for us is to antagonise

America. Without Roosevelt's backing we might be overwhelmed in a war.[27]

When the two officials met Eden at Dover on 15 January, he immediately agreed with their views. Chamberlain's unencouraging reply seemed to jeopardise the advances made in 1937. The trade negotiations and the naval talks seemed to Eden to indicate the gradual modification of America's 'psychological withdrawal' from world affairs. American public opinion would react violently if news of the rejection leaked out and good relations would be fatally damaged. Eden believed that public opinion would become more favourable to the idea of Anglo-American cooperation if the dictators rejected the initiative while Britain welcomed it.[28] His insistence on the importance of accepting the American proposal developed into a government crisis in the next few days. On 16 January he visited Chamberlain and attempted to persuade the Prime Minister to withdraw his rejection. Eden argued that Roosevelt's proposal should have priority because Britain's own approaches to the dictators were not certain to achieve results. American friendship must come before talks with Berlin or Rome.[29] This conversation can only have confirmed Chamberlain's suspicions about Foreign Office obstruction and achieved nothing. The Prime Minister remained determined to defuse Roosevelt's 'bombshell' before it destroyed his own plans.[30]

The Americans were shocked by the outright rejection of the Welles plan. It seemed that Chamberlain wished to exclude the United States from all participation in a European settlement. The British preference for bilateral negotiations aroused suspicions that the kind of agreements which might emerge would not favour American interests. The news that Britain was considering *de jure* recognition of the Italian position in Abyssinia was particularly unpleasant. Roosevelt believed that recognition should be a collective act conceded as part of the American peace plan. It must be accompanied by agreements establishing a new system of international law. Chamberlain seemed to be condoning an Italian breach of international law without insisting on the establishment of new codes of conduct. The American reply to the British note, handed to Lindsay on 17 January, emphasised that while Roosevelt was prepared to defer his initiative for 'a short while', he believed that recognition should only be considered as part of his own appeasement plan.[31] The President insisted on this point because he feared that an Anglo-Italian agreement about Abyssinia would have damaging effects in the Far East where non-recognition was the basis of American policy towards Japanese conquests. There was a great difference in American eyes between recognition as part of general settlement which isolated Japan and recognition as part of an Anglo-Italian bargain. The first would deprive Tokyo of allies and force it to observe the terms of the Nine Power treaty in China. The second would only encourage the Japanese to press ahead with the construction of a Closed Door system in the Far East, in the hope that they could eventually play the other powers off against each other and strike similar bilateral bargains. Hull warned Lindsay on 17 January that Japan would interpret British action as a 'universal precedent'.[32] The same day Welles informed the ambassador that American public opinion would view recognition as a 'corrupt bargain' at the expense of American interests in the Far East.[33]

This strong American reaction gave weight to Eden's arguments. He was in any case opposed to *de jure* recognition of the Italian position in Abyssinia[34] and used American objections to support his case. On 18 January he sent another memorandum to Chamberlain, arguing that the United States might 'withdraw more and more into isolation' if Britain pursued the Italian negotiations on a basis repugnant to American opinion. Roosevelt did not seem to have the same objections to British discussions with Germany which could be coordinated with his own plan.[35] This insistence on accepting the American initiative placed Chamberlain in a difficult position. If the Prime Minister stood by his own policy, ignored Roosevelt and pressed ahead with the Italian talks, the cabinet would support him. He did not, however, wish Eden to resign and cause a controversy in the middle of approaches to Berlin and Rome. Chamberlain, therefore, reached a compromise with his Foreign Secretary on 21 January. Britain would agree to cooperate with Roosevelt's plan. It would also delay approaching Italy 'for at least a week'. At the same time Lindsay was to explain the danger to the British position in the Mediterranean if Italy remained hostile and to invite a further exchange of views with the President about Abyssinia.[36] The Foreign Office saw this development as a 'great victory' for its views.[37] Privately, however, Chamberlain still hoped to surround Roosevelt's 'bombshell . . . with blankets sufficient to prevent its doing any harm'.[38]

This sudden reversal of British policy pleased the Americans since it seemed to guarantee the United States a role in European appeasement. Welles informed Lindsay on 22 January that the British decision would 'make a good impression on the President'. The concession to American views on Abyssinia was particularly welcome. According to Welles, Roosevelt believed that recognition of the Italian Empire was 'an unpleasant pill which we should both swallow and . . . he wished we should both swallow it together'.[39] Despite the belated promise of British support, however, Roosevelt delayed launching the Welles plan. The main reason for the postponement was the internal crisis in Germany at the beginning of February which resulted in the dismissal of Blomberg, Fritsch, Neurath and many other 'moderates' from their posts. It was clear that political and economic discontent was coming to a head and Roosevelt was at first hopeful that the crisis would result in a victory for moderation. He informed the cabinet on 11 February that he had recently talked with Brüning, the ex-Chancellor of Germany. According to Brüning, the army officers were 'very powerful' and wanted 'a say about the Government'. Roosevelt believed that the army could 'upset Hitler's applecart in short order'. He felt that the Nazi system was being 'seriously tested from the inside' and there might be a 'break in the log jam'.[40] It rapidly became evident, however, that Hitler and the 'extremists' had emerged triumphant from the internal power struggle and that any opposition to the changes in the army high command had been overcome. Brüning had warned that if the conservative generals were removed Hitler would follow a policy of adventure.[41] Events following the purge seemed to confirm this impression. On 14 February Schuschnigg, the Austrian Chancellor, visited Hitler. On 15 February the American chargé in Vienna reported that the interview had been alarming. According to Schuschnigg, Hitler wanted to annex Austria. He was 'undoubtedly a madman and in complete control of Germany'. Wiley felt that the situation was most 'unfortunate and menacing'.[42] Roosevelt, therefore, postponed his initiative until Hitler's aims in Austria became clear. The Führer seemed determined to escape German economic problems not by negotiation but by military expansion in Central Europe.

American reluctance to act was confirmed by the resignation of Eden on 20 February, since he was known to be a firmer supporter of Anglo-American cooperation than Chamberlain. The postponement of Roosevelt's plan put an intolerable strain on the already uneasy relationship between the two men. The Prime Minister was anxious to open negotiations with Germany and Italy. Until Hitler began to threaten Austria, Eden did not object to the German discussions although he doubted if they would achieve much and feared that Chamberlain would give an impression of British weakness by failing to be firm enough with Berlin.[43] It was his objections to Anglo-Italian negotiations which led to an open breach with the Prime Minister. Eden wanted to delay an approach to Mussolini and to 'do nothing without Roosevelt's approval'.[44] Chamberlain was increasingly irritated by this obstructionism and the Austrian crisis brought matters to a head. The Italians claimed that an agreement should be rapidly concluded because of the German threat and Chamberlain agreed.[45] Eden, however, suspected that Mussolini secretly supported Hitler's designs on Austria and was merely blackmailing Britain into an agreement which would not bring lasting peace in the Mediterranean. He demanded some evidence of Italian good faith as the price of negotiations, such as a withdrawal of 'volunteers' from Spain. The Prime Minister insisted on opening talks on his own terms and accused the Foreign Secretary of losing 'chance after chance' with the dictators. Attempts to settle the differences between the two failed and Eden resigned on 20 February.[46] While the Italian talks were the immediate cause of Eden's action, the dispute between the two men had been touched off by Chamberlain's attitude to Roosevelt's initiative in January 1938.[47]

The internal crisis in Britain had an immediate impact on Anglo-American relations since it was believed to precede some immoral deal with the dictators. The United States had been aware of an emerging division between Eden and Chamberlain since the beginning of 1938. The Americans suspected that the Prime Minister was the agent of selfish City interests which maintained that Britain would benefit 'financially and commercially from coming to terms with Berlin'. An Anglo-German deal was possible which would grant Germany domination of Central Europe in return for abandoning an aggressive policy in the West. The British Empire would be thus secure and the threat of communism contained. Eden and the Foreign Office resisted this approach on the grounds that, while it might bring temporary material gains, this would be at too great a cost to principle and British interests might ultimately be endangered by bolstering up the Nazi system.[48] A similar division of opinion was thought to exist with regard to Italy. Eden's resignation was taken as a sign that the City group now controlled British policy and would attempt to reach agreements with both axis nations about spheres of influence. In the process, the American desire for a freer world trading system and equal access to raw materials would be ignored. British attempts to reassure the United States that policy would remain unchanged were unsuccessful. On 21 February, Cadogan informed the American chargé that press rumours to the effect that Britain would now reach an agreement with the dictators 'at any cost were absolutely nonsensical'.[49] The State Department was sceptical. Moffat believed that Chamberlain now intended to 'play ball with Hitler and Mussolini' and characterised British reassurances as 'patter'. A selfish clique now controlled British policy which intended to concede German domination of South and Central Europe as the price of political and economic security.[50] Roosevelt appeared to share this view of the Prime Minister. In a letter to Cudahy on 16 April 1938, the President equated Chamberlain's supporters with the 'economic royalists' who were opposing the New Deal in the United States. He remarked

> Over here there is the same element that exists in London . . . They would really like me to be a Neville Chamberlain – and if I would promise that, the market would go up and they would work positively and actively for the resumption of prosperity. But if that were done we would only be breeding more serious trouble four or eight years from now.[51]

The belief that Chamberlain might make immoral bargains for economic reasons was coupled with the belief that Germany might prove ultimately unappeasable. This was a view which gained weight as a result of the February purge and the pressure against Austria. Messersmith suspected that Hitler intended to annex Austria before moving against Czechoslovakia. The Germans had a definite programme aimed at domination of the Balkans and ultimately the whole of Europe. With the restraining influence of the generals removed there was no internal opposition to this policy of ruthless expansion.[52] In these circumstances Chamberlain seemed to be running a grave risk in pursuing appeasement. On 9 March 1938, Roosevelt set out his own views of the inherent dangers of Chamberlain's policy

> If a Chief of Police makes a deal with the leading gangsters and the deal results in no more hold-ups, that Chief of Police will be

called a great man, but if the gangsters do not live up to their word, the Chief of Police will go to jail. Some people are, I think, taking very long chances.[53]

Despite the Austrian crisis, Chamberlain went ahead with his approaches to Germany and Italy. It was clear that with Eden gone the Prime Minister intended to minimise American involvement in the negotiations. On 4 March 1938 Chamberlain informed Kennedy, the new American ambassador, that the time had come to make 'concrete concessions' to Hitler and Mussolini. Once that had been achieved Roosevelt might perhaps take action along the lines discussed with Britain in January. Kennedy noted, 'He does not really expect America to do anything'.[54] On 8 March 1938, Lindsay saw Welles and informed him that Britain hoped to reach 'regional agreements' with Germany and Italy which would avert war 'at least for a period'. Lord Halifax, the new Foreign Secretary, hoped that the United States would support British policy. If the political negotiations proved successful, the Americans might extend economic assistance to help Germany and Italy return to normal 'commercial and financial' system. When Welles pressed him for a more precise definition of the American role, Lindsay replied on his own initiative that:

> In the judgement of his Government the only constructive program which had been put forward over the past five years had been the Hull trade agreements program . . . and enlargement of the scope of that program would, in the opinion of the British Government, be the most effective way that had yet been devised of assisting Italy and Germany through the transitional phase back to normal relationships with the other powers of the world.

This promise of an Open Door in Europe might earlier have met with unqualified American approval. By this stage, however, Welles was sceptical and remarked caustically that it had taken Britain 'a good many years to realise this'. He went on to warn Lindsay in strong terms about the American commitment to freer world trade and the reduction of tariff walls.[55] Welles was clearly suspicious that 'regional agreements' might mean 'spheres of interest' and preferential trading systems which would discriminate against American commerce. This was the kind of European settlement which the United States believed Chamberlain, and the

City interests which supported him, really desired. Welles did not trust the Prime Minister and simply discounted reassurances given by Lindsay on his own authority. Moreover, following the February purge, the Americans were not convinced that appeasement would prove ultimately successful, no matter what 'concrete concessions' were made to Hitler. The United States, therefore, refused to support Chamberlain's policy. As Welles made plain, Roosevelt was holding his own plan in abeyance while reserving the right to a voice in any settlement which might emerge as a result of the British initiative.

American fears of an Anglo-German bargain and the creation of a Closed Door in Europe were never realised. Hitler spurned Chamberlain's offer to discuss the colonial question and other outstanding issues. Instead of opening talks to remove German grievances peacefully, he annexed Austria on 12 March. Chamberlain was forced to admit that he found it impossible to 'come to grips' with the Germans and 'have them state what they want'.[56] The British, however, had not abandoned hopes of an Anglo-German settlement despite their condemnation of the forceful methods used by Hitler to obtain the *Anschluss*. The element of suspicion injected into Anglo-American relations by the departure of Eden was exacerbated in the following months by British attempts to remain on good terms with Germany and to promote an agreement between Hitler and Benes on the status of the Sudeten minority in Czechoslovakia.

6 The United States and the Sudeten Crisis

American policy after the *Anschluss* was founded on two main assumptions. The first was that the 'extremists' were in complete control of Germany and that Czechoslovakia was the next target of Nazi expansion. The second was that Chamberlain would be prepared to bargain with Hitler at the expense of the Czechs. British policy was interpreted in the light of conclusions reached during the Eden-Chamberlain quarrel. It was assumed that Chamberlain's victory meant the triumph of selfish City interests which stood for a policy of 'peace at any price'. As Roosevelt informed the French ambassador, the Prime Minister was a 'City man' who had abandoned France in the hope of making a 'business deal' with the dictators.[1] The United States, therefore, maintained its distance from Anglo-German negotiations after the *Anschluss*. Roosevelt would not endorse an immoral bargain reached at the expense of Prague and hoped to restrain Hitler by leaving the American position undefined. There remained some ambiguity about his position at this point however. While disapproving of Chamberlain's actions and claiming that they would merely stimulate German greed, the President put forward no alternative and seemed content to couple public coolness with private condemnation of British policy. The domestic political situation was undoubtedly an inhibiting factor. Roosevelt was faced with a rebellious Congress and a public opinion which was unwilling to see the United States become involved in European quarrels on behalf of the Czechs. In these circumstances the easiest course was to let Chamberlain make the running and assume the political risks. If he failed he could be condemned for trying to deal with the 'leading gangsters', while if he succeeded the United States could renew its demands for a new 'Congress of Berlin'. American 'appeasers' such as Welles and Berle were perfectly willing to lend an American 'moral' tone to an 'immoral' British policy if Chamberlain appeared to be on the verge of success. The President himself sometimes approached this position and attempted to seize some of the credit for Munich during its brief period of public popularity.[2] American policy after the *Anschluss*, therefore, was opportunist and Roosevelt's attitude could best be described as 'watchful waiting'.

Despite the *Anschluss*, Chamberlain had not abandoned hope of reaching a settlement with Germany and Italy which would free Britain to defend its interests in the Far East. He looked for American support of his approaches to both countries. Negotiations with Italy were concluded on 30 March 1938. Under the new agreement Britain would press the League to free its members to recognise the Italian empire in Abyssinia. The terms, including *de jure* recognition, would come into force once Italian 'volunteers' had been withdrawn from Spain.[3] Chamberlain saw the settlement as a major step towards breaking up the Berlin-Rome-Tokyo axis since it would relieve Britain of the threat to imperial communications in the Mediterranean. The Prime Minister was anxious to secure American approval of his efforts and asked Halifax to ensure that Roosevelt was 'specially treated' in receiving information about the negotiations.[4] On 6 April Halifax asked Kennedy if the President would issue a public statement in support of the agreement.[5] This request was based upon a combination of foreign policy and domestic political considerations. At a time of poor relations with Germany, an expression of American interest in peace might deter the Nazi 'extremists' while impressing Mussolini by showing that powerful forces were ranged in support of Britain. In domestic terms an American statement would help to justify the agreement in the eyes of public opinion and counter any claim which Eden might make that the government had placed appeasement of Italy before solidarity with the United States. Chamberlain carefully emphasised that Roosevelt had endorsed the agreement when he defended his policy in the Commons on 2 May.[6]

The British request for a statement of approval divided the Roosevelt administration. Hull and Moffat opposed any close identification with British policy while Welles believed that the United States must endorse a move designed to weaken the axis.[7] He was supported by Kennedy and Phillips who emphasised that a unique opportunity existed to divide Mussolini from Hitler because of the unpopularity of the *Anschluss* in Italy.[8] Welles felt that the advantages of the Anglo-Italian agreement in breaking up the European axis would more than balance any ill effects in the Far

East. Whereas in January he had argued that *de jure* recognition of the Italian position in Abyssinia would undermine the Stimson doctrine, encourage the Japanese and weaken Chinese resistance, his views had changed as a result of the European crisis caused by the annexation of Austria. The shift of attention away from China was further encouraged because a settlement on Japanese terms seemed less likely by the spring of 1938. The Chinese began 'making a good showing' and displayed fewer signs of accepting a settlement dictated by Japan, an outcome which had seemed possible after the fall of Nanking.[9] As a result the Far East had 'subsided from page one to page five' in American priorities.[10]

Welles finally persuaded Roosevelt to issue a statement about the agreement on the grounds that 'silence would seem almost like a rebuke',[11] to the disgust of Hull who was on leave and could not make his opposition felt. There were rumours that the Secretary intended to resign over the issue but in the end he decided to remain at his post.[12] Hull may have feared that his going would leave Welles with a clear field and weaken the cause of anti-appeasement at the highest levels of the administration. The President, however, was not prepared to go further and, as Welles desired, prevent members of his cabinet from publicly condemning fascism. Welles attempted to dissuade Ickes, the Secretary of the Interior, from making several unflattering references to fascism in a speech which he was to deliver at Chicago on the grounds that condemnation would alienate Mussolini and make it 'more difficult for Great Britain to pry Italy loose from its alliance with Germany'. Roosevelt, however, suggested only minor changes in Ickes' draft and 'made it very clear that he thought it was all right to discuss fascism in a critical vein'.[13]

British hopes of an early general settlement with Berlin were dashed by German rejection of Chamberlain's colonial offer and the *Anschluss*. It was obvious that Hitler intended to 'solve' the problems of Central Europe and that the next area of tension would be Czechoslovakia with its Sudeten German minority. Since France was pledged to defend the Czech state against aggression and the USSR had a similar commitment, contingent upon the French fulfilling their obligations towards Prague, the Sudeten question contained the seeds of a European war. In London opinions differed about the Führer's ultimate aims and the British response to tension in Central Europe. Some, such as Churchill, believed that Hitler intended to destroy Czechoslovakia as the first step in the creation of an autarkic *Mitteleuropa* which would provide the base for further conquests. According to Churchill, 'the Nazification of the Danube States' would be 'a danger of the first capital magnitude to the British Empire' and he called for Britain to join with France and the Soviet Union in a 'grand alliance' against further German expansion.[14] The government, however, did not believe that Hitler's aims were limitless.

Chamberlain had never aimed at contesting German political and economic predominance in Central Europe but had attempted to ensure that revision was carried out by peaceful means. This was the reason for requesting guarantees of German good behaviour in the area as part of the March proposals. The essential change after the *Anschluss* was that hopes of solving political and economic problems at a stroke by offering Germany colonies in return for political guarantees and the termination of autarky were temporarily abandoned. Piecemeal solutions to immediate problems were sought instead. Talks on the Sudeten issue were paralleled by discussions of Anglo-German economic relations. Chamberlain believed that Hitler was interested only in justice for the German minority and that if the Sudeten problem could be solved peacefully a broad general agreement with Hitler would yet prove possible.[15] As Kennedy noted, 'He hopes that the Czech matter will be adjusted without difficulty and that in the fall . . . they will start negotiations with Germany.'[16] France, therefore, must be persuaded to play down the Czech alliance lest its existence encourage intransigence in Prague. The Soviet Union must remain completely isolated. On 24 March, in pursuit of this goal, the Prime Minister announced that Britain was adopting no new commitments as a result of the *Anschluss*.[17]

The economic situation undoubtedly influenced the government in avoiding a confrontation with Germany. The recession worsened in the spring of 1938 and economic advisers predicted the onset of another 'world depression period'.[18] The alternative to appeasement, Churchill's plan for a 'grand alliance' against Germany could only worsen the British economic position. It would damage business confidence and mean the suspension of normal trade for increased armaments. It would also mean the collapse of the Anglo-German payments agreement and the loss to Britain of trade worth £20.6 million a year. Moreover, quite apart from the dangerous ideological implications of an alliance with the Soviet Union, Churchill's plan would make the British Empire dependent on the goodwill of the United States which had long displayed an ambition to dismantle imperial preference. In these circumstances the best course seemed to maintain contact with Berlin in the hope that, once the Sudeten problem was solved, the payments agreement could be broadened to provide the economic basis for a more general settlement. When the agreement was extended to cover Austria in July 1938, Hudson, of the Department of Overseas Trade, noted that in further economic talks

> We might get a comprehensive agreement covering not only mutual trade . . . but our competitive positions in third markets . . . if the chances for making such an agreement emerged, it would obviously have great possibilities as a stepping stone to political appeasement.

Ashton-Gwatkin, of the Foreign Office agreed. As he remarked to Halifax, further talks might lead to

> further extension of mutual trade. With the extension of trade, the extension of further credits to Germany should become possible, resulting in more trade and so on. This is a practical advance towards economic appeasement.

Britain might have to make certain concessions such as the lowering of tariff walls and the alteration of colonial quotas, but Germany in return might be persuaded to enter the international coal cartel and conclude marketing agreements in foreign markets, lessening the pressure of subsidised competition on British exports. Ashton-Gwatkin concluded that Britain benefited from good economic relations with Germany and emphasised the payments agreement as a means of increasing British exports.[19] American critics, therefore, were justified in suspecting that economic self-interest had a large influence on British policy. Cartels and marketing agreements contradicted the ideal of the Open Door and raised the spectre of two closed industrial systems in subsidised competition against US trade. Even if such arrangements were characterised as mere stages on the road back towards free trade, that goal was sufficiently vague and distant as to arouse American suspicions about Chamberlain's real commitment to an open world economy. The schemes circulating in the Foreign Office and the Department of Overseas Trade were to be a fertile source of Anglo-American dispute when Chamberlain attempted to carry them out after Munich.

British contacts with Germany after the *Anschluss* were with the group thought to favour some form of Anglo-German economic agreement. Unlike the Americans, the British were not alarmed when the conservatives were ousted from power in February 1938. When Schacht's influence began to decline in 1937, Chamberlain had started to cultivate the new party leader in charge of the German economy, Reichsmarschall Göring. It was believed that Göring, influenced by officials of the Reichsbank and the Ministry of Economics, represented a 'moderate' force within the Nazi party itself, opposed to the forceful methods advocated by 'extremists' such as Ribbentrop. Chamberlain hoped that through Göring, Hitler might yet be persuaded to accept a peaceful settlement of German claims.[20] The successful revision of the payments agreement was taken as evidence that the 'moderates' could still influence German policy.[21] If the Sudeten problem could be solved it would strengthen their position further by proving to Hitler that negotiation was a viable alternative to force in gaining 'justice' for the Reich. By contrast the Americans had few contacts with the party 'bosses'. While Henderson was on good terms with Göring, Dodd had branded all party leaders as extremist thugs after the Röhm purge.[22] His successor, Wilson, was never in Berlin long enough to become acquainted with the most powerful figures in the party hierarchy. As a result American information about Germany after the February purge tended to come from opposition figures such as Brüning and later Goerdeler, who had little faith in the goodwill of any Nazi. This was to have an effect on Anglo-American relations since it conditioned the United States to take a generally more pessimistic view of Hitler's intentions than Britain.

British policy after the *Anschluss* attempted to warn off the 'extremists' from an armed coup against Czechoslovakia, while trying to demonstrate that a negotiated settlement of the Sudeten problem was possible. The government adopted no new commitments but did warn that it might prove impossible to localise any way in Central Europe.[23] Chamberlain hoped to create uncertainty amongst the other powers. Germany would not know whether Britain would remain neutral if Czechoslovakia were attacked, while France and Czechoslovakia would be unsure about British support in the event of hostilities. Ideally, therefore, both sides would exercise caution and work for a reasonable solution of the

Sudeten problem.[24] At the end of April 1938 the French agreed to support Britain in promoting a negotiated settlement between Czechs and Sudetens.[25] Both powers would urge Benes to make concessions to the German minority. Britain would point these efforts out in Berlin and repeat the warning that if a war broke out over the issue, it might prove impossible to contain.[26] In practice, pressure on Prague was more evident than warnings to Hitler. As Henderson pointed out, Britain and France must avoid committing 'the folly of urging Benes not to make concessions and to stand pat'.[27]

The United States had a role to play in this strategy. Although Chamberlain remained sceptical about American support in the event of war, he felt that Roosevelt could play a part in preserving peace by publicly endorsing British efforts. This would not only restrain 'extremists' within Germany but could also be used to counter critics of appeasement at home. Washington, therefore, was kept informed about the aims of British policy. On 23 March Lindsay informed Welles that Britain intended to adopt no new international commitments as a result of the *Anschluss*. This decision had been influenced by 'misgivings as to the present military situation'. Britain did not have the resources to protect Czechoslovakia which could not defend itself and was bound to be defeated in any war with Germany. In these circumstances the government felt that every possible step should be taken

> both by the French . . . and by themselves to help remove the causes of friction . . . by using their good offices with the Government of Czechoslovakia to bring about a settlement of these questions affecting the position of the German minority.[28]

This message failed to inspire American confidence. After Eden's resignation, the Roosevelt administration had little faith in Chamberlain's good intentions. His policy towards Czechoslovakia was fitted into a preconceived picture of the Prime Minister as the agent of selfish economic interests which stood for a policy of 'peace at any price'. As one British diplomat remarked, 'the Americans could not understand the PM and disliked him'.[29] After the Anglo-French talks in April, Moffat noted that Daladier had

> returned to Paris with an understanding of how deep-seated is the British desire to . . . maintain peace. The lodestar of British

policy seems to have remained constant, namely that everything possible shall be done to draw Germany out of herself and back into the community of Western Powers.[30]

It was suspected that neither France nor the USSR would support Czechoslovakia without British backing and that Chamberlain was more concerned with exerting pressure on Benes than in issuing strong warnings to Hitler. As Moffat remarked on 17 May:

> The news from Europe looks increasingly dark and the clouds seem to be gathering daily over Czechoslovakia. The French Government is in an unenviable situation with England continuing to . . . try to dominate her entire foreign policy without at the same time giving any commitment to support France if she has to move by virtue of her treaty with Czechoslovakia.[31]

From Washington, a 'sell-out' of Prague seemed inevitable.

The Roosevelt administration was divided over the wisdom of Chamberlain's approach to the problems of Central Europe. There were many in Washington who, like Churchill, feared that Hitler's aims were unlimited and that he planned to establish an autarkic *Mitteleuropa* as a base for further conquests. Even before the *Anschluss* Messersmith had characterised expansion towards the south-east as the first stage in a plan to dominate Europe. After the annexation of Austria Moffat recorded a similar impression in his diary:

> British reaction to what has been going on is the key to the whole situation and with each day that passes it becomes clearer that England is willing to surrender Eastern Europe to German ambitions. . . . When Germany has consolidated these gains [they] will make her a far more dangerous foe to Britain throughout the world.[32]

It was suspected that fear of communism blinded Chamberlain to the German danger,[33] a feeling which seemed to be confirmed when the Prime Minister rejected Churchill's 'grand alliance' scheme and a Soviet proposal for a European security conference. On 14 April Davies reported from Moscow that only 'a London-Paris-Moscow axis' could contain Germany. The 'Fascist Powers', however, were trying 'to isolate the Soviet Union from the Western Powers by raising the bogey of Communism [and] they are getting away with it'.[34] It was recognised that American as well as British interests might ultimately be menaced by indefinite German expansion. By 1938 the State Department was becoming concerned about the growth of German political and economic influence in Latin America, a development encouraged by the bilateral barter deals concluded between Berlin and many of the South American republics since 1934. As Messersmith noted

> If Germany gets . . . control . . . of south-eastern Europe, she will be in a position to put England and France into a secondary place . . . This can only mean the gradual disintegration of the British Empire . . . which I believe we in this country cannot look upon with unconcern. I am confident that in the end we would have our own troubles in South America where Germany, Italy and Japan are already so active and where they have their definite objectives – particularly Germany.[35]

This warning was underlined by an attempted coup in Brazil in May 1938 which it was believed had been instigated by Berlin to consolidate German influence in that country.[36] Hull was soon arguing that the threat to US interests in South America could only be averted if German expansion in Europe was contained.[37] The German embassy in Washington correctly attributed deteriorating relations after the *Anschluss* to American fears of a Closed Door economic system dominated by Germany, Italy and Japan which would exclude the United States from world markets and undermine its position in Latin America.[38]

American spokesmen began to adopt an overtly anti-axis tone designed to raise uncertainties in Berlin about American policy in the event of a war provoked by German expansion. On 17 March Hull warned: 'Isolation is not a means to security, it is a fruitful source of insecurity' and emphasised that the United States would not abandon the rule of law.[39] In a speech written for him by the State Department, Kennedy also stressed that any assumption of automatic American neutrality was mistaken. In the event of war the United States would be found strongly armed and alert. Its policy could not be decided for it in advance, an obvious warning to Germany not to rely on the existence of the Neutrality Act.[40] Wilson, the new ambassador in Berlin, made a similar statement on 14 April.[41] Further warning statements followed the May crisis over Czechoslovakia. On 28 May Hull made a speech condemning international anarchy and emphasised American interest in the rule of law.[42] His Assistant Secretary of State, Francis Sayre, put the position more bluntly on 7 June when he remarked that the United States was prepared 'if necessary, to withstand the aggression of lawlessness'.[43] On 7 July, before the German ambassador returned to Berlin on leave, Hull summoned him to the State Department to discuss the deteriorating relations between the United States and Germany. At the end of the interview he warned Dieckhoff that if militarism led to war there would in the end 'scarcely be left a trace of the people who brought it on'.[44]

As before the *Anschluss*, the problem for the 'anti-appeasers' was to lend weight to such warning statements by concrete acts. As in late 1937 two main lines of approach were considered which would not fall foul of isolationist opinion: naval manoeuvres and trade negotiations. After the Brazilian crisis and the war scare over Czechoslovakia of May 1938, increasing emphasis was laid upon the ability of the fleet to defend either the Pacific or the Atlantic coasts of the Western Hemisphere against attack. On 18 June news leaked to the press that the annual fleet exercise in 1939 would be held in the Atlantic and that the objective would be to defend the Americas against a hypothetical European attack. Roosevelt was considering bringing forward the date of the manoeuvres to the summer of 1938 in the light of European tension and the attempted coup in Brazil.[45] After reviewing the fleet at San Francisco on 14 July, the President stressed that the navy was 'not merely a symbol' but a 'potent ever ready fact in the national defense of the United States'.[46] This statement was a warning to both Germany and Japan that the United States intended to defend its interests. Simultaneously Washington increased pressure on London to bring the Anglo-American trade negotiations to a successful conclusion. Hull believed that a 'broad basic trade agreement' would contribute to international stability in both Europe and Asia. Failure to conclude a treaty would merely encourage German and Japanese aggression and strengthen 'the forces of isolation within the United States'.[47] At the same time the United States condemned bilateral Nazi trading methods and protested against the extension of autarky to Austria.[48] The British, however, continued to feel that the Americans were demanding too great a sacrifice of imperial perference and agreement proved elusive. By July 1938 it was clear that nothing substantial could be achieved until after the summer recess. On 24 July Hull expressed his 'keen disappointment' with the progress of discussions.[49] The United States commented unfavourably on the delay in this area while Britain simultaneously extended the Anglo-German payments agreement to meet the new situation created by the *Anschluss*.[50] Chamberlain seemed more concerned to guarantee British markets in *Mitteleuropa* than to join the United States in condemning bilateralism and constructing an open world economy.

In the spring of 1938, therefore, American 'anti-appeasers' were attempting to stiffen British policy and promote some form of united front which would deter Hitler from further expansion. The obvious American contribution to such a system of containment was repeal of the Neutrality Act. Administration spokesmen hinted at such a departure in March and Dieckhoff warned Berlin to expect repeal.[51] Roosevelt himself hinted privately at some modification of the act. In January 1938 a French purchasing mission, headed by Baron de la Grange, visited the United States to investigate the possibility of buying large numbers of aircraft. de la Grange explained that the French government, worried by the growth of German air power and lagging French production, wished to make up the deficiencies in its airforce by purchases from the United States. He was naturally concerned, however, lest the Neutrality Act cut France off from supplies and spares in the event of war. Roosevelt expressed approval of the purchasing scheme and remarked that Britain, France and the United States would have to stand together to contain Germany. France, therefore, could expect modification of the Neutrality Act.[52] Despite some sentiment for reform in Congress, however, neither Hull nor Roosevelt was prepared to put administration support behind new legislation. On 22 March revision was shelved until the following session. Dieckhoff attributed Roosevelt's inaction to fear of a bitter political struggle with Congress.[53] This failure to support repeal had its effects on French hopes. On 17 May Bullitt informed the French Air Minister that contrary to de la Grange's report, France 'could not count on receiving a single American plane after a declaration of war'.[54]

In default of neutrality revision the 'anti-appeasers' had little hope of stiffening the policies of the Western powers. Chamberlain could continue to argue that Britain would receive little assistance from the United States in the event of war.[55] French leaders took a similar line. Bonnet later justified deserting Czechoslovakia on the ground that France could expect no aid from the United States.[56] There is evidence that the efforts of the 'anti-appeasers' made a limited impression on German diplomats. Dieckhoff warned his government on 31 May that in the event of a war over Czechoslovakia, the United States 'would enter the conflict against us'.[57] On 19 June the official publication, *Diplomatische Politische Correspondenz*, asked if the United States must be included amongst those agitating for war against the axis in the light of Hull's recent speeches and rumours of US fleet manoeuvres.[58] The impact of American threats in Berlin, however, was vitiated by divisions within the administration over policy. If Hull, Messersmith and others had little faith in the prospects of a European settlement after the *Anschluss*, others remained undecided and hoped that Hitler might yet be contented with limited gains.

Bullitt remained obsessed with the communist danger and felt that in the event of war, Roosevelt should seek some means of helping France to evade its obligations. If Germany invaded Czechoslovakia, the President should summon a great power conference at the Hague. If Prague refused to accept its decisions, France would be justified in refusing to fight. The United States would be accused of 'selling out a small nation . . . to produce another Hitler triumph' but this was preferable to seeing 'an Asiatic despotism established on fields of dead'.[59] In London, Kennedy continued to take a soft line towards Germany despite the stiffening attitude of Hull. In July 1938 he informed Dirksen, the German ambassador, that he would like to visit Germany to speak with someone of importance about the prospects of a European settlement. According to Kennedy, he had the full support of the President who sympathised with German demands for 'justice'. Roosevelt desired a settlement which would revive world trade, restore international stability and reduce unemployment within the United States.[60] This bid for an invitation to visit Hitler reflected Kennedy's belief that free institutions and free enterprise within the United States could not survive a prolonged world recession or the economic dislocations which would accompany war.[61] It is unclear how much encouragement he received from within the State Department where appeasement sentiment continued to exist. As Berle noted on 19 March

The State Department is divided. About half of it is following a Wilsonian moral line which in my judgement would lead eventually to our entry into a war on the British side. The other half, headed by Sumner and myself, is still endeavoring to steer matters into an ultimate conference.[62]

Although shaken by the purge of the German conservatives on whom their previous peace plans had been based, Welles and Berle hoped that Nazi extremism could be satiated by political and economic expansion to the south-east. Berle argued that the 'reconstruction of the Austrian Empire unit under Germany' was 'probably necessary and . . . not alarming'.[63] Its ambitions satisfied in this area, Naziism would become a moderate force and Hitler would have to collaborate in American plans for a new world order. Although both men distrusted Chamberlain, therefore, they sympathised with his attempts to promote a settlement in the Sudetenland. Once the Prime Minister had solved the Czech problem the United States, by summoning a world conference, could ensure that his efforts did not ultimately result in a narrow Anglo-German deal at American expense.[64]

The confusion in the State Department over American policy was compounded by Roosevelt's failure to adopt a definite line towards Europe. While he privately characterised Chamberlain as a 'City man' who had abandoned France and emphasised the risks of dealing with 'gangsters', he took few steps to promote the united front against aggression which he sometimes claimed was the real answer to German expansion. He backed away from neutrality revision, the one major American contribution to collective security and was unwilling to propose even an accelerated programme of rearmament. Indeed some of his own speeches, while emphasising American preparedness, expressed the hope that world industrial capacity could be put to more productive uses following a general agreement on arms limitation.[65] If Roosevelt was uncertain about the prospects of appeasement after the *Anschluss*, he was unwilling to take the political risks involved in wholehearted pursuit of the strategy advocated by the 'anti-appeasers' and may even have given some tacit encouragement to their opponents such as Kennedy and Welles. The suspicion remains that the President wished to leave his options open lest Chamberlain's efforts prove successful. He would not, however, endorse British policy in advance of that point. As Offner concludes, therefore, American policy before Munich 'remained ambiguous at best, on the side of misguided appeasement at worst'.[66]

Chamberlain's desire to act as an 'honest broker' in the Sudeten question and Roosevelt's reluctance openly to endorse British policy were clearly revealed in July 1938 when the Runciman mission was sent to Czechoslovakia. Although London had been advising the Czechs to grant reasonable concessions to the Sudetens throughout the spring and talks had actually begun between Benes and minority leaders, it was increasingly obvious that the problem was not going to be solved without direct outside intervention. During June Halifax became suspicious that the Czechs were not wholly sincere in their negotiations with the Sudetens.[67] It was recognised in London that if the talks collapsed, Germany might intervene, facing Britain with the prospect of a European war. In order to avoid such an outcome Halifax proposed on 16 June that Britain appoint a 'distinguished mediator' between Czechs and Sudetens.[68] On 20 July this solution was suggested to Benes.[69] Two factors dictated the timing of the British initiative: The visit of Captain Wiedemann to London and the failure of negotiations within Czechoslovakia about a minorities statute to produce results. In July 1938 several feelers were put out from Berlin apparently aimed at securing an understanding with Britain. Oliver Hoare and Lady Snowden both received reports that Hitler desired an Anglo-German agreement and wished to send Göring to London to continue the talks initiated at Berchtesgaden in November 1937. Hoare persuaded Halifax to discuss the matter with Hitler's aide-de-camp, Captain Wiedemann, when he visited Britain on 18 July. The German made 'a good impression' on Halifax. He explained that he had come to London on Hitler's authority to discuss the possibility of a visit by Göring. The Führer still desired a final settlement with Britain. Halifax replied that the Sudeten problem would have to be solved before Anglo-German discussions could take place. Wiedemann then promised that Germany would not attack Czechoslovakia unless a massacre of Sudetens took place. He also stated that Ribbentrop was losing his influence with Hitler. Only Göring and Neurath knew about the visit to London.[70]

Halifax was gratified by the news that the 'moderates' were influencing German policy. It was his aim to maintain them in a dominant position. This was the background to the Runciman mission. It was believed that Hitler would continue to listen to the 'moderates' only if negotiations between Czechs and Sudetens were shown to work. When it was reported that talks between Prague and the minority were collapsing, Britain was forced to intervene. On 18 July it was decided to offer Lord Runciman's services to Benes as an independent arbiter. The Czechs were warned that the British initiative would be made public even if they rejected it.[71] Under this pressure Benes accepted and the offer was announced in parliament on 26 July. The Runciman mission was designed to encourage the German 'moderates' and to check 'the war party'.[72] It was envisaged as a means of coercing the Czechs into a settlement of the Sudeten problem acceptable to Germany.[73] Once this end was achieved, Chamberlain hoped to take up Wiedemann's offer of a comprehensive Anglo-German settlement.

The government wished the United States to endorse the Runciman mission as it had endorsed the Anglo-Italian agreement. On 29 July Halifax informed Sargent that: 'the cabinet hoped . . . we might be able to get some commendatory message out of Roosevelt about Runciman'. Sargent was asked to raise the subject with the American embassy. Kennedy was on leave but on 2 August Sargent saw Millard, the First Secretary. He explained that Halifax was most anxious to keep Roosevelt informed about British attempts to prevent 'a dangerous crisis developing out of the Sudeten problem'. If the President 'could find some means of expressing approval . . . of Lord Runciman's mission it would be . . . extremely helpful'.[74] Runciman himself wrote personally to Roosevelt about his mission, remarking that Britain was trying 'a new method of preserving the peace . . . the method of agreed investigation and conciliation'.[75]

The President, however, made no statement about the Runciman mission. The Americans remembered that Roosevelt's approval of the Anglo-Italian agreement had been used 'for partisan purposes by Chamberlain in the House of Commons and for diplomatic purposes by Halifax at the League of Nations'. They wished to avoid a similar attempt to involve them in a scheme designed to put pressure on Czechoslovakia. It was recognised in Washington that although the mission was described as independent it was in fact the vehicle of British policy. Britain and any other country which supported the mission would assume responsibility for its findings and thereby become entangled in the Sudeten problem. If Roosevelt endorsed the British initiative and the Czechs subsequently rejected Runciman's findings, there would be diplomatic pressure on the United States to support the imposition of Runciman's terms on Prague. The Americans were anxious to avoid direct implication in such a potential 'sell-out' of Czechoslovakia.[76] Hull was incensed when Wilson, the ambassador in Berlin, visited Prague in August 1938, giving rise to press speculation that he was cooperating with Runciman.[77] Far from Roosevelt publicly supporting the Runciman mission as Chamberlain desired, therefore, the United States was anxious to avoid even the appearance of indirectly endorsing British efforts.

In retrospect, American aloofness from the Sudeten problem after the *Anschluss* depended on the assumption that Hitler would allow Chamberlain to 'sell' the Czechs. As long as the Prime Minister was acting as an 'honest broker' and there was no war crisis over Czechoslovakia, Roosevelt could leave his options open. If Britain succeeded in establishing lasting peace at the expense of Prague, the United States could demand a voice in the permanent settlement of European problems. If 'selling' the Czechs provided only a temporary respite in a programme of indefinite German expansion, the President could adopt the policy of the 'anti-appeasers' with a better expectation of public support. The sudden collapse of British mediation in September, however, forced Roosevelt to make a definite choice between appeasement and anti-appeasement, since it seemed that Hitler might not after all allow a negotiated solution of the Sudeten problem, however generous to Germany. The United States had either to encourage the Western powers to resist or itself directly intervene in favour of peace, risking, as Bullitt had predicted in May, accusations of having 'sold-out' a 'small nation in order to produce another Hitler triumph'. Bullitt accepted this responsibility as the price of a higher moral end: the preservation of peace and civilisation. It was characteristic of Roosevelt, however, that he ultimately chose Bullitt's course while simultaneously absolving himself from any responsibility for the sacrifice of Czech integrity.

7 Munich

In August 1938 tension again began to grow over the Sudeten problem. In the ensuing crisis British policy passed through three stages. The first stage, dating from mid-August until 14 September, saw an intensification of previous efforts. Hitler was warned that a war against Czechoslovakia might ultimately involve all of Europe, while Benes was urged to reach a speedy solution of minority grievances. During the second stage, after Hitler's speech at Nuremberg, there was direct intervention to save the peace, the two visits to Hitler at Berchtesgaden and Godesberg. In the third stage, between 24 and 28 September, the British role of 'honest broker' collapsed in the face of German intransigence and a deadlock emerged which it seemed could only be broken by war. During the first two periods Roosevelt was able to avoid direct intervention in European affairs but he was forced to take positive action in the third stage when British efforts were exhausted. Forced to make a choice between appeasement and anti-appeasement, the President put the preservation of peace before the integrity of the Czech state and called for a conference on the Sudeten issue. As a result the United States was finally unable to avoid implication in a 'deal' at the expense of Prague despite Roosevelt's previous efforts to maintain his distance from Chamberlain's policy.

At the beginning of August 1938 Germany began to take steps which could be interpreted as preparations to solve the Sudeten problem by force.[1] When a British request to suspend such military measures was ignored, an indirect warning was delivered to Berlin. In a speech at Lanark on 27 August, Simon stated that a war in Central Europe might prove difficult to limit. Nobody could predict who might ultimately become involved.[2] Chamberlain, however, had to decide if he would go further and state definitely that Britain would support France in the event of an attack on Czechoslovakia which brought French treaty obligations into effect. The German opposition had been urging the government to issue such a warning, arguing that otherwise Hitler would attain his aims by force. Carl

Goerdeler, the ex-mayor of Leipzig, had been in contact with London since 1937 through secret meetings with the British businessman, Arthur Young. Young's unofficial activities had been instigated by Vansittart, Chief Diplomatic Adviser to the government and an opponent of Chamberlain's German policy. On 6 August 1938 Goerdeler warned Young that Hitler intended to smash Czechoslovakia by military action in the near future. He had obtained this information from friends in the Foreign Office and the army who were unhappy about the decision to risk a war over the Sudetenland. According to Goerdeler, Britain must not rely on the restraining influence of Göering. The 'moderates' were powerless and only a definite statement that Britain would fight could have any effect on Berlin. If Hitler ignored such a warning he would be overthrown by the army.[3] Similar advice reached the Foreign Office from other opposition sources.[4] Vansittart sympathised with Goerdeler's suggestions but they were rejected by Chamberlain at a meeting of ministers on 30 August. The Prime Minister did not wish to provoke Hitler nor to make the Czechs intransigent and continued to hope for a negotiated settlement. It was, therefore, decided to 'keep Germany guessing' while doing everything possible to 'forward the success of the Runciman Mission'.[5] Despite renewed pressure for a warning during the first week in September, this remained Chamberlain's position. The Führer was to address the Nuremberg rally on 12 September and the Prime Minister was reluctant to take any step which might drive Hitler to make 'a violent speech instead of a conciliatory one'.[6] Moreover Chamberlain had evolved a plan of his own for use in the event of a crisis. He hoped to fly to Germany and win Hitler's support for a peaceful solution by a direct personal appeal. The Führer would be tempted to accept British mediation by hints of a general settlement once the Sudeten problem had been solved. In pursuit of this goal, the Prime Minister crushed all sentiment for a warning which would have led Britain into a direct confrontation with Germany and damaged the chances of building a bridge to Hitler.[7]

The results of Hitler's speech at Nuremberg on 12 September led to the early implementation of Chamberlain's plan. The address, although leaving the way open to a negotiated solution by calling for self-determination in the Sudetenland, was followed by widespread rioting in the area the next day which was suppressed by the Czech army. It was feared that this would provoke German military intervention.[8] In these circumstances Chamberlain requested a meeting with Hitler. It was hoped that his initiative would 'make it easier' for the Führer to 'choose the way of negotiation rather than of force' and 'strengthen the moderates in Germany'. It was also intended to pave the way towards Chamberlain's dream of 'an all-round . . . Anglo-German settlement'.[9] It was clear even before the Prime Minister left for Berchtesgaden that he intended to accept the German demand for self-determination. As he informed the cabinet, he doubted if peace could be preserved as long as Czechoslovakia contained a German minority.[10] At Berchtesgaden on 16 September Chamberlain agreed to promote self-determination for the Sudetens. Hitler in return agreed to postpone a military solution while the Prime Minister worked out the details of the scheme with his colleagues and the French.[11] On his return to London Chamberlain persuaded the cabinet and Daladier to agree to the transfer of the Sudetenland and an international guarantee of the remainder of the Czech state.[12] On 19 September details of the Anglo-French scheme were sent to Prague. The Czechs were warned that if they rejected the proposals the Western powers could take no responsibility for the outcome. Britain and France would 'wash their hands' of Benes.[13]

This result was not unexpected in Washington where Chamberlain had long been suspected of putting appeasement ahead of the integrity of Czechoslovakia. The administration remained divided, however, about the wisdom of his efforts. Roosevelt and Hull responded to German military measures at the beginning of August by issuing warning statements. In a radio address of 16 August Hull condemned aggression and emphasised American interest in the rule of law.[14] On 18 August, in a speech at Kingston, Canada, Roosevelt gave 'an assurance' that the United States would not 'stand idly by if domination of Canadian soil is threatened by any other Empire'.[15] His words were intended to deter Hitler from the use of force while remaining within the politically unassailable limits of hemisphere solidarity. They were also intended as a warning to Japan. Roosevelt continued to assume that Tokyo was acting in concert with Berlin and would seize the opportunity of a European war to impose its own solutions in the Far East. At this point the President believed that Chamberlain should adopt a firmer line in the face of German military preparations, an opinion which perhaps owed something to Goerdeler's message which reached the United States at the end of the month.[16] In a letter to Bowers on 31 August Roosevelt remarked: 'I do wish that our British friends would see the situation as it seems to be – but as you know they are doing everything to stall off controversy and possible war'.[17] Hull adopted a similar position. Goerdeler's warning made 'a deep impression on him'. He was convinced that the 'German program' was 'indefinite' and that Britain, therefore, should take a strong stand against aggression.[18]

At the beginning of September the President authorised naval measures which were clearly intended both to deter Hitler and encourage a firmer British line. On 1 September the US Atlantic Squadron was established, based on seven of 'the newest and most formidable cruisers in the world'.[19] On 10 September two of these warships were sent to British ports, an act which coincided with Britain's own precautionary measures and which was obviously designed to raise the possibility of American intervention.[20] The same day Kennedy approached Halifax and suggested that the Russians be requested to make a similar military demonstration, moving air squadrons to their forward bases.[21] Simultaneously Roosevelt ordered Morgenthau to investigate the possibility of placing British and French gold stocks in the United States in a special fund which could be spent on war materials. The President thought 'it would help psychologically to indicate to the world that the democracies had gold resources in a safe haven'.[22] The British embassy was impressed by these moves. On 12 September Lindsay noted that American opinion was in favour of 'making a strong stand against German aggression'. In the event of war the United States itself would eventually become involved.[23] Roosevelt's actions, however, made little impact in London. While they may have encouraged rebels such as Duff Cooper who wanted to send a definite warning to Berlin, they were simply ignored by Chamberlain and the inner group which dictated policy.[24]

Although Roosevelt seemed to be pursuing a policy of anti-appeasement, contradictory tendencies existed within the administration. Bullitt continued to argue that in the event of a crisis the United States should summon a conference.[25] Kennedy hoped that the United States would support Chamberlain's efforts to preserve peace. He planned to emphasise his own approval of the Prime Minister in a speech at Aberdeen on 2 September when he intended to state that there was nothing in the Czech issue 'remotely . . . worth shedding blood for'.[26] Such views enjoyed support at high levels in the State Department. Welles was on leave at this stage in the crisis, but on 1 September his assistant, Berle, sent a memorandum to Roosevelt complaining about the anti-German feeling at the White House. The United States must not allow itself to be drawn by dislike of the Nazi domestic system into a war 'to maintain a situation which was untenable from the time it was created by the treaties of Versailles and Saint Germain'. Only the Russians could benefit from such a struggle. Instead of stiffening the Western powers, the United States should sponsor a 'general peace conference' although only after the 'sell out' of Czechoslovakia was 'complete'.[27] Welles was to take up Berle's argument when he returned to duty on 26 September.

Before 12 September, however, the President ignored the advice of the appeasers. He continued to criticise Chamberlain and refused to lend his policy American support. Bullitt was not consulted about his conference plan and Kennedy was ordered to strike the projected passage from his speech because it could be interpreted as meaning 'the United States would never fight and England should not'.[28] Roosevelt was increasingly suspicious that Chamberlain planned to place responsibility for a 'sell-out' of Czechoslovakia on the United States and that Kennedy was collaborating with the Prime Minister. His misgivings were first aroused by a message from London on 31 August. Kennedy reported that Halifax had enquired about the American attitude if Czechoslovakia were invaded and Britain stood aside. The ambassador noted 'Chamberlain and Halifax would appreciate your reaction and judgement on this'.[29] News of the British approach leaked to the press the following day. The President was enraged and believed that the leak had been concerted between Kennedy and Chamberlain to put pressure on the administration. He complained that the Prime Minister was 'slippery' and

> could not be trusted under any circumstances . . . [he] was playing the usual game of the British, peace at any price, and would try to place the blame on the United States for fighting or not fighting.

Kennedy had engineered the press reports. The ambassador was 'pro-British' and 'playing Chamberlain's game'. Roosevelt considered ordering Kennedy to issue a formal denial of the newspaper stories, but finally took less extreme action.[30] The State Department merely announced that the American attitude towards the crisis had been made clear in recent speeches by the President and Hull.[31]

If Roosevelt disapproved of appeasement, however, he did little to stiffen Chamberlain's policy beyond sending the *Nashville* and the *Honolulu* into British ports. Indeed at a press conference on 9 September he disclaimed any association with the construction of a united front against Germany. Ironically this statement was provoked by misreporting of a speech delivered by Bullitt on 4 September. At a ceremony in Bordeaux, the ambassador had emphasised the sentimental ties between the United States and France and concluded, 'Today we are working together to preserve peace. May we be as successful in that task as . . . when we marched together under the flags of war.' This was hardly the blunt warning to Hitler requested by the French and represented a plea for a peaceful solution. The Associated Press, however, misreported Bullitt's words and claimed he had stated, 'France and the United States are united in war as in peace.'[32] This version was widely circulated and Roosevelt, fearing isolationist reaction, felt compelled to issue a disclaimer. On 9 September he made a statement denying that the United States was promoting a 'stop Hitler movement'. Such interpretations of American policy were 'one hundred percent wrong'.[33] Nothing could have been better designed to undermine the effects of the Kingston speech and the naval moves. Roosevelt's public repudiation of American involvement encouraged Hitler to discount the alarmist reports of his embassy in Washington while confirming Chamberlain's belief that Britain could not count on American support in the event of war. Hull did nothing to prevent this Presidential retreat. Indeed he argued that rather than provoke the isolationists, the movement of US warships into British ports should be cancelled to prove the truth of Roosevelt's statement. The President, however, refused to go this far and the cruisers were sent to Portland and Gravesend.[34]

Hitler's speech of 12 September and the rioting which followed in the Sudetenland next day seemed to Roosevelt like 'the beginning of the end for European peace'.[35] As long as Chamberlain was making the running the United States could enjoy the benefits of peace while condemning British policy. The threatened breakdown of Chamberlain's mediating role forced Roosevelt to reconsider his position. The President had to decide if the United States should encourage a firm stand by the Western powers or whether, as the 'appeasers' in his own entourage argued, America should intervene to preserve peace, a course which might mean the sacrifice of Czechoslovakia. Typically Roosevelt attempted to pursue both courses at once. After listening to Hitler's speech on his radio, the President sent Harry Hopkins to California to investigate the capacity of the aircraft industry there.[36] He obviously recalled French fears of German air superiority and in the following week developed the idea, first suggested by de la Grange, of the United States acting as the 'arsenal of democracy'. Roosevelt believed that public opinion would support such a scheme if war broke out and intended to encourage anti-axis sentiments.[37] Simultaneously, however, he investigated the possibility of an American peace initiative. On 13 September the President telephoned Bullitt and discussed the idea of an American sponsored conference.[38] Roosevelt was saved from intervention at this stage, however, by Chamberlain's decision to fly to Berchtesgaden. He only reconsidered Bullitt's scheme after the Godesberg meeting when Chamberlain's mediating role appeared to have collapsed for good.

Despite the Anglo-French scheme for cession of the Sudetenland which emerged from the Berchtesgaden meeting war remained a possibility. The main danger was that the Czechs would reject the proposals for an orderly transfer and that Hitler would then use force.[39] On 17 September Roosevelt remarked that if the Czechs remained intransigent they would be overwhelmed in 'a swift and brutal war'. Hitler would seize what he wanted while Britain and France stood aside and 'washed the blood from their Judas Iscariot hands'. Public opinion, however, might force the Western powers to intervene. In the event of hostilities Britain and France should fight defensively. If he were conducting the war 'he would announce that every frontier of Germany would be closed tight regardless of consequences . . . surrounding countries would be rationed if they did not come into the alliance voluntarily'. German morale would quickly collapse in the face of such a blockade combined with an allied bombing campaign.[40] He was aware that German air strength might be used to counter this strategy and subject the populations of Britain and France to a 'pounding' from the air. The President, however, intended to remedy any deficiencies by supplying the Western powers with the products of American industry. At this point Hopkins was already in California investigating the potential of American aircraft factories. Although the Neutrality Act continued to exist, Roosevelt planned to evade the legislation by exporting aircraft in parts or as partly finished raw materials. Such supplies would be paid for by the liquidation of British and French investments in the United States.[41] The President intended to inform the British of his plans but not through Kennedy who could not be trusted. Instead he hoped to arrange something through Lindsay, 'the old boy up at the British embassy'.[42] The President was convinced that his scheme was in America's strategic interests. Britain and France kept Germany 'bottled up'. If the United States allowed them to be defeated Hitler and his axis partners would attempt to penetrate Latin America, undermining American strategic and economic security.[43]

It might seem, therefore, that Roosevelt had finally opted for anti-appeasement and intended to encourage a firm stand against further German threats by promising Britain material support in the event of war. His position, however, remained equivocal, a fact which became evident when he expressed his views to Lindsay at a secret meeting on 20 September. The President outlined his scheme for an economic blockade and promised that the United States would cooperate in cutting off supplies to Germany. He also indicated his willingness to evade the Neutrality Act in the event of war. On the other hand, Roosevelt seemed unconvinced that Hitler's aims were indefinite and required the construction of a united front against aggression. He called the Berchtesgaden terms 'the most terrible remorseless sacrifice that had ever been demanded of a state' and claimed that they would arouse 'a highly unfavourable reaction on the part of public opinion'. He was not, however, disposed to blame Chamberlain and talked 'in a most friendly and appreciative manner of the Prime Minister's policy and efforts for peace'. If Chamberlain were successful, Roosevelt would be 'the first to cheer'. He was uncertain how the United States could help in the current situation. He dare not express approval of the Anglo-French proposals but hesitated to condemn Germany lest this encourage the Czechs to 'vain resistance'. He would, therefore, refrain from any public comment. If Prague rejected the Berchtesgaden terms and Hitler attacked, Britain and France should summon a conference to consider disputed borders. If this were held outside Europe, for example in the Azores, the United States would attend.[44] Clearly the President was anxious to preserve peace while evading direct implication in the 'terrible remorseless sacrifice' which would have to be forced on the Czechs as the price of avoiding war. In the last resort Roosevelt, like Chamberlain, was prepared to buy peace by conceding the

Sudetenland, even if Hitler resorted to force. His anti-appeasement plans would only come into force if the Führer finally proved that Nazi aims were indefinite by demanding more. As the crisis developed after 20 September the President's scheme to support the allies faded into the background and he placed increasing emphasis on securing a negotiated solution, to the distress of 'anti-appeasers' such as Hull.

American fears that the Czechs would reject the Berchtesgaden terms proved to be unfounded. On 21 September, after Britain and France had threatened to withdraw their support and leave Czechoslovakia to face invasion alone, Prague accepted a plebiscite. Chamberlain then flew to Godesberg to discuss the details with Hitler. The meeting proved to be a rude shock for the Prime Minister. Hitler demanded military occupation of the Sudetenland by 1 October. The Czechs were to be given no indemnity for lost resources. A plebiscite might subsequently be held but military occupation was a prerequisite.[45] Chamberlain was shocked but returned to London prepared to accept these new terms. As he informed his colleagues on 24 September, he had at first been angered by Hitler's attitude but had subsequently 'modified his views'. He continued to believe that the Führer was interested only in racial unity and had no claims beyond the Sudetenland. It would be a 'great tragedy' if Britain 'lost this opportunity of reaching an understanding with Germany'.[46] The Prime Minister clearly remained determined to subordinate the Sudeten issue to the larger goal of an Anglo-German agreement which would preserve peace and stabilise the British economy. In the ensuing debate Halifax played a key role. On 24 September he horrified Cadogan by agreeing with Chamberlain but next day he came out against recommending the Godesberg terms to Prague as a result of overnight consideration. The Foreign Secretary provided leadership for a group of junior ministers unhappy with Chamberlain's policy which had been largely ineffectual at an earlier stage in the crisis. As he revealed at Cabinet on 25 September Halifax had begun to doubt the possibility of a lasting agreement with the Führer as a result of Hitler's insistence on a military solution in the Sudetenland. He recalled the earlier warnings and recommendations of the German opposition which he had ignored. Halifax now felt that if the democracies rejected German demands and Hitler went to war 'the result might be to bring down the Nazi regime'. Halifax's intervention and the uneasiness of other ministers ensured that the Godesberg terms were not recommended to Prague as suggested by Chamberlain at the beginning of the meeting.[47]

A new departure followed this British decision. Hitler was warned for the first time that France would receive British military support in the event of a war arising out of French treaty obligations to Czechoslovakia. On 26 September Sir Horace Wilson was sent to Berlin with this warning and a personal letter from Chamberlain to Hitler suggesting a conference between Germany and Czechoslovakia to discuss methods of ceding the Sudetenland. The letter was delivered on the evening of 26 September. Hitler's reaction to the idea of a meeting with the Czechs was so hysterical that Wilson hesitated to deliver the warning. The same night, in a furious anti-Czech tirade at the Sportpalast, the Führer demanded surrender of the Sudetenland by 1 October.[48] Wilson finally delivered his warning next morning when Hitler was in a calmer mood. He accompanied this action by emphasising that Chamberlain remained anxious to conclude a broad general agreement which would provide the basis for 'great economic prosperity throughout the world'. The only prerequisite was a peaceful settlement of the Sudeten problem. Hitler, however, was unmoved by the British warning and refused to modify the Godesberg terms. It seemed that he would accept no other solution than military occuption of the Sudetenland.[49]

Despite Hitler's rebuff to Wilson's overtures Chamberlain had not abandoned hope of preserving peace. Although the fleet was mobilised on 27 September, the Prime Minister was still seeking some solution which would avert war by meeting German territorial demands. Chamberlain was convinced that Hitler desired military occupation of the Sudetenland, not because he intended to smash Czechoslovakia but because he distrusted Prague and wished to liberate the Sudetens from the outrages which he claimed were being perpetrated by the Czechs. Despite his insistence on a military solution, the Führer's aims were essentially limited. The Prime Minister, therefore, remained willing to accept the Godesberg terms, a fact which became evident at Cabinet on 27 September when Wilson reported the results of his visit to Berlin. According to Wilson the only course which could now avert war was to 'advise the Czechs to evacuate th~ [Sudeten] territory', allowing the Germans to march in unopposed. Chamberlain supported Wilson's recommendation, arguing that the Empire opposed war and that the Czech army was in no condition to fight. Once again, however, acceptance of the Godesberg terms was opposed by Halifax who had 'lost all his delusions about Hitler' and rejected the idea of such a 'complete capitulation'.[50] The deadlock over the Godesberg terms was only resolved that evening as the result of a letter from Hitler offering to guarantee the Czech state minus the Sudetenland.[51] This confirmed Chamberlain's belief that his demands were limited and that his intransigence sprang from fundamental distrust of the Czechs. On 28 September the Prime Minister replied to the Führer suggesting an immediate conference in Berlin. Britain, France and Italy would attend as well as Germany and Czechoslovakia but the USSR would be excluded. Chamberlain offered to guarantee that the Czechs would accept any solution which emerged, hoping that Hitler would see the British pledge as an alternative to immediate military occupation. Simultaneously Mussolini was asked to intervene with Hitler in favour of peace.[52] Italian influence proved decisive and on the afternoon of 28 September Chamberlain was invited to attend a conference at Munich next day. The agreement which emerged from this four power meeting seemed an improvement on the Godesberg terms since German military occupation was to take place in stages under international supervision. Since the international commission 'quickly collapsed', however, Hitler had been granted the essence of the Godesberg demands while conceding to Chamberlain the empty form of an orderly transfer.[53]

Between 24 and 28 September, with the British role as 'honest broker' apparently breaking down, Roosevelt was faced with hard decisions which he had been able to avoid earlier in the crisis. Equivocation was no longer possible and there seemed to be a clear choice between appeasement and anti-appeasement. There were proponents of both courses within the administration. On 24 September Kennedy reported that while Chamberlain remained committed to 'peace at any price' the Cabinet was split and many ministers were opposed further concessions to Hitler.[54] The ambassador's own inclination was to support Chamberlain and at this point he was spreading information about overwhelming German air strength in the hope of exerting an influence in favour of accepting the Godesberg terms.[55] The same day Bullitt informed the President that with the impasse at Godesberg, the time had come to issue an appeal for a conference at the Hague.[56] In Washington opinions were divided as they had been throughout the crisis. The difference was that events were now forcing the President to make a clear choice. Hull was reluctant to act on Bullitt's advice. He was convinced that Hitler was 'bent on widespread aggression' and that 'nothing short of . . . force or complete capitulation' would halt him 'in pursuit of his plans'. American intervention would throw the United States 'into the same appeasement camp with Chamberlain [and] sooner or later attract the same obloquy that Chamberlain received'. Moreover if successful, it would encourage the complacent notion at home and abroad that German aims were limited, interfering with rearmament and weakening the capacity of the democracies to resist the next set of Nazi demands.[57] Welles, however, adopted a contrary position. He had returned from leave on 26 September ensuring that for the first time in the crisis the appeasers had a powerful spokesman next to the President. Welles did not subscribe to Hull's belief that German aims were indefinite. He argued that Hitler could be satisfied and Nazi extremism defused by revision of Versailles and supported Bullitt's plea for American action to save the peace.[58] With the assistance of Berle, Welles drew up a proposal for American mediation which, like his earlier scheme of October 1937, hinted at revision of Versailles. Welles hoped to transform any conference on the Sudeten issue into a forum for a general European settlement. There was a heated debate about his plan in the State Department and in the end Roosevelt himself rejected 'the idea of revision' as 'too dangerous'.[59] The President was also reluctant to propose mediation and instead, on 26 September, issued a general appeal to all parties to the Sudeten dispute to avert war by continued negotiation.[60] This appeal received the same reply from Hitler as the similar plea made by Sir Horace Wilson, a catalogue of German grievances and Czech 'crimes'.[61] In this situation Welles renewed his pressure for an American sponsored conference. Once again he attempted to transform the Sudeten dispute into the basis for a general settlement. Roosevelt should call a conference at the Hague which would be accompanied by parallel economic discussions in which the United States would play a major role. While the European powers solved their border problems, the United States would remodel the world economy.[62] Once again, however, the President modified Welles' proposals. On 27 September he called for a conference at the Hague but avoided any suggestion that the United States would attend. Economic talks were not mentioned.[63] Roosevelt remained anxious to avoid any personal involvement in the dissolution of Czechoslovakia which was bound to be the result if

Hitler agreed to the meeting. Mussolini was requested in a separate message to support the American effort to solve the crisis by 'negotiation . . . rather than by resort to force'.[64] While the President was urging continued discussions, Hull was pursuing his own course designed to demonstrate American support for Britain in the event of war. On the morning of 28 September he summoned Lindsay to the State Department and pledged that if war broke out, the United States would not take advantage of the situation to displace British trade in world markets.[65] The Secretary was clearly unhappy about the prospect of a 'capitulation' to Hitler and this intervention may have been designed to strengthen the hands of the 'anti-appeasers' in the Chamberlain Cabinet.

Under pressure of events Roosevelt had moved very far from his previous condemnation of Chamberlain as a 'Judas Iscariot' who was 'selling' Czechoslovakia. However much the President might later readopt that line and disclaim any responsibility for the Munich settlement, his appeal for a conference was an implicit acceptance of the dismemberment of the Czech state, a solution which he had earlier seemed to oppose. When Roosevelt intervened, all sides had already accepted the principle of cession. Further talks could only be about the method and timing of transfer. It was the realisation of this fact which dictated the President's refusal to become directly involved in any peace conference held as a result of his intervention. It would seem that despite his doubts about appeasement after the *Anschluss* and his disparagement of Chamberlain, Roosevelt was not yet entirely convinced that Hitler's ambitions could not be satisfied short of European domination. The evidence suggests that faced with the threat of war after 24 September, Roosevelt made a final gamble on appeasement hoping, like Chamberlain, that the sacrifice of Czechoslovakia might provide the basis of a lasting peace. The President may have reasoned that if this gamble failed, it would nevertheless place responsibility for war clearly on Hitler and thus reconcile public opinion to the idea of assisting Britain and France. Fundamentally, however, Roosevelt wanted to believe that a settlement was possible. The phased occupation of the Sudetenland agreed at Munich at first convinced him that Hitler's aims were limited. As he had promised Lindsay on 20 September, he was 'the first to cheer'. In the immediate aftermath of the crisis the President sent his famous 'good man' telegram to Chamberlain and in a letter of 5 October remarked 'I wholly share your hope and your belief that today there is the greatest opportunity in recent times to establish a new order based on justice and right.'[66] With the 'sell out' of Czechoslovakia completed, the United States was clearly anxious to participate in any wider settlement along such lines.

In retrospect the Munich crisis marked the last phase of one American policy and the beginnings of another. Roosevelt's intervention in the final stages of the crisis was a final attempt to pursue the appeasement line which had characterised policy before the *Anschluss*, a line based on the assumption that Hitler's aims were limited and that Germany could be reintegrated into the international system by a policy of judicious concessions. When it was revealed later in October that Hitler did not regard Munich as a final settlement, the President abandoned the policy. The failure of appeasement brought him back to the idea first evolved during the Czech crisis, of containing further German expansion by placing the economic resources of the United States behind Britain and France. This approach was based on the assumption that Hitler's aims were unlimited and that Germany could only be restrained by the threat of force. The conception of the United States as the 'arsenal of democracy', a limited liability role which envisaged the deployment of American economic rather than military power against the axis, was to characterise American policy until 1941.

8 The Failure of Appeasement

The Americans, like the British, at first believed that Munich might provide the basis for a world settlement. The suspicion that Hitler's aims were unlimited vanished briefly. The administration, however, soon concluded that Munich had been merely a truce and by November Roosevelt was admitting to shame at his association with that settlement. American disillusion was based upon developments in German foreign and domestic policy. Hitler's Saarbrücken speech and the *Kristallnacht* pogrom convinced Roosevelt that no permanent settlement was possible while the Nazis remained in power. Ribbentrop's attempts to strengthen the Anti-Comintern Pact confirmed fears of an axis conspiracy aimed at world domination. In November 1938 Britain was faced by a similar impasse in relations with Germany. A measure of Anglo-American cooperation followed which had been absent in the period before Munich. Hitler's intransigence forced both powers to replace appeasement with a show of force designed to deter further German expansion.

The immediate American reaction to Munich was one of cautious optimism about the future. The construction of a stable world order based upon disarmament, free trade and the rule of law appeared possible. The appeasement group in the State Department began to lay plans for American participation in this effort. The task was not to be left to the four powers which had met at Munich. Welles hoped that the United States could promote a settlement which would defuse Nazi extremism by granting Germany a stake in the system while simultaneously remodelling the world economy along American lines. In a radio address of 3 October he claimed that an opportunity existed to found a new world order based on justice and law.[1] This clearly implied revision of Versailles. It also implied economic justice in the form of equal access to raw materials and the creation of the Open Door world which had long been the aim of American diplomacy. Berle was equally optimistic and argued that the United States could best promote peace and prosperity by sponsoring a general disarmament conference.[2] The most outspoken appeaser of all was Kennedy. At a Trafalgar Day in London on 20 October he called for cooperation between dictatorships and democracies and international action to end the arms race.[3] Significantly his text had been cleared by Welles and annoyed officials such as Hull who were less convinced about the prospects of a lasting settlement with Germany.[4]

This group continued to express unease about Hitler's ultimate intentions and in particular emphasised the danger of an Anglo-American economic deal which would strengthen the Nazi system. In a memorandum of 29 September Messersmith argued that despite Munich, Hitler had not abandoned his expansionist programme. He feared, however, that Chamberlain might extend economic aid to Hitler as the price of peace, an act which would only bolster rearmament and intensify German trade competition in Latin America. The liberal trade system promoted by the United States since 1934 would collapse in the face of such a development and America would be left with the 'crumbs' of world trade. Messersmith concluded

> I am fearful that in the arrangements about to be made, and which may be made in the near future growing out of the Munich meeting, someone other than ourselves may give away something precious that belongs to us.[5]

As before Munich, Messermith's formula was to leave Hitler to 'stew in his own juice' in the belief that economic difficulties would produce a collapse of the regime and the creation of a more trustworthy government headed by conservatives. Instead of strengthening autarky, therefore, Chamberlain should contribute to the containment of Germany by signing the Anglo-American trade teaty.[6] Morgenthau shared Messersmith's doubts about German intentions and advocated positive measures against the Reich. He wanted to exploit Hitler's economic difficulties by imposing heavy duties on German exports to the United States, thus curtailing imports vital to German rearmament. He also wished to extend financial assistance to Latin American to combat German trade in the area. Morgenthau believed that firm action along such lines would rally 'anti-appeasers' in Britain and fatally weaken the German war machine.[7]

Roosevelt called Morgenthau's ideas 'bully' but showed no signs of implementing them.[8] The President adopted a middle position between Welles and Morgenthau, neither ruling out action against Germany nor a further attempt to appease Hitler. While praising Morgenthau's scheme, he did not condemn Welles' statements about American support for a world settlement. The President wished to leave his options open and to avoid a definite policy decision until the results of Munich became clear. If a general settlement proved possible, Roosevelt was clearly anxious to participate,[9] but Chamberlain was to assume all the risks of further approaches to Berlin. The only positive step taken by the President after Munich was to discuss a rearmament programme designed to strengthen American air power. Roosevelt was convinced that the possession of overwhelming air strength had allowed Hitler to dictate his terms during the recent crisis and wished to remedy Western weakness in this area. At a conference on 20 October he called for the expansion of the American aircraft industry to produce 15,000 machines per year. Part of this total would be used to equip the US army and the remainder would be made available to the Western powers and the Latin American states.[10] It was known that France in particular was anxious for access to American production to re-equip its obsolescent air force and would take advantage of such an opportunity. Roosevelt left the political aims of his scheme deliberately ambiguous. Rearmament could be used as a lever to secure a final settlement or as a means of deterring further German expansion pending the collapse of the Nazi regime. At the very least it could be regarded as an insurance lest appeasement fail. Rearmament, therefore, did not imply the adoption of a definite policy towards Germany. It left Roosevelt's hands free until Chamberlain had sounded out the prospects in Europe, while safeguarding the United States against the consequences of British failure.

There were dangers, however, in concentrating on rearmament and allowing Chamberlain to take the lead in approaching Hitler. As Messersmith suspected, plans were being considered in London for an economic bargain with Germany as part of an Anglo-German settlement. Chamberlain hoped that outstanding political and economic issues could be discussed and four power cooperation established as a result of Munich. The Germans were to be led towards a comprehensive settlement by promises of economic assistance. On 19 October 1938 Leith-Ross outlined a plan for economic cooperation to a German trade delegation. He informed the Germans that Britain was interested in reaching an agreement with the Reich. Europe would be in danger of American domination if the four great powers continued to work against each other. Leith-Ross then outlined a scheme to stimulate reciprocal trade. The Balkans needed British and colonial goods which could not be supplied by Germany, but procured no foreign exchange from their barter trade with the Reich to purchase such imports. If the Western powers could allocate to Germany up to 25 per cent more foreign exchange this could be used by Berlin to purchase Balkan exports. The Balkans could use the foreign exchange thus secured to buy British and colonial goods and world trade would receive a stimulus.[11] Such a scheme had several advantages for Britain. Not only could London concede political domination of Central Europe to Germany whilst guaranteeing its markets in the area, it could achieve this goal in a way which would bolster the purchasing power of commodity producers, thus stimulating its entire export trade. Domestic unemployment would be reduced by economic expansion. Chamberlain, moreover, still hoped for a general Anglo-German agreement on prices and markets which would meet the problem of German dumping and through a cartel system guarantee fair returns to both British and German exporters. This possibility had first been raised in July 1938 and was seriously explored after Munich.[12]

The Leith-Ross plan has been interpreted as an attempt to establish a four power economic bloc to combat American trade competition.[13] Leith-Ross certainly implied this and Dirksen subsequently emphasised that Britain desired friendship with Germany to avoid political and economic dependence on the United States.[14] It is difficult to know how far Dirksen was exaggerating to attract the attention of Berlin, or how far Leith-Ross exaggerated anti-Americanism to arouse German interest. Britain certainly resented the economic sacrifices it was being forced to make for political reasons in the Anglo-American trade negotiations and would have welcomed a greater degree of independence in relations with the United States. A European settlement would have placed London in a stronger position to resist American demands for economic concessions. Although Leith-Ross hinted that the Americans might be persuaded to support his scheme, it is difficult to see how the plan could have met with Roosevelt's approval. The United States opposed economic blocs and even if something less was intended, at the very least the plan recognised a German sphere of interest in Central Europe and a British sphere of domination in the Empire. A general Anglo-German marketing agreement was open to the same objections. Both ideas were totally contrary to the American concept of the Open Door and would have been as unpopular in Washington as the Ottawa preferences. Any Anglo-German economic agreement would have confirmed existing American suspicions that Chamberlain was the tool of 'England's Wall Street' anxious only to gain a 'reprieve' for 'private profits' and 'private investment'.[15] The extreme secrecy surrounding Anglo-German contacts implies that London was well aware of this fact, despite vaguely expressed hopes of eventual American cooperation.

While hoping to reach a European settlement which would make Britain less vulnerable to American economic pressure, the government was anxious to remain on good terms with the United States. It was recognised that Anglo-American friendship might deter Hitler from any attack in the West and was valuable in restraining Japan from extreme action against British interests in China.[16] As Halifax revealed, ideally Britain desired the friendship of both Germany and the United States, conceding Hitler *Mitteleuropa* while defending the Empire and Western Europe with the moral support of the Americans.[17] London would be dependent on neither power and would preserve its freedom of manoeuvre. As an added bonus, the Soviet Union would be safely contained. The problem for British policy was that neither Germany nor the United States was satisfied with the concessions which Britain offered and increasingly Chamberlain was forced to abandon balancing and to choose between them. The problem emerged soon after Munich when Hitler spurned British advances while the United States pressed for an early conclusion of the Anglo-American trade treaty. As Dirksen noted, German intransigence forced concessions to the United States which might not otherwise have been considered. Both the Board of Trade and the Exchequer were unhappy about inflexible American demands which it was felt involved too great a sacrifice of imperial preference. Stanley noted that Britain could not 'pay a price out of all proportion to the benefits we are to receive' while Simon felt that 'it would be a misfortune if we were unable to conclude a treaty, but there was a limit to the demands which we could concede'.[18] The Foreign Office, however, recognised that the treaty was vital on political grounds. As Halifax remarked, 'I am afraid . . . the political reasons for getting a treaty through must outweigh trade and economic considerations. And I suppose the Americans have a shrewd realisation of this too.' A breach between London and Washington would only encourage Japan and make Hitler more intransigent.[19] A treaty was, therefore, finally signed on 2 November which was characterised as 'highly unsatisfactory from the point of view of our foreign trade and our inter-Imperial commercial relations'.[20] Economic talks with Germany designed to lead to a European settlement and restore Britain's freedom of action were in progress even as Anglo-American negotiations entered their final stages. Hitler's actions, however, made Britain more rather than less dependent on the United States. He refused to investigate British offers and in a series of speeches at Saarbrücken and elsewhere attacked British rearmament.[21] London, therefore, welcomed the beginnings of American rearmament and the deterioration of American-German relations as factors likely to restrain Germany.[22] Chamberlain, however, had not abandoned hopes of avoiding an unhealthy dependence on the United States through a deal with Hitler. While forced to place more emphasis on conciliating Roosevelt, he held open the economic offers made to Germany in October.[23]

The Americans were disturbed by German actions in October which seemed to show that Hitler would pursue a policy of blackmail and intrigue rather than detente. The State Department was concerned about Hitler's statements at Saarbrücken and remarked that the speech left 'no illusion that the Munich Accord has established all these conditions . . . necessary for a lasting peace'.[24] Tension in Europe was accompanied by reports of an attempt to strengthen the Anti-Comintern Pact and fresh revelations about axis designs on Latin America. On 12 October Grew learned from Craigie, the British ambassador in Tokyo, that the German ambassador had 'definite instructions to strengthen the Anti-Comintern pact' and was 'bringing pressure to bear' on the Japanese government.[25] This attempt to solidify the axis alliance was accompanied by a German trade offensive in South America and reports of German political designs in the area. Vargas claimed to have discovered a plot to secure the secession of four Brazilian states and the establishment of a government under Nazi influence.[26] These developments revived American suspicions of a world axis conspiracy with ultimate designs on the Western Hemisphere. Roosevelt abandoned his initial optimism about Munich and even Welles began to adopt a harsher tone towards Germany. While not for the moment going as far as Morgenthau desired in the direction of positive action, the President gave clear warning that the United States intended to defend its interests and emphasised the deterrent value of rearmament. On 26 October Roosevelt delivered a radio address designed to reply to the Saarbrücken speech. He warned that 'peace by fear has no higher or more enduring quality than peace by the sword. There can be no peace if the reign of law is to be replaced by the recurrent sanctification of sheer force.' Armaments were necessary to defend the Western Hemisphere and there could be no unilateral disarmament.[27] On 2 November Messersmith stated that the United States would take steps to defend its economic position in Latin America and on 6 November Welles called for hemisphere solidarity against outside attack. At a press conference on 15 November Roosevelt called for a defence programme which would make the whole continent impregnable against air attack.[28] The columnist Anne McCormick commented on the new apprehension about German policy:

> Nobody in Washington is quite sure whether we are at the beginning of another Napoleonic era or of a period of appeasement. They are taking no chances . . . the watchword is: Never mention armament without expressing willingness to talk disarmament, but arm.[29]

As German-American relations deteriorated, Roosevelt took steps to strengthen ties with Britain and reassured Chamberlain of American support in the event of war. On 21 October he gave Colonel Murray, an old British friend, a message for the Prime Minister which reiterated the promises given to Lindsay on 20 September. The President stated that in the event of war he would provide Britain and France with partly finished raw materials for an aircraft construction programme sufficient to establish air superiority over Germany. He wanted Chamberlain to feel that he had 'the industrial resources of the American nation behind him in the event of war with the dictatorships'. The Prime Minister should not say this publicly but he might use the phrase 'Great Britain, in the event of war, could rely upon obtaining raw materials from the democracies of the world'. Roosevelt believed that public opinion was becoming less isolationist and was coming to realise that the axis represented an ultimate danger to the United States. He could conceive of 'events' which might involve America itself in war. He did not specify what such 'events' might be but he was clearly thinking of some form of coordinated assault on the British position in Europe and the Far East.[30] Roosevelt perhaps hoped that his message would persuade Chamberlain to reply to the German-Japanese rapprochement and Hitler's rhetorical attacks with a statement of his own emphasising democratic solidarity. This would have paralleled Roosevelt's speech of 26 October and would have threatened Germany with the combined resources of the United States and the British Empire.

The *Kristallnacht* pogrom destroyed any remaining American illusions about the prospects of a general settlement. Even appeasers such as Welles now accepted Messersmith's thesis that Nazism was a revolutionary movement based on extremism at home and expansion abroad. The series of events after Munich, beginning with the Saarbrücken speech, convinced Welles that Hitler did not wish to revise the existing international system but to impose his own solutions. There could be no lasting peace until Nazi expansionism had been contained.[31] Bullitt had already been converted to this view by German conduct during the Munich crisis and after September 1938 believed that Hitler was a greater menace to American security than Stalin.[32] Only Kennedy remained to argue the appeasement case and he no longer enjoyed the sympathy of powerful figures in the State Department.[33] The pogrom, therefore, finally crystallised official opinion in favour of anti-appeasement. Wilson was recalled from Berlin and Dieckhoff left Washington.[34] At a press conference Roosevelt publicly condemned Nazi excesses, not only out of genuine horror but also out of a desire to educate the American people about the German danger and thus win support for the rearmament programme.[35] Simultaneously pressure was brought to bear on Chamberlain to adopt a stiffer line towards Berlin. On 15 November Kennedy warned Halifax that *Kristallnacht* had led to a 'violent reaction against appeasement' in the United States. Opinion was now 'definitely less sympathetic to Britain'.[36] In a letter to his ambassador in Lisbon Roosevelt remarked that the time had come for Chamberlain to 'fish or cut bait'. He plainly felt that Hitler should no longer be allowed to take the initiative in international affairs.[37]

Kristallnacht pushed Britain into closer relations with the United States. Hitler's intransigence and public reaction to the pogrom denied Chamberlain the opportunity to strike a bargain with Germany which would have freed Britain from dependence on American goodwill. The events of October and November forced the government to adopt a stiffer line towards Germany. Hoare recognised this fact in a speech on 24 November in which he remarked that *Kristallnacht* 'made much more difficult the discussion of many questions that we wish to see settled between Germany and ourselves'.[38] Chamberlain himself admitted that a settlement was less likely at the Foreign Press Association dinner on 13 December. While it condemned German intransigence, the government emphasised the friendship of the United States. In the Press Association speech Chamberlain praised the Anglo-American trade treaty as an expression of Anglo-American solidarity.[39] He repeated his remarks in parliament on 19 December.[40] The Prime Minister stressed the importance of the trade treaty because the Germans saw it as more than a symbol of economic cooperation and believed that it contained 'secret military clauses'.[41] Dirksen, the German ambassador, was worried by the new mood of Anglo-American rapprochement. He informed Berlin that the difficulty of reaching a European settlement was forcing London to rely on Washington. In the absence of an Anglo-German agreement the 'only possible alternative' for Britain was to 'foster closer political ties with the United States'.[42]

Chamberlain was encouraged in pursuing a stronger line towards Germany by Murray's message from Roosevelt which reached him on 14 December. The Prime Minister welcomed Roosevelt's promises and clearly hoped that American sympathy with Britain would restrain Germany. He informed Murray that the message was 'most important'. There was 'no question . . . but that in certain circumstances a statement which really brought it home that the vast resources of the United States would be behind Great Britain might have a properly deterrent effect'. While Hitler might try to ignore it, it would have a 'powerful' impact 'on the rest of them and on the army, and make them do their best to put a brake' on the Führer. He was 'very grateful' to the President for his support.[43] Chamberlain subsequently noted on Murray's memorandum, 'To be carefully preserved. Note the formula on second page which may be used.'[44] This was an unexpectedly positive response to a Presidential initiative and reveals how far Anglo-

German relations had deteriorated since Munich. Even Chamberlain realised that appeasement was for the time 'bankrupt'.[45] In a letter to his sister he complained about the 'venemous attacks of the German Press and the failure of Hitler to make the slightest gesture of friendliness'.[46] In these circumstances, American moral support was invaluable in restraining the 'extremists' in Berlin. Moreover the beginnings of rearmament and the deterioration of American-German relations lent Roosevelt's statements some credibility for the first time. Clearly Chamberlain hoped that close Anglo-American relations, symbolised by the trade agreement, would déter a German 'mad dog act' and bring Hitler back to the conference table.

After *Kristallnacht* Britain and the United States pursued parallel policies towards the three axis powers designed to counter Hitler's attempts to use the axis bloc as an instrument of blackmail. What emerged in this period was a threat to use the economic strength symbolised by the Anglo-American trade treaty against Germany and Japan. Simultaneously an attempt was made to weaken the ties of Italy with its axis partners. Germany and Japan depended on the British Empire and the United States for raw materials. Both were already experiencing economic strains, Germany because of autarky and rearmament, Japan because of the crushing burden of the China war. An Anglo-American embargo, therefore, would strike a severe blow at axis war potential. The United States could legally restrict trade with Germany by discriminating against German exports on the grounds that they were subsidised. Since Germany relied upon exports to America to finance purchases of American raw materials, such a move would in effect embargo trade with the United States. Britain could deal an even more serious blow to the German economy by abrogating the Anglo-German payments agreement which gave Germany access to the British and colonial market. Japan, by its flagrant violation of Western rights in China, had given both powers ample grounds for retaliation against Japanese trade.

There was, however, a certain ambiguity about such a joint policy of deterrence. Chamberlain had not abandoned hopes of an Anglo-German agreement and appears to have viewed deterrence as a short-term expedient designed to bring Hitler back to the conference table by proving that Germany had much to lose by enmity with Britain. In Washington it was assumed that the Anglo-American trade treaty marked the end of British offers to Germany.

As Messersmith noted: 'The British agreement means that they are not able to go ahead with any plans that Chamberlain and his friends may have had for far-reaching economic understandings with Germany.'[47] This, however, was not the case. The Prime Minister continued to hint that the economic concessions offered in October were still open if Hitler moderated his policy. In December a preliminary meeting took place between representatives of the Federation of British Industries and the Reichsgruppe Industrie looking towards a marketing agreement between British and German industry. According to a German report the British delegation was anxious for a settlement and 'afraid of being led into a position of economic and therefore political dependence on the USA'. The same month Schacht visited London for unofficial talks about economic relations and was seen by Chamberlain.[48] The Prime Minister, therefore, remained prepared for a deal with Germany even at the expense of American interests. If he was ready to use the United States to deter the Nazi 'extremists', he was also anxious to maintain and increase the influence of 'moderates' such as Göring in the hope that they could persuade Hitler that German self-interest lay in a settlement. Roosevelt by contrast, envisaged deterrence as a longer-term policy. He was not ready to abandon it at the first conciliatory approach from Berlin. The President believed that any future negotiations with Hitler must be conducted from a position of strength. This meant establishing a Western air deterrent while allowing the progressive weakening of the German economy. In the end Hitler would be forced to negotiate on Western terms or be overthrown by mass discontent. Any talks in advance of this development would be regarded by Berlin as a sign of weakness. Unlike the British, the Americans did not believe that 'moderates' such as Göring should be encouraged by economic offers. Bankers and industrialists, such as Mooney of General Motors, who argued along such lines were discouraged by the State Department.[49] Roosevelt himself condemned the 'philosophy of some of our industrialists . . . [that] we can do business with Hitler'.[50] The differing approaches of Roosevelt and Chamberlain were hidden for the time being because Hitler's intransigence left the Prime Minister no opening. Anglo-American dissension did not emerge until a conciliatory speech by the Führer in January 1939 brought to fruition British plans for an economic deal with the Reich.

Morgenthau was the main advocate of economic warfare in the Roosevelt administration. In effect he demanded that the President carry out the policy threatened in the 'quarantine' speech, embargoing aggressors and extending aid to countries such as China which were resisting invasion.[51] Such a development was much feared in Berlin, both by the diplomats and by Göring who was in charge of the war economy. Germany did not break off relations with the United States, despite Roosevelt's hostile attitude, because of the effects on the rearmament programme if this were followed by an American trade boycott.[52] Morgenthau's scheme for economic retaliation, however, was opposed by the State Department and hindered by Roosevelt who refused to lend it positive support. Hull argued that action was inadvisable on both political and economic grounds. He did not believe that public opinion would support retaliation and was sensitive to the reaction of Southern Congressmen to any interference with cotton exports. Hull also feared that if Germany were denied raw materials in the United States it would intensify its efforts in Latin America where German trade competition was already severe.[53] Roosevelt himself would take no positive decision in Morgenthau's favour and asked the Justice Department to delay a ruling on whether German exports were subsidised and, therefore, liable to countervailing duties.[54] The President believed that for the moment he had gone far enough by recalling Wilson from Berlin. He needed public support for his rearmament plans and dared not couple rearmament with offensive action against Germany. This would only have provided the isolationists with ammunition. Roosevelt was also considering neutrality revision and hesitated to alienate the powerful Southern bloc in Congress, whose support was vital for success. On an international level there were further reasons for delay. Economic discrimination might persuade Hitler that he must seize sources of raw materials by force. Once used, countervailing duties would lose their deterrent value. It was better to hint to the Germans that they had something to lose in the event of another international crisis rather than openly to provoke one. The administration, therefore, kept Germany guessing about the future of economic relations with the United States by leaking the fact that countervailing duties were under consideration. Simultaneously the State Department discouraged any idea of financial assistance to an unreformed Germany. The commercial attaché in Berlin informed American bankers, who were thinking of granting credits to the Nazis, that this would be 'contrary to public policy'.[55]

The British pursued a parallel policy after *Kristallnacht*, threatening Germany with economic retaliation but hesitating to translate words into action for fear of forcing Hitler into a 'mad dog act'. German trade with Britain was more important than German trade with the United States. Anglo-German economic relations were based on the payments agreement of 1933. Germany had a favourable balance of trade with Britain and under the agreement was committed not only to purchase a certain ratio of British goods but also to utilise a proportion of the foreign exchange earned in the British market to purchase colonial goods.[56] This placed Britain in a dilemma because, although German purchases boosted the buying power of colonial producers and thus stimulated British exports, many of the raw materials secured by the Reich were used for rearmament. The commercial attaché in Berlin advocated denouncing the agreement for this reason, believing that German rearmament would immediately collapse.[57] The government was unwilling to go this far. Magowan was reprimanded and ordered to confine his reporting to commercial matters.[58] Chamberlain, like Roosevelt, had no wish to provoke Hitler into war by boycotting Germany. Denunciation would affect the British balance of payments directly by cutting off British exports worth £20.6 million per year, and indirectly by decreasing the purchasing power of colonial producers.[59] Since Chamberlain believed that financial strength would be Britain's main asset in the event of war, he sought a less drastic means of showing Hitler that Britain could defend its interests. At the end of November 1938 the government introduced the Export Credit Guarantee Bill designed to provide support for British manufacturers against subsidised German competition. The bill gave clear warning to Berlin that Britain had the resources to win a trade war and to persuade the Germans that more was to be gained by compromise than by force.[60]

While cooperating to restrain Germany in Europe, Britain and the United States had also to devote some attention to the Far East. In that area Japan was not only contemplating closer ties with the European axis, but was also making clear its determination to drive Western interests from China. The 'democracies' had to consider what could be done to make Japan less useful to Germany and to deter Tokyo from further assaults on the Western position in Asia. The two powers went as far as discussing joint sanctions against Japan. It was felt, however, that sanctions might lead to war in the Far East and play into Hitler's hands by distracting the 'democracies' from Europe.[61] It was, therefore, merely hinted in

Tokyo that sanctions were under consideration in the hope of making Japan think twice about further anti-Western measures.[62] As an alternative the two powers extended loans to China in order to prolong Chinese resistance and absorb Japanese energies.[63] Anglo-American cooperation in the Far East consisted largely of a holding action pending a solution of the German problem.

While a policy of deterrence' was pursued towards Germany and Japan, a policy of appeasement was adopted towards Italy, the weakest of the axis partners. Britain and the United States based their hopes of cultivating Italy on Mussolini's 'moderate' attitude during the Czech crisis and his mediating role at Munich. It was thought that Italian economic difficulties and a desire to avoid subordination to Germany might push Rome into closer relations with the 'democracies'.[64] The British agreed to bring the Anglo-Italian agreement into force in October 1938 and after *Kristallnacht* decided to concentrate their efforts on Mussolini.[65] The Cabinet was informed on 30 November that Chamberlain and Halifax were to visit Rome in January 1939. On 21 December Chamberlain remarked that the main purpose of the visit was to secure Mussolini's good offices at Berlin:

> For some time it had been impossible for Great Britain to take any useful action in Berlin . . . He hoped that Signor Mussolini could be persuaded to prevent Herr Hitler from carrying out some mad dog act.[66]

Roosevelt followed Chamberlain's lead in cultivating Mussolini. It was hoped to interest the Italians in a scheme to settle Jewish refugees in Abyssinia with American economic assistance. This was obviously intended to 'drive a wedge' between Mussolini and Hitler by playing upon the chronic shortage of settlers and capital to develop the new Italian empire.[67] It was perhaps unrealistic of Roosevelt to suggest Jewish settlement in Abyssinia at a time when Italy itself was introducing anti-semitic measures. The Duce rejected the American scheme when Phillips broached the question on 3 January 1939.[68] Moreover too much was made of Mussolini's 'moderation' by both Roosevelt and Chamberlain. The Italians had no real intention of weakening the axis. It was, however, believed in Washington and London that it would be unwise to threaten all three 'dissatisfied' powers simultaneously. This could only assist Ribbentrop's efforts to strengthen the Anti-Comintern

Pact. It seemed worthwhile to cultivate Mussolini in the hope that he might restrain Hitler or at least hamper German attempts to consolidate the axis. In the background was always the recollection of Italy's defection to the highest bidder in 1915.

Roosevelt's reluctance to arouse controversy by a policy of economic warfare is perhaps best understood in relation to his plans for rearmament and neutrality revision. The President regarded rearmament and the opening of American industry to the Western powers as the main deterrents to further axis expansion. The 'democracies' were to strengthen themselves while the deterioration of the German economy weakened Hitler's position. This process could be assisted without sanctions simply by guaranteeing that Germany received no economic assistance, something which seemed to have been achieved with the signing of the Anglo-American trade treaty. Roosevelt regarded Anglo-American diplomatic action to restrain Germany and Japan as a holding action pending the completion of rearmament when the West could face the axis from a position of overwhelming strength. The President never clearly explained what he expected to happen at this point. Presumably he believed that confronted with a collapsing economy and superior military force, Hitler would be forced to abandon his aggressive policy or risk the overthrow of his regime. Roosevelt, therefore, placed the main priority on securing Congressional support for the basic elements in his containment programme rather than becoming entangled in the fight with domestic pressure groups involved in a policy of economic retaliation.

The President emphasised the importance of rearmament at a conference on 14 November immediately after *Kristallnacht*. Roosevelt informed his advisors that he intended to ask Congress to provide funds for an air force of 12,000 planes and a production capacity of 24,000 per year. He would combine rearmament with relief measures by granting funds to the Works Progress Administration to finance seven government plants which would augment private production capacity and soak up unemployment. Roosevelt argued that rearmament was essential to American security

The recrudesence of German power at Munich had completely reorientated our own international relations; for the first time since the Holy Alliance . . . the United States now faced the possibility of an attack on the Atlantic side in both the Northern and Southern Hemispheres . . . this demanded our providing immediately a large air force so that we did not need to have a large army to follow up that air force. He considered that sending a large army abroad was undesirable and politically out of the question.

The President felt that such an air force would deter German expansion and prevent another Munich

> I am not sure that I am proud of what I wrote to Hitler in urging that he sit down around a table and make peace. That may have saved many, many lives now, but that may ultimately result in the loss of many times that number later. Had we this summer 5,000 planes and the capacity . . . to produce 10,000 per year, even though I might have had to ask Congress for authority to sell or lend them to the countries of Europe, Hitler would not have dared to take the stand he did.[69]

Roosevelt regarded rearmament as a political weapon. He wanted the largest number of aircraft in the shortest possible time in order to impress Hitler. In this he faced the opposition of the armed forces. The army favoured rearmament in depth rather than breadth and feared that by concentrating solely on the production of large quantities of aeroplanes Roosevelt might eventually saddle the air corps with obsolescent types and a shortage of pilots. It recommended a more balanced programme, with less expenditure on aircraft and more on airfields and training. It also wanted funds devoted to the ground forces.[70] The President grumbled that he wanted 'airplanes and was being offered everything except airplanes', but he was forced to take professional arguments into account.[71] Moreover Congress would not approve an air force of 12,000 planes because public opinion was not conscious of a state of emergency grave enough to warrant such expenditure. As Morgenthau had always expected, the President had to modify his ambitious plans.[72] Roosevelt's message to Congress on 12 January envisaged an air fleet far inferior to the 12,000 planes mentioned on 14 November and requested only 3000 aircraft. The Germans concluded correctly that this modified programme reflected 'the views of the Armed Forces'.[73] Roosevelt, however, did secure his secondary objective of opening the resources of the American aircraft industry to the Western powers. He overruled army opposition at the end of December and allowed the French to place orders in the United States. This not only allowed France to build up its own air force, it also encouraged American manufacturers to expand capacity which could be used in the American rearmament programme.[74]

It was recognised in the White House that to be really effective as a deterrent, rearmament must be accompanied by revision of the Neutrality Act. The retention of the act could only encourage Hitler to doubt Roosevelt's capacity to intervene decisively in European affairs. Conversely revision of the act might convince Hitler that the American public would support a more active foreign policy and that American military force might be used against Germany. On 7 November the State Department recommended repeal of the arms embargo and the supply of arms to belligerents on a cash and carry basis.[75] Roosevelt probably had this recommendation in mind when he spoke on 14 November of seeking authority from Congress to 'sell or lend' aircraft to the Western powers. The President clearly felt that his freedom of action had been severely circumscribed during the Munich crisis by the existence of the act and wished to secure greater latitude in the future. Revision would guarantee that the United States was taken seriously as a world power both by the axis and by the 'democracies'.

On 4 January 1939 Roosevelt's message to Congress drew together all the elements of deterrence initiated since *Kristallnacht*. The President spoke of methods 'short of war but stronger and more effective than mere words' of resisting aggression. This expression echoed the ambiguous statements of the 'quarantine' speech and was widely interpreted as a threat to impose sanctions against the axis powers. Like the 'quarantine' speech it was meant to restrain the axis by leaving Germany and Japan uncertain about future American action. Roosevelt also called for rearmament and for revision of the Neutrality Act which he claimed endangered American security rather than protecting it.[76] Like many of Roosevelt's statements on foreign affairs, this speech had both a domestic and an international aim. It was designed to rouse the American people to action against the axis. It was also intended to underline in Berlin and Tokyo Roosevelt's intention to pursue a more active role in foreign affairs.

By the beginning of 1939 American policy was committed to containing the axis. Roosevelt's efforts since *Kristallnacht* could be regarded as reasonably successful. A measure of cooperation had been established with Britain and while the President had not secured his full rearmament programme, a beginning had been made. Under administration prompting, Congress was moving towards revision of the Neutrality Act. Time, however, was not on Roosevelt's side. There would inevitably be a time lag before measures such as rearmament and neutrality revision could become effective. The American plan depended for success upon Hitler remaining passive during the critical period. It was thought that the threat of economic retaliation might serve to restrain Germany but it was perhaps unrealistic to believe that if Hitler were really determined he would calmly await the creation of a situation in which Germany was weaker than the Western powers and could not dictate its terms. In 1939 Roosevelt's new policy was overtaken by German action.

9 The January Crisis

At the beginning of January 1939 Roosevelt appeared satisfied with the measures he had taken to restrain Hitler and was optimistic about the future. By the end of the month, however, the whole situation had changed. A war scare about a German plan to invade Holland coincided with a domestic crisis which paralysed the administration at a crucial point in world affairs. Moreover Britain, in the face of the German threat, seemed to be abandoning the strong line pursued after *Kristallnacht* and reverting to a policy of appeasement. The fragile nature of Anglo-American cooperation was revealed. Both countries had collaborated to restrain Hitler, but it became evident that disagreement existed as to whether he had been effectively deterred and whether talks could safely be opened with Berlin. The result was renewed American suspicion of Chamberlain's policy. By the end of February 1939, therefore, it was obvious that Roosevelt had lost the initiative in foreign affairs which he believed had been won at the start of the year. Instead of implementing policies designed to restrain Hitler the President found himself once again merely responding to German actions.

In the two weeks after his address to Congress Roosevelt was confident that his words were being taken seriously in Berlin. At Cabinet on 15 January he boasted that his policy was succeeding. He remarked to Hull that he had been 'doing some straight talking to Hitler'. Hull 'indicated his awareness of that fact and said that it had been doing some good'.[1] American confidence was probably stimulated by a report from Warsaw that the Polish Prime Minister, who had recently visited Hitler, had found the Führer 'furious and worried' as a result of the President's speech.[2] Moreover although Berlin had hinted that diplomatic relations would be broken off if the United States continued to criticise Germany,[3] no action was taken despite Roosevelt's address to Congress. Instead, at a meeting with an American official on 21 January, Göring spoke about his desire to restore cordial relations with the United States.[4] This was attributed to fear of American economic strength and seemed to prove the value of standing firm in the face of threats.[5] Roosevelt was doubtless also encouraged by the British response to his speech which indicated a willingness to join the United States in seizing the diplomatic initiative from the dictators. On 5 January Chamberlain praised Roosevelt's message to Congress and remarked, 'the sentiments expressed by the President will be welcomed as yet another indication of the vital role of American democracy in world affairs'.[6] *The Times*, in an editorial, emphasised that the United States, guided by the ideals expressed by Roosevelt, could 'make a decisive contribution to the maintenance of international order'.[7] Dirksen warned Berlin that Britain felt its position 'vis-à-vis the totalitarian states' had been 'strengthened' as a result of Roosevelt's speech.[8]

The position was rapidly transformed, however, at the end of January 1939. On 23 January a bomber being tested by a French purchasing mission crashed in California with French officers on board. The isolationists seized upon the incident to launch a spirited attack against the secret diplomacy of the administration.[9] On the same day as Roosevelt faced this domestic crisis the international situation deteriorated dramatically. A secret report reached the British Cabinet from Carl Goerdeler of the German opposition that Hitler planned to overcome Germany's desperate economic situation by military force. According to Goerdeler, Schacht had recently warned Hitler that Germany faced financial ruin unless the budget was balanced. Rather than accept this advice and abandon rearmament, Hitler intended to create an international crisis by mobilising on the Dutch border. He hoped to terrorise the West by threats, and if necessary by invading Holland, into conceding German demands for economic assistance. Goerdeler recommended that the West stand firm and call Hitler's bluff otherwise further demands would follow.[10] Halifax was alarmed by this report and remarked that the economic situation might be 'compelling the mad dictator . . . to insane efforts'. He recommended that the government inform Roosevelt about Hitler's intentions 'and also tell him what action we proposed to take'. Vansittart 'thought that it would be of very great value if President Roosevelt could be persuaded to make some announcement on the subject before the speech which Herr Hitler was to deliver on January 30'. Chamberlain agreed about the desirability of an American statement.[11] A note was therefore sent to Washington informing Roosevelt about the threat to Holland. It remarked that it was

> impossible as yet for the Prime Minister to decide whether he himself will utter any public warning to Germany before Hitler makes his speech on 30 January . . . if the President were disposed to take the occasion for any public announcement it might be the more valuable if he were to do so before January 30.[12]

It might at first seem strange that Chamberlain should request an American statement while evading any commitment to make one of his own. There is, however, an explanation for his action. As he revealed at Cabinet on 25 January, the Prime Minister was a 'long way' from accepting Goerdeler's report as an accurate account of Hitler's plans.[13] He continued to distrust the German opposition and did not wish to worsen Anglo-German relations by delivering a warning based on insufficient evidence. If a blunt statement was indeed necessary to restrain the Nazi 'extremists' it should come from the United States while Britain stood ready with the carrot of economic appeasement to encourage the 'moderates'. This approach was clear in the Prime Minister's speech at Birmingham on 28 January. Despite the urgings of Halifax[14] this contained no specific reference to the Low Countries and emphasised American rather than British warnings against any attempt to dominate the world by force. The bulk of the text was devoted to arguing that German economic difficulties could be overcome without war.[15]

The British note about Hitler's plans alarmed the White House. Fears were immediately expressed about the security of Latin America and about the repercussions in the Far East of another German coup. A further extension of the Nazi economic system was seen as a dangerous threat to American military and economic security. The issue was first raised at cabinet on 27 January. Ickes noted:

> If Hitler breaks loose . . . and if he attains his objective, this country is going to suffer tremendously. As the President pointed out, Hitler will not have to control all of Europe . . . in order to make it difficult for us economically. For instance the Argentine now exports eighty per cent of her products to Germany and other European countries. If Hitler can dominate the major part

of Europe, he can serve notice on the Argentine that unless it accepts fascist principles and yields to fascistic economic domination, all of her exports to Europe will be cut off . . . And the same situation would exist with respect to other South American countries. They would be turned against us and we . . . would be powerless to do anything except to retire within our own territory, there to get along as best we could.[16]

If Roosevelt feared the effects of renewed German expansion in Latin America he was also concerned about its possible impact in Asia. The President suspected that Hitler would demand the Netherlands East Indies as part of a settlement with Holland. The islands would then be handed over to Japan as the price of Tokyo's adhesion to the new tripartite pact.[17]

Despite his fears for international stability, however, Roosevelt made no statement about the threat to Holland as Chamberlain desired. He was due to testify before the Senate Military Affairs Committee on 31 January about the sale of aircraft to France and felt that in the circumstances he could go no further than his 4 January message to Congress. Another speech would lay him open to accusations of warmongering and endanger the chances of neutrality revision. It had already been agreed on 7 January that Senator Pittman should raise the question of revision during the current Congressional session.[18] Hull informed the British chargé on 27 January that the domestic situation made it necessary to proceed with extreme caution. Mallet noted that Roosevelt's relations with Congress were 'passing through a critical phase . . . the isolationists are full of fight and many critics are accusing the President of being abnormally alarmist'.[19] Roosevelt himself was highly conscious of this fact. On 29 January he discussed the axis threat with Ickes and remarked that 'It would be absolutely impossible for him . . . to go on the air and talk . . . as we were talking. The people simply would not believe him.'[20]

Although Roosevelt felt unable to act he believed that Britain should do something and resented Chamberlain's attempt to push the United States out in front. His resentment burst out on 29 January as the result of an interview with Lord Lothian, who was to replace Lindsay as British ambassador later that year. Apparently Lothian remarked that since Hitler could not be appeased, the United States must intervene to save 'Anglo-Saxon civilization' from destruction.[21] According to Ickes the President replied that 'while he was willing to help all that he could, he would do nothing if Great Britain cringed like a coward'.[22] Roosevelt was clearly angered by British policy. In a letter to Professor Merriman on 15 February, which also mentioned the Lothian interview, the President noted:

> What the British need today is a good stiff grog, inducing not only the desire to save civilization but the continued belief that they can do it. In such event they will have a lot more support from their American cousins.[23]

It is important to note that these statements were made after Chamberlain's speech at Birmingham on 28 January. Roosevelt believed that he had gone as far as possible in supporting Britain which nevertheless seemed unwilling to stand up for itself. Chamberlain, like Lothian, had asked for American assistance rather than taking a forthright stand against aggression. His conciliatory policy risked tempting Hitler to gamble on British weakness and endangered Roosevelt's entire strategy. It was useless for the President to attempt to repeal the Neutrality Act or educate the American people about the axis danger if Chamberlain denied that any threat existed. The administration would simply appear wildly alarmist. This was what Roosevelt meant by the remark that a stronger British stand would evoke greater American support.

Hitler's speech of 30 January brought Anglo-American differences to a head.[24] Chamberlain and Roosevelt interpreted German intentions differently on the basis of two contrasting passages in the speech. Chamberlain seized upon the section devoted to economics and in particular upon the phrase 'We must trade or die', to argue that fears of a German coup had been exaggerated and that it was now possible to negotiate with Berlin. The Prime Minister believed that 'Hitler and Ribbentrop, so far from hatching schemes against us, are searching round for some means of approaching us without the danger of a snub'.[25] He intended to give them their opportunity. Roosevelt placed greater emphasis on the section devoted to foreign affairs and Hitler's pledge to support Italy in the event of war. This interpretation was reinforced at 'the beginning of February when the State Department received its own copy of the Goerdeler memorandum which argued that the threat to Holland was only a first step and that afterwards Hitler would support Italian claims against France.[26] Washington believed that far from seeking a peaceful way out of German financial difficulties, Hitler was attempting to blackmail the West into extensive economic concessions. Chamberlain should take a strong line with Germany and as Goerdeler recommended there should be no concessions to Berlin. As Messersmith noted, 'I am not one of those who gets any comfort out of Mr Hitler's speech . . . My one hope is that we will all stand up [to Germany] and that there will be no further giving in, for I think it is our best chance really to avoid war.'[27]

Chamberlain, however, assumed that Hitler, under the influence of the 'moderates' was responding to the offer of economic cooperation contained in his Birmingham speech. The goal of European stability seemed within reach and Britain must seize the opportunity to guide Germany away from autarky towards a more liberal political and economic system. As the Prime Minister informed the Commons on 31 January, the policy of appeasement was 'steadily succeeding . . . It seemed . . . that there were many passages in [Hitler's] speech which indicated the necessity of peace for Germany as well as for other countries.'[28] Britain's economic position must have influenced Chamberlain in reaching this conclusion. At the end of 1938 the adverse balance of trade stood at £70 million and unemployment had risen to over 2,000,000. Marketing agreements with German industry would have eased the strain on the export sector of the economy and a return of confidence might in itself have stimulated trade and employment. Chamberlain clearly believed that Britain too 'must trade or die'.[29]

The Prime Minister thought that Anglo-American cooperation after Munich had played a large part in bringing Hitler to the point of negotiation. He noted on 5 February, 'Roosevelt is saying heaven knows what but anyhow something disagreeable to dictators and there is an uneasy feeling that in case of trouble it would not take much to bring US in on the side of the democracies'. Germany could not count on the assistance of Japan since American rearmament and Anglo-American cooperation in China made Tokyo unwilling to 'offend US and UK'. Hitler was increasingly isolated and war had become unpalatable as a solution to German economic problems.[30] Dirksen encouraged this view. He informed Halifax on 23 February that Roosevelt's message to Congress had convinced Hitler that 'in the event of war the United States would come to the aid of the Allies in two days not two years'.[31] As far as Chamberlain was concerned, therefore, deterrence had succeeded and must now be replaced by a more flexible policy which offered Germany a solution to its economic problems.

Chamberlain moved quickly to follow up Hitler's speech. It was hoped that the signature of an Anglo-German coal agreement on 28 January would pave the way to further industrial talks. It was agreed that British and German representatives should meet at Dusseldorf to discuss marketing agreements amongst other export industries. A visit to Berlin by the President of the Board of Trade was also arranged.[32] In a speech at Blackburn on 22 February Chamberlain responded to Hitler's Reichstag address. He declared that international tension was the chief cause of unemployment since it undermined business confidence and reduced international trade. Hitler's statements on 30 January had stimulated foreign trade and the government hoped that this trend would continue. If tension were reduced and trade flourished this would provide a greater impetus towards reducing unemployment 'than all the artificial remedies which anyone has ever thought of'. Chamberlain welcomed the coal agreement and stated that the quickest way to improve Anglo-German relations was further economic discussions. Such talks would eventually lead to arms limitation and peace.[33] The speech reveals the importance attached by Chamberlain to economic talks both as a bridge to a political settlement and as a means of escape from the British trade recession.

In mid-February Ashton-Gwatkin of the Foreign Office Economic Department visited Berlin and talked to several prominent Nazis. His report was to provide the basis for Stanley's visit. Ashton-Gwatkin found Göring anxious to agree on economic cooperation in the Balkans as the basis for political discussions. Funk desired to remove exchange controls and grant economic concessions to Britain. Ashton-Gwatkin believed that the state of the economy demanded peace and that the Germans were turning to Britain for concessions. He recommended that: 'We should not ignore the possibilities of a more peaceful development and we should not put Hitler into a position to say that once again he had made an offer of cooperation and Britain had pushed it aside.'[34] Henderson endorsed this report on 28 February and advocated the extension of economic assistance to Hitler. This should be 'just sufficient to encourage Germany to hope for more provided . . . she reduces her present armaments programme'. Halifax marked this section and endorsed the policy recommendation as 'about right'. He asked that Stanley's 'special attention' be drawn to Henderson's report before he visited Berlin.[35] On the basis of Ashton-Gwatkin's information, Chamberlain concluded that no new adventure was imminent and that the Germans had a genuine desire for economic cooperation with Britain. He assumed that Hitler himself had prompted the statements on the necessity of loosening exchange control.[36] This concession was important since it represented the first step towards dismantling autarky and returning to a more liberal political and economic system. The few British diplomats who argued that the Nazis would never go so far as to abolish the entire apparatus of the totalitarian state in return for British financial assistance were simply ignored by the Prime Minister.[37]

The Americans were puzzled by Chamberlain's optimism. It was suspected in Washington, as after the *Anschluss*, that Britain was trying to buy Hitler off by some unprincipled bargain. Messersmith remarked on 3 February 'the stupidities which are being committed are so great that they are more than criminal' and he accused Chamberlain of 'criminal participation' in Hitler's aggressive plans.[38] Kennedy, who was on leave in January, was hurriedly sent back to London by Roosevelt to ascertain what lay behind British policy.[39] His enquiries did nothing to stimulate American confidence in Chamberlain. At a meeting on 17 February the Prime Minister painted a reassuring picture of international developments. The situation was 'much better' than it had been in January. He saw 'no definite indication of moves towards Holland or Switzerland or elsewhere to the West or to the Ukraine'. Chamberlain felt that Britain could 'do business' with Hitler and hoped to achieve something by means of trade talks. Henderson had been sent back to Berlin as an indication of a 'more pliant attitude' on the part of Britain. The Prime Minister did not believe that Germany was encouraging Italy to attack France. 'In fact . . . Hitler is urging Mussolini to play down the issues with France rather than to make too great a fuss about them.' Mussolini might even be persuaded to put forward disarmament proposals once the Spanish Civil War had ended, an event which could not be long delayed.[40]

This view did not square with information in American hands about axis intentions. Washington was no longer concerned about the supposed German threat to Holland which had never materialised but believed that Hitler's attention had shifted to another area mentioned by Goerdeler as a possible target, the Mediterranean. It was thought that the Führer was encouraging

Mussolini to attack France. This in itself was merely part of a wider conspiracy involving Japan which was to pursue its own aims in the Far East. On the basis of reports from Moscow, the Americans assumed that a strengthened tripartite pact was about to be signed which provided for a coordinated attack on the Western powers at some point in the spring.[41] Undoubtedly Roosevelt was much influenced by his ambassador in Paris. The French froze Bullitt's blood with tales of German military movements in support of Italy. As Berle noted 'The French have been scaring Bullitt almost to death, talking of war at any moment and of the certainty that the American embassy will be bombed.'[42] Since Bullitt was trusted and Kennedy was not, such reports carried greater weight in the White House than reassurances from London. On 16 February it was reported from Paris that Mussolini intended to go to war with France if his demands in Corsica, Nice and Tunis were not met. Hitler had promised him military assistance. Italy was now mobilising. There were 100,000 troops in Libya and a large number of German soldiers were serving with the Italians. The axis was about to begin a 'campaign of intimidation and . . . would strike at the end of March'. Bullitt felt this information, which came from the Deuxième Bureau, should be taken 'most seriously'.[43] On 17 February the military attachés in Berlin, Rome and Paris were asked to check on the authenticity of this report.[44] The attachés in Berlin and Rome could detect no evidence of preparations for war. The attaché in Paris, however, reported that France had unconfirmed evidence that two German divisions were being prepared for service in North Africa.[45]

Washington was not reassured by the calming reports of the military attachés in the axis capitals nor by the despatches of Phillips in Rome, who doubted whether Mussolini intended to do more than put diplomatic pressure on France.[46] The Japanese occupation of Hainan Island on 10 February confirmed fears of an axis conspiracy. Bullitt reported on 11 February that the French believed Japan was well informed about the Berlin–Rome timetable. The occupation was connected with the German–Italian threat to French security and was designed to distract the democracies. It was 'one of the final steps preparatory to the precipitation of events by Mussolini'.[47] Moffat noted on 17 February that Welles was 'very apprehensive of the role which the seizure of the Island of Hainan plays in the timing between Italy, Germany and Japan'.[48] Lindsay suffered for the optimism of his government. On 20 February Welles questioned him closely about the views expressed by Chamberlain on 17 February. Welles remarked that the United States had received 'disquieting' information pointing towards a new crisis. The Italians and mobilised 300,000 men and were being supported by the Germans who had sent mechanised units to Libya. Japan was about to sign a new axis pact and all three were prepared to 'play into each others hands'. The occupation of Hainan was an example of this. Welles expected a new crisis in the middle of March and predicted that by the end of that month war was 'more likely than peace'. He asked Lindsay to justify Chamberlain's optimism in the light of this information. Lindsay could only reply rather lamely that 'he doubted whether Mr. Chamberlain's colleagues in the cabinet shared his feeling of reassurance, and he, the Ambassador, knew as a positive fact that the Foreign Office was exceedingly apprehensive'.[49]

The Americans also expressed concern about the Anglo-German trade talks initiated by Chamberlain. On 21 February Davies sent a memorandum to Hull and Welles containing information about the economic discussions and the projected visit of Stanley to Berlin. Davies felt that any marketing agreement between the two powers would have 'very extensive repercussions' upon American policy and 'upon the interests of our exporters'. It would be 'the direct antithesis of free competition and the free flow of trade' desired by the United States.[50] Hull expressed similar concern and doubted that Britain seriously wished to promote the open world economy sought by the State Department.[51] It was feared in Washington that an Anglo-German economic agreement would not only threaten American trade interests but would also strengthen Germany without gaining any guarantees for the future. It was thought that any bargain involving a British loan would only put Hitler into a better position to arm and threaten. In a message to Kennedy on 7 March Welles remarked that he had informed Lindsay of the strong American interest in

both the political and the economic connotations of any arrangements which may be worked out between England and Germany . . . What form of arrangements [British] efforts may result in is not at all clear. If any arrangements should be established which would facilitate the operation of the German trade system while Germany continues to arm and threaten aggression, this could not fail at the present time to attract attention in the United States and to affect public sentiment with regard to European affairs.[52]

Chamberlain had no desire to alienate the United States. On the assumption that American sympathy with the democracies had forced Hitler to negotiate, a breach in Anglo-American relations would only encourage him to spurn British offers. Attempts were, therefore, made to reassure Washington about the general international situation and the Anglo-German trade talks. The Foreign Office was as anxious to calm American fears of axis intentions as the Prime Minister. While not so optimistic as Chamberlain, the Foreign Office feared that Roosevelt was being unduly alarmist, perhaps with French encouragement. It was feared that Paris, by crying 'wolf' too often without good reason, might deprive the democracies of American support in a genuine crisis.[53] On 27 February, therefore, a despatch was sent to Lindsay arguing that British information did not confirm American reports. Hitler seemed to have abandoned the idea of precipitating an immediate crisis. Halifax did not believe that Mussolini intended to attack France. There was no evidence that Japan intended to sign a new tripartite pact. Halifax admitted, however, that Germany would support Italy in the event of war and that the axis powers would play into each others hands when it suited them to do so.[54] This despatch reflected the Foreign Office view of the situation, which was half way between Roosevelt's pessimism and Chamberlain's optimism. Halifax himself was uncertain what to think. In the presence of permanent officials, such as Harvey, he was less optimistic than in the presence of Chamberlain. His ambiguous attitude towards the idea of an axis conspiracy was revealed at a meeting with Dominion representatives on 17 February. Halifax admitted at this point that he was concerned about Italian military measures and the Japanese occupation of Hainan. Nevertheless he did not feel that a crisis was imminent. Such moves were 'part of a policy of keeping us frightened'. Halifax admitted, however, that his predictions might be proved false 'the very next day'.[55] Chamberlain never made such reservations. As he remarked on 19 February, while Roosevelt was expressing concern, 'I myself am going about with a brighter heart than I have had for many a long day'.[56]

Halifax's message failed to carry any conviction in Washington, where some form of German-Italian coup was still expected. The administration remained under the influence of alarmist reports from France. Bullitt informed Hull on 28 February that Mussolini intended to 'try some flamboyant blackmailing act about the 7th of March'. Bonnet believed that Italy would back down if France refused to be intimidated, but Daladier and the General Staff were not 'nearly so optimistic' about the possibility of avoiding war.[57] The sense of gloom in Washington was further stimulated by an émigré Italian source. On 2 March Davies reported that Count Sforza, the cousin of the King of Italy, had warned him that Hitler was backing Mussolini's claims against France. The signal for war would be a contrived 'incident', such as the murder of the Italian consul in Tunis.[58] The Americans believed information from such sources rather than reassurances from London about the international situation. On 2 March Welles informed Moffat that he was 'most apprehensive' about the future and thought that the British were 'living in a fool's paradise'.[59]

British attempts to reassure the United States about the Anglo-German trade talks also met with a signal lack of success. Johnson reported from London on 2 March that there was 'a complete awareness, in leading business circles, of the need for not antagonising the United States in regard to any settlement reached either by British industries with their complementing German organisations or by any joint Government understandings'.[60] Hudson, of the Department of Overseas Trade, approached Kennedy on 3 March to 'reassure' the ambassador 'that the British were not attempting by their trip to Germany to interfere at all with American trade and that when they found out anything definite about the position' they would immediately 'get in consultation' with the United States.[61] It is unclear what the British wanted beyond general American approval of economic appeasement. Hudson seemed to envisage eventual American participation in marketing agreements. London may also have hoped that, following an Anglo-German agreement, the United States would grant credits and favourable trade terms to the Reich. Whatever the British wanted it soon became clear that the United States disapproved of economic appeasement. On 20 March Welles again expressed concern about the trade talks and the marketing agreement reached between British and German industrialists at Dusseldorf. Kennedy was ordered to inform Stanley that 'from the beginning [the United States] has been disturbed lest the outcome should serve to strengthen the present German system of trading and handicap the type of commerical policy which this

Government has sought to advance'. The cartel agreements envisaged at Dusseldorf did not 'make a happy impression' in Washington.[62]

Besides expressing its fears for the future and disapproval of the Anglo-German trade talks the administration attempted to pursue the policy of deterrence initiated after *Kristallnacht*. On 31 January Roosevelt met the Senate Military Affairs Committee and justified the sale of aircraft to France on the grounds that a strong France was essential to American security. This statement leaked to the press in a garbled form and emerged as a pronouncement that America's frontiers were 'on the Rhine'. Despite the controversy which this aroused, Roosevelt was not displeased since he felt the remark added to the effect of his 4 January speech. He noted on 4 March that the episode had exerted 'a definite effect on Germany and only a slightly less effect on Italy'.[63] On 18 February, after receiving alarming reports about axis designs against France, the President made another attempt to restrain the dictators. Before embarking on a cruiser to attend the spring fleet manoeuvres Roosevelt delivered two radio addresses at Key West which condemned the use of force in international affairs and called for hemisphere solidarity in the face of totalitarian threats. He also stated at a news conference that disturbing reports had reached him about the international situation and that he might have to cut short his cruise to deal with the crisis.[64] The *New York Times* believed that the President hoped to remind the dictators of American interest in 'the continued political independence of the world democracies'.[65]

It was hoped that the American fleet manoeuvres would have a restraining effect on the axis. The presence of an American fleet in the Atlantic was itself an expression of United States interest in European affairs. Roosevelt ensured that the exercises were publicised and emphasised that their purpose was to prove that the United States could defend the Western Hemisphere against European attack.[66] Beyond such indirect actions, however, Roosevelt refused to go. He resisted Morgenthau's renewed demand for the imposition of countervailing duties on German goods when he returned to Washington at the beginning of March, although he did agree to inform Berlin that such measures were under consideration.[67] Perhaps, like Hull, he feared that economic retaliation might push Hitler over the edge into war. It is also likely that the President felt constrained by the domestic situation. His statement to the Military Affairs Committee and his warnings about a new crisis on 18 February had aroused some controversy. If the isolationists could couple these two statements with an act of 'aggression' against Germany they would gain greater public support and might perhaps be able to prevent the passage of revised neutrality legislation.

At this point the President felt frustrated by Chamberlain's return to appeasement and by the dictates of domestic politics which prevented him from taking stronger action to restrain Germany. At a meeting with Baron Rothschild, whom he met during his February cruise in the Caribbean, Roosevelt complained bitterly about British policy. He remarked that Germany, Italy and Japan had concerted their plans for aggression and intended to strike very soon. Despite American warnings, however, Chamberlain believed that Hitler was 'bluffing'. The President was 'disturbed' by this attitude. Britain 'seemed quite unwilling to listen to the cold facts. Either her Intelligence Service had completely gone to pieces or the Administration was wilfully blind to reality'. The United States could not take a more prominent role in restraining the axis because of public opinion. He was doing his best to warn the Americans of the threat to their security but 'the people disliked war and would not hear of any probability that it might happen, nor would they take any positive steps to prepare for it'. In the event of a two ocean war, however, the United States would eventually become involved and from the start he intended to interpret the Neutrality Act in favour of the Western powers.[68]

Britain and the United States continued to differ about axis intentions until the German seizure of Prague on 15 March. Chamberlain was not deflected from his purpose by American warnings about Hitler's plans or complaints about the Anglo-German trade talks. On 10 March the press published 'rosy accounts' of future developments by the Prime Minister. At an interview with lobby correspondents he stated that Franco-Italian difficulties would soon be settled and described Anglo-German relations as promising. He hoped that it would soon be possible to end the arms race.[69] The same day, in a speech at Chelsea, Hoare predicted 'a new Golden Age' for Europe.[70] The invasion of Czechoslovakia, therefore, came as a surprise to London.[71] The Americans were less astonished since they had always predicted an axis coup in March. By 10 March the administration believed that events in Europe and the Far East were building towards a climax. Axis preparations in Europe were accompanied by rumours of

Japanese activities in the Far East. Grew reported that the docks at Darien had been closed to civilian shipping and that rumour predicted 'an event of international importance' within the next ten days. This might mean war with Russia.[72] This despatch was mentioned at cabinet on 13 March. Morgenthau noted that Roosevelt wished to postpone countervailing duties because events abroad were 'building toward new crises. Japan had closed various docks to public use . . . the Germans were threatening to absorb the Czechs'.[73] The administration, therefore, did not doubt that a crisis would soon occur, but there were uncertainties as to the form it would take—a Japanese attack on the Soviet Union, a German-Italian attack against France, a German thrust into Central Europe or some combination of these moves.

The uncertainties were resolved by the occupation of Prague. The United States immediately made its displeasure known to Germany. It was decided to impose countervailing duties on German goods. Morgenthau noted: 'The President is tickled to death he has a weapon and tickled to death to use it.'[74] The American-Czech trade treaty was suspended so that Germany would not benefit from its terms and Roosevelt investigated the possibility of freezing Czech assets in the United States.[75] At a press conference on 17 March Welles made it clear that Washington did not intend to recognise the German conquest and condemned the use of force in international affairs.[76] Roosevelt hoped that public reaction to the German outrage would benefit his own policy of deterrence. In particular he hoped that it would lead to an early modification of the Neutrality Act. Welles informed Bullitt on 15 March that there was every prospect of revision 'coming along satisfactorily in the near future'.[77] Roosevelt did not wish to take a direct hand in the matter but he did encourage action by remarking at a press conference on 17 March that revised legislation was now more necessary. He hoped that Congressional leaders would work out a satisfactory bill.[78] Roosevelt evidently believed that public opinion would galvanise Congress into action without direct intervention on the part of the administration. He was probably encouraged by a poll published on 12 March showing that 72 per cent of the American people favoured aiding the democracies with food supplies and 52 per cent favoured sending war materials. The *New York Times* remarked that the poll displayed widespread support for the 'short of war' policy announced on 4 January and revealed that public opinion had 'gone beyond some of the provisions of the present Neutrality Act'.[79]

By these actions Roosevelt felt that he had gone as far as possible in demonstrating hostility to the axis and awakening public opinion to the totalitarian danger. It remained to see what action Britain would take as a result of the German coup. If Hitler were to be effectively restrained, Chamberlain must play a leading role. The events of March proved that warning statements by Roosevelt alone were insufficient. Moreover, if Chamberlain continued to pursue appeasement, it might be difficult to persuade public opinion to support a policy of neutrality revision and sympathy with the democracies. As the letter to Merriman reveals, Roosevelt believed that American assistance was conditional on self-help by the Western powers. In the following weeks the attention of the administration was concentrated on London, to ascertain if Chamberlain intended to abandon appeasement, or if he would continue to seek an agreement with Germany.

10 The United States and the Guarantee System

The question mark over British policy seemed to be effectively removed in March and April by the guarantees to Poland, Greece and Rumania and the negotiations for an alliance with the Soviet Union. The United States contributed to this 'peace front' against further axis aggression. At the beginning of April the American fleet was moved into the Pacific to deter Japan, freeing the Western powers to concentrate their resources on Europe. An attempt was made to restrain Italy by making it clear to Rome that American sympathies lay with the democracies which would receive supplies from the United States in the event of war. In a series of public pronouncements the administration attempted to raise doubts in Hitler's mind about American non-involvement in a European struggle. In April 1939 Roosevelt tried to alienate the German public from Hitler by proposing a just settlement which the Führer was bound to reject. Despite such acts of solidarity with the Western powers, however, Washington was at first by no means convinced that Chamberlain had abandoned appeasement or that British policy was stiff enough to deter the axis. Scepticism was displayed about British intentions and the administration made attempts to add to British commitments, particularly over conscription, which ultimately proved successful.

It did not seem at first as if Chamberlain intended to change his policy, despite the Prague coup. On 15 March he informed the Commons that since the Czech state had broken up a British obligation to Czechoslovakia no longer existed. He also announced that appeasement would not be abandoned despite Hitler's action.[1] Halifax, however, was disturbed by this muted response and many Tory MPs evidently shared his feelings.[2] The Foreign Secretary no doubt used beckbench feeling to persuade Chamberlain to adopt a stiffer line in his Birmingham speech of 17 March. There was more, however, than fear of party reaction behind Halifax's advocacy of a firmer policy. He clearly felt a sense of moral outrage at Hitler's action, which broke the solemn pledges given to Chamberlain at Munich. Halifax had been uneasy about the morality of dealing with the Nazi regime since *Kristallnacht* and believed that the time had come to resist evil. Moreover Hitler had shown that his aims were indefinite. Halifax informed Dirksen on 15 March that the Führer aimed at world domination.[3] His fears were confirmed on 16 March when the Rumanian ambassador brought a warning that Hitler was now threatening Bucharest.[4] In this new situation a settlement with Germany was impossible and Britain had to make a stand. If Hitler were to be resisted, the government required as many friends as possible and could not afford to alienate the United States. The administration was known to favour a firmer British policy[5] and there was also American public opinion to consider. If Britain remained inactive, support for Roosevelt's 'short of war' policy might fade away. These were powerful considerations, particularly since resistance to German designs in Europe would make Britain dependent on the United States to defend Western interests in the Far East against Japan. Such arguments had been used before by critics of Chamberlain's policy, such as Eden, but to no avail. After Prague there were rumours of a similar split between Halifax and Chamberlain.[6] Halifax, however, was in a better position to press his arguments than Eden since, as a result of the Prague coup, the appeasement option no longer existed. Chamberlain could hardly argue, as in January 1938, that there was a good chance of reaching an agreement with Hitler. Nor could he contend that the United States was hopelessly isolationist. The public had shown itself willing to support the 'short of war' policy and there was a possibility that the Neutrality Act would be revised. Lastly, in party terms, Halifax was more powerful than Eden had been in 1938. His resignation on the appeasement issue could fatally damage the position of the Prime Minister. Chamberlain, therefore, was willing to listen to advice from the Foreign Secretary about the text of a speech to be delivered at Birmingham on 17 March and broadcast to the Dominions and the United States.[7]

At Birmingham, the Prime Minister was clearly anxious to create a new image. He stated that he wished to correct the mistaken impression conveyed by his statement to the Commons and emphasised that British policy must be reconsidered in the light of the Prague coup. Britain and other peace loving nations must now decide if Germany intended to 'dominate the world by force'. Any such challenge would be resisted. Nor would Britain stand alone. States 'outside the confines of Europe' were also reconsidering their policies because of Hitler's action. Chamberlain was warning Germany to go no further and attempting to meet criticism from within his own party. His speech, however, had broader aims than these. The Prime Minister was attempting to influence the United States by emphasising that Britain had not 'lost its fibre'.[8] He was aware of Roosevelt's argument that approval of support for Britain was conditional upon British standing up for itself[9] and was trying to consolidate public opinion behind the President's policies. Chamberlain was also reminding Hitler that London had powerful friends. The reference to states 'beyond the confines of Europe' which were reconsidering their position was a thinly veiled allusion to Roosevelt's 4 January speech and American condemnation of the Prague coup.

Chamberlain did not specify what commitments Britain would adopt to contain Germany. Halifax was similarly vague about the correct course to pursue beyond withdrawing the British ambassador from Berlin. In a talk with Kennedy on 17 March about the threat to Rumania the Foreign Secretary was not prepared to say whether Britain 'would or would not go to the rescue of Rumania or Poland at this time'. Kennedy reported that ministers were 'going to start educating public opinion . . . to the need of action. They are suspicious that Hitler will keep on moving and that rather quickly.'[10] Halifax, however, soon abandoned this ambiguous position. On 17 March telegrams were despatched to Ankara, Athens, Belgrade, Moscow, Paris and Warsaw, asking for the reaction of these capitals to a further German move. By the morning of 18 March Halifax himself had reached a definite conclusion as a result of overnight consideration. He informed Kennedy that Britain 'must fight if Hitler enters Rumania'.[11] Kennedy replied that Chamberlain's speech the previous evening had been 'first rate'. The United States

> would be more readily moved to support action [against German designs on Rumania] than if, having done nothing as regards Rumania [Britain] then became involved in some trouble consequent upon aggression upon Greece and Turkey, when American opinion would be disposed to say that [the British] were only looking after [their] own interests.[12]

This conversation had a significant effect on Halifax. It is unclear what kind of support Kennedy was talking about but he probably meant that the end of appeasement would make it easier for the administration to secure repeal of the Neutrality Act. Halifax naturally found this prospect attractive. He also realised that if Britain were to resist Germany successfully it would have to rely upon the United States to safeguard Western interests in the Far East. The day after the Kennedy interview he asked the Americans to reactivate the staff contacts which had lapsed after Ingersoll's visit in January 1938 and on 22 March he asked if Roosevelt could move the US fleet into the Pacific in case of need.[13] Halifax clearly wished to convey an image of determination to the United States in order to secure such cooperation. The importance which he attached to Kennedy's words about the necessity of standing up to aggression was revealed at cabinet on 18 March when the threat to Rumania was discussed. Halifax remarked that Kennedy had 'warmly welcomed' the Birmingham speech but 'had added that it carried with it the connotation that this country would not submit to further aggressive action on Germany's part'. Halifax himself believed that Britain must resist any attack on Rumania. Chamberlain agreed that the government could not allow another German coup. Britain should seek allies against further Nazi expansion.[14] As a result of this meeting enquiries were made to Poland, France and Russia, in the hope of reaching some kind of four power agreement.[15] The Americans were kept informed about these developments. On 20 March Halifax informed Kennedy that Poland, France and Russia had been approached. An agreement to consult in the event of aggression would constitute a warning to Hitler.[16]

The United States was expected to make a solid contribution to the emerging 'peace front'. On 19 March Lindsay was instructed to ask Roosevelt for an exchange of naval views since the European crisis meant that Britain could not spare forces for the Far East. Halifax himself approached Kennedy on 21 March and asked if the US fleet could be moved back into the Pacific to restrain Japan.[17] The President was not unwilling to entertain these British requests but felt that he had to move carefully in order not to run ahead of public opinion. He did not wish another confrontation with the isolationists over foreign policy like the one caused by the bomber crash in January, particularly since Pittman had recently introduced revised neutrality legislation. On 21 March Welles visited the British embassy in secret. He informed Lindsay that the President was 'prepared to resume naval conversations'. Talks must be held in secret, however, to avoid a press leak which would endanger neutrality revision.[18] Roosevelt was also willing to consider moving the American fleet back into the Pacific. On 24 March Lindsay was informed that the British request was receiving attention and a 'definite answer' might be expected 'about April 25'.[19]

Besides American moves to restrain Japan and a generally anti-German policy designed to keep Hitler guessing, the British hoped for Roosevelt's support in dealing with the third axis partner, Italy. Chamberlain hoped to weaken the Anti-Comintern grouping by an appeal to Mussolini. He informed the cabinet on 20 March that the Duce might 'put the brake' on Hitler and proposed sending a private letter to Rome.[20] This was despatched the same day. It stated that any further German expansion would make 'another major war' inevitable and asked Mussolini to use his influence for peace.[21] That evening Halifax requested parallel American intervention in Rome.[22] Roosevelt knew that the Prague coup had been an unpleasant surprise for the Italians[23] and was prepared to make an approach to Mussolini which might weaken the axis. His method, however, unlike Chamberlain's was threatening rather than conciliatory. On 22 March when the new Italian ambassador came to present his credentials, the President read the astonished diplomat a 'curtain lecture'. He warned Colonna that in the event of war the democracies would receive American material support and attempted to sow distrust between Berlin and Rome by emphasising that German expansion would ultimately endanger Italy. 'Europe could not contain two overloads at the same time.'[24]

Although the United States was prepared to cooperate with Britain in containing further axis expansion, the old distrust of Chamberlain had not disappeared. Despite the collapse of Anglo-German economic talks after Prague, Hull remained suspicious of the Dusseldorf agreements. He complained that although Britain was doing 'lip service' to free trade 'yet in practice she was encouraging clearing agreements, exchange controls, preferential tariffs and international cartels'.[25] On 24 March Messersmith revealed his own deep distrust of the Prime Minister when he informed a British visitor that the United States would prefer Eden to Chamberlain as British premier. Chamberlain's 'weak and vacillating leadership' might 'easily deal an irreparable blow to

Anglo-American friendship'.[26] Moffat questioned British determination to build a front against further German aggression. He was suspicious of Chamberlain's failure to adopt firm new commitments and characterised the British consultation scheme as 'inept'.[27] The administration was particularly concerned about the failure to introduce conscription as a symbol of British determination to intervene on the continent. Roosevelt raised this question on 26 March in a conversation with Sir Arthur Willert, an old British friend. The President informed Willert that he was 'depressed about Europe' and felt that the chances of war were fifty–fifty. The situation might improve, however, if Britain adopted conscription and threatened Germany with a vast bombing offensive in the event of hostilities. He knew the Germans. They were bullies who would back down if faced with determined resistance. Roosevelt explained that he was doing everything to demonstrate American sympathy with the democracies in the hope of restraining Hitler. He was propagandising isolationist Senators about the dangers to American security posed by German air power and Nazi activities in Latin America. He complained that he was being helped in this campaign 'by Hitler and Mussolini' but not by Chamberlain. Roosevelt 'asked for a lead' from Britain.[28]

Washington, therefore, was impatient with the lack of urgency about British efforts to construct a 'peace front'. Apart from a series of enquiries in East European capitals, London seemed to be following a policy of business as usual. Roosevelt believed that a greater sense of crisis was necessary to secure neutrality revision and convince the American people of the German danger. The French shared the belief that Britain was not going far enough. Bonnet complained to Bullitt on 25 March that London had brushed aside a proposal to guarantee Poland and Rumania and had instead substituted the 'idiotic' policy of the four power declaration.[29] The French were also desperately anxious to persuade Chamberlain to introduce conscription. It was felt that Hitler would not take the threat of British intervention seriously without national service and that in the event of war France would bear the main casualties. The French raised the issue, without success, when Daladier and Bonnet visited London on 23 March.[30] Halifax was more sympathetic to French demands than Chamberlain. Unlike the Prime Minister, he was prepared to accept a degree of economic disruption for the sake of reassuring France and restraining Germany. He also wanted to conduct a bipartisan foreign policy which meant securing Labour support. The TUC, however, opposed national service. Halifax hoped that a consultation agreement with other powers might persuade the Labour leaders to drop their opposition. It could then be argued that conscription was necessary to support the new security system.[31]

American and French complaints about the dilatory nature of the British negotiations were perhaps unjustified. The delay was due to the difficulty of persuading Poland to cooperate with the Soviet Union and the source of the problem lay in Warsaw rather than in London. The Russians agreed to support the British consultation scheme, but the Poles objected to any association with the USSR as liable to provoke Hitler. Beck proposed instead a secret Anglo-Polish agreement to consult in the event of further aggression.[32] Britain rejected this approach but decided to meet Polish objections to association with Moscow. On 27 March it was decided that Polish support was vital to any 'peace front' in Eastern Europe. The Russian negotiations should be abandoned in favour of securing a Polish commitment to defend Rumania.[33] The French remained unhappy about the delay in reaching a security arrangement, perhaps suspecting that Chamberlain was procrastinating. On 28 March Léger requested American intervention in London, pointing out that unless new commitments were soon adopted 'all the countries in Central and Eastern Europe' would fall to Hitler. Bullitt suggested that Roosevelt speak with Lindsay on the subject.[34] It is uncertain whether Roosevelt would have acted as suggested by his ambassador. The President's impatience with British delays and his later intervention over conscription, suggest that he might have been persuaded to put pressure on Chamberlain. In the event, however, the administration did not have to adopt such extreme measures. On 29 March Biddle reported from Warsaw that a German invasion of Poland was imminent. This information was passed on to London.[35] It was later revealed that the source of Biddle's warning was a journalist attached to an American press agency in Berlin who had proved 'reliable on previous occasions'.[36] Simultaneously Ian Colvin, a British journalist in Germany, arrived in London with a similar warning.[37] Halifax took Colvin to see the Prime Minister and discussed the information which had arrived pointing to imminent German action. The decision to fight for Poland without awaiting Beck's reply to the proposals of 28 March was taken on the evening of 29 March as a result of the American message and Colvin's information.[38] At a Cabinet meeting on 30 March Halifax informed his colleagues of the new threat and proposed a unilateral guarantee of Poland. Chamberlain hoped to associate the guarantee with a statement offering British assistance in settling German-Polish differences. Halifax, however, objected to this idea.[39] He perhaps believed that public opinion in the United States and elsewhere would draw a parallel with the Czech crisis and suspect the preparation of another Munich at Polish expense. Chamberlain subsequently abandoned the proposal and it was not mentioned in his statement to the House next day, announcing the British guarantee.[40]

The United States welcomed the British guarantee to Poland which showed that Chamberlain was at last prepared to take firm deterrent action against Hitler. Moffat noted that Britain was committed to 'positive action in Eastern Europe, which she has never before been willing to consider'.[41] Kennedy informed Harvey on 31 March that the President thought the guarantee 'excellent and said that in his judgement it would have a very great effect'. Roosevelt believed that the American public would 'consider that war was imminent . . . but did not think that this would do any harm'.[42] The guarantee was the lead from Britain which Roosevelt had always claimed he required. Chamberlain had shown that Britain was prepared to help itself and provided the answer to critics who claimed that the President was being unnecessarily alarmist. As the *Times* correspondent in Washington reported on 5 April

> In Congress voices were heard saying that a too impulsive policy was drawing the United States forward to a position which neither tradition nor immediate interest would support . . . Great Britain's pledge to Poland, with all it implies of positive action at a time of grave emergency, has brought the Government and public together again . . . When the American people see European nations . . . courageously taking the leadership which they strongly feel must not be American, their disquiet gives way to unstinted approval.[43]

The guarantee to Poland did nothing to calm the international situation which moved towards a fresh crisis when Italy invaded Albania on 7 April. The British were not unduly alarmed by the Italian action which it was believed had a partly anti-German character. While Chamberlain, therefore, was prepared to consider

British commitments to Greece and Rumania in the light of the Italian action, he was not prepared to denounce the Anglo-Italian agreement or to take military measures which might alarm Rome. The Prime Minister continued to hope that if Britain remained on good terms with Mussolini he would act as a restraining force on Hitler.[44] Great care was taken to quiet any suspicions which might be aroused in Washington by the decision to maintain the Anglo-Italian agreement. It was emphasised that while Britain did not want to alienate Mussolini, further Italian aggression would be resisted and Kennedy was asked to keep the American press 'as steady as possible' in its interpretation of British policy.[45] While continuing to stress its determination to resist aggression, the government redoubled its efforts to secure a tangible American contribution to the emerging 'peace front'. If Britain were to adopt new commitments in the Mediterranean as well as in Eastern Europe, its position in the Far East would be even further weakened. The defence of Australia and New Zealand had to be assured and the Western position in China maintained. The movement of the US fleet from the Atlantic to the Pacific, therefore, had become a matter of urgency. On 11 April Halifax again requested Roosevelt to redeploy the navy, emphasising the necessity for speed in view of Britain's projected new commitments in the Mediterranean.[46]

In the event, Roosevelt was prepared to move the fleet, but his decision was as much a response to French panic as to Halifax's request. In the wake of the Albanian coup the situation in January 1939 was repeated. France and the United States expected a coordinated axis offensive on three fronts and were unable to understand British optimism. The alarmist reports of the Deuxième Bureau caused panic in Paris which was quickly communicated to Washington by Bullitt. The French believed that the seizure of Albania had been coordinated with Germany and predicted an imminent German assault on Poland timed to coincide with an Italian offensive in the Mediterranean and a Japanese attack on Singapore. Bullitt accepted such predictions at face value in his messages to the White House.[47] The sense of impending disaster in the reports from Paris prompted Roosevelt to issue another warning to the dictators. On 9 April, as he left Warm Springs for Washington, the President informed the press that he would return in the autumn 'if we don't have a war'.[48] The use of the ambiguous term 'we' seems to have been carefully calculated to exercise an effect on Berlin and Rome. Welles followed up Roosevelt's statement in a speech of 13 April which emphasised American determination to resist agression and called for increased rearmament and neutrality revision.[49] Krock, of the *New York Times*, felt that the administration was joining the democracies in a show of 'preponderant force' against the axis.[50]

There was strong pressure on Roosevelt to go beyond more rhetoric. On 10 April Bullitt urged the President to ask Chamberlain to introduce conscription and to send ships to Corfu. Such firm action would deter Germany and Italy.[51] The ambassador was responding to the promptings of the French who were desperate to secure American intervention in London. It was suspected in Paris that, in the absence of American pressure, Chamberlain would abandon France in the event of a coordinated axis offensive in the Mediterranean. On 10 April Léger complained that the British 'in response to pressure from the City of London, had decided . . . [to] divide their fleet and send a considerable portion of it to Singapore to prevent possible Japanese action'. France was 'appalled' and considered this 'a fatal error'.[52] On 11 April Daladier repeated the story and warned Bullitt that if the British fleet sailed to the Far East 'France would have nothing more to do with resistance in Central and Eastern Europe'. In an urgent message to the President, Bullitt recommended that Roosevelt immediately move the US fleet to deprive Chamberlain of any excuse for abandoning France.[53] This advice, based on a complete misunderstanding of British strategy, was decisive. Admiral Leahy was ordered to prepare a redeployment to the Pacific in the afternoon of 11 April, before Halifax's message was received. The President believed that he was saving the entire 'peace front' from collapse due to Chamberlain's abdication of British responsibilities in the Mediterranean.[54] The British guarantees to Greece and Rumania announced on 13 April, quietened suspicions in Paris and Washington. The fleet movement went ahead, however, on 15 April.[55] It was interpreted, as it was meant to be, as a gesture of support for the guarantee system. In conversations with prominent Japanese, Grew reinforced its deterrent effect by emphasising American sympathy with the democracies and the repercussions on American-Japanese relations of any action in support of Germany and Italy.[56]

Roosevelt accompanied the fleet move with an initiative designed to place the dictators on the defensive and to silence domestic critics of the 'short of war' policy; the peace appeal of 14 April 1939. The aim of this scheme appears to have been to divide the German people from Hitler by offering to sponsor a conference which would discuss legitimate German claims. If Hitler rejected such an offer, as he was expected to do, he would be revealed as a warmonger both before his own people and the American public. The conference plan was first suggested by Carl Goerdeler and represents one of the few occasions on which the German opposition influenced the policy of a major Western power. The British businessman A. P. Young had been passing Goerdeler material to the Roosevelt administration since the Munich crisis. It had reached the White House and the State Department via Messersmith who knew Goerdeler from his time as US consul in Berlin and was the leading American 'anti-appeaser'.[57] Goerdeler's reports had contributed to Roosevelt's alarmist view of the international situation during the January crisis, but his greatest impact came after the German seizure of Prague. On 16 March 1939 Goerdeler drew up a memorandum proposing 'a positive plan of action' in the light of the new German coup. He emphasised that the Western powers must display no sign of weakness but must form a firm front against further agression. At the same time, however, he argued that Hitler had made a major blunder in seizing Prague. For the first time the Führer had moved beyond Versailles grievances and undermined his moral position by annexing non-German territory. He was clearly bent on conquest rather than justice. This fact could be brought home to the German people if the democracies proposed a conference to discuss legitimate German claims. The conference was to be held under strict preconditions. There must be no further aggression and Hitler must give firm guarantees that he would keep his word. The Führer would be bound to reject these conditions but the act of rejection would brand him as an aggressor before the world. The effect on the German people would be 'profound'. Public reaction would undermine the position of the 'extremists' and force Hitler 'within the complete embrace of the Generals' who opposed war. 'The ultimate repercussions inside Germany' might 'well prove to be the death warrant of the Hitler regime'. In order to ensure that the Goebbels propaganda machine did not distort the peace appeal, the full text should be broadcast in German, particularly by the United States which was regarded as a disinterested power.[58] As an added precaution Goerdeler later suggested that the Pope be persuaded to endorse the initiative to lend it further moral force.[59] The recommendations in this document were brought to the attention of Messersmith by Young on 24 March 1939. Ostensibly Young was in the United States to attend an industrial conference but his real mission was to influence American policy. In this he was entirely successful. Messersmith saw the importance of Goerdeler's message immediately and forwarded the memorandum to Hull. In a covering letter he emphasised that the recommendations came 'from the best informed man on the situation in Germany and one who has contacts in high places . . . particularly in the army and industrial and financial circles'. The document was worthy of 'careful reading'.[60] Hull, who had already received a copy of the 'X document' from another source, noted that he had read the material 'with much interest'.[61]

Goerdeler's suggestions appealed to Roosevelt and provided the basis for the President's peace plan. Roosevelt seized the opportunity to take an anti-Nazi initiative while simultaneously posing as a mediator, thus minimising the political risks. Moreover Hitler's inevitable response to any initiative hedged with guarantees could only improve the chances of neutrality revision. The American peace initiative of 14 April was strongly marked by Goerdeler's influence and was clearly designed to undermine Hitler's domestic position. It recalled the Führer's previous claims of devotion to peace and called on him to match his words with actions. If Hitler were willing to guarantee neighbouring states against agression, the United States would be willing to sponsor a conference on disarmament and equal access to raw materials. The peoples of the world desired peace and their leaders would be held responsible if they led their countries into war.[62] The administration took steps to ensure that the text of Roosevelt's speech was translated and broadcast to Germany.[63] Simultaneously an attempt was made through 'high Catholic circles' in the United States to persuade the Pope to endorse the American appeal.[64] There was no doubt in administration circles that the 'peace plan' was an offensive weapon rather than a return to appeasement. Ickes noted that Roosevelt had 'put Hitler . . . in a hole . . . if war now comes the whole world will know who is responsible'.[65] Morgenthau hoped that German rejection of the American offer would pave the way for further anti-axis measures.[66] The British also welcomed Roosevelt's intervention because it was recognised as an anti-Nazi move. As Chamberlain noted on 15 April 'the appeal is very carefully framed and has put H[itler] into a tight corner'. He would 'refuse to reply' but 'world opinion and particularly American opinion' would be consolidated against the axis and the German people would be 'disappointed'.[67]

It was uncertain how Hitler intended to reply to Roosevelt. At first it was predicted that the American initiative would be flatly rejected, but it was then announced that the Führer would make a formal reply before the Reichstag on 28 April. It was by no means clear that peace would be preserved until this date. The French still expected an incident in the Mediterranean and redoubled their efforts to persuade Chamberlain to introduce conscription as a deterrent and a symbol of British determination to uphold the guarantee system. Roosevelt supported these demands. On 19 April Bullitt dined with Phipps and informed the British diplomat that the President

> felt very strongly that it was absolutely essential for [Britain] to introduce compulsory national service at once . . . [Roosevelt] could not understand how [Britain] could hesitate when this step might still save peace.

He implied that the United States expected such a move in return for moving the American fleet into the Pacific.[68] Simultaneously the President asked Léon Blum to use his influence with the British TUC to overcome its opposition to conscription.[69] Roosevelt's intervention, coupled with French appeals, had a decisive effect on Chamberlain. He had previously resisted pressure for conscription from Halifax and Hore-Belisha, but it was now plain that something had to be done to preserve British credibility. On 20 April Wilson informed Hore-Belisha, the War Minister, that it had been decided to introduce national service.[70] The new departure was formally announced at cabinet on 22 April. Chamberlain informed his colleagues that conscription was being introduced as

> an earnest of British determination to resist agression . . . there was great pressure on this country to introduce some scheme of compulsory military training, not only from France but also from the United States.[71]

Roosevelt was informed of the British decision before parliament was told on 26 April.[72]

The main aim of American support for the 'peace front' and

pressure for British conscription was to deter Hitler. The goal of Roosevelt's peace initiative was to deprive Hitler of public support for any attempt to smash the new security system before it was firmly established. Hitler, however, was astute enough to turn the tables on the President and avoided Roosevelt's trap. He informed the Reichstag on 28 April that none of the states mentioned by Roosevelt felt threatened by Germany or in need of a guarantee. He went on to warn the German people that they had received offers of justice from a previous American President, Woodrow Wilson. Wilson's fourteen points had been a fraud and had led directly to the Versailles *Diktat*. He implied that Roosevelt harboured similar designs against Germany. In the same speech Hitler announced the Anglo-German naval agreement and the German-Polish non-agression pact on the grounds that Britain and Poland were attempting to encircle Germany, a policy which he clearly believed enjoyed American support. It was a masterly performance which attained its aim of preserving German unity while rejecting Roosevelt's offer of justice.[73] As Brüning later remarked 'the linking . . . of Roosevelt with Wilson and his fourteen points had been almost entirely successful'.[74] Moreover, by denying that Germany had any designs on the United States, Hitler gave the isolationists ammunition with which to fight neutrality revision. The President's initiative had been transformed into a weapon against him. It was generally accepted, however, despite Hitler's denunciation of two treaties on 28 April, that a pause had taken place as a result of British conscription and Roosevelt's intervention. Daladier informed Phipps on 28 April, that Hitler had been 'greatly impressed' by British national service. Without this his speech 'would have been much more extreme'.[75] The new air of calm in Paris ended Anglo-French differences about axis plans and it was agreed that a further crisis was unlikely until after the harvest.

In March and April, as a result of Prague and Albania, Britain and France had moved further and faster than could possibly have been imagined in January. The United States had played a large part in this process by making it clear that American support would only be forthcoming to those who helped themselves. The United States extended moral support to the new security system by making clear its sympathy with the democracies and provided physical assistance by moving the fleet into the Pacific to restrain Japan. A new world system had emerged among the democratic powers to counter the tripartite axis alliance with the United States undertaking the leading role in the Far East while Britain and France attempted to stabilise Europe. In the remaining months before the outbreak of war, Roosevelt tried to carry support of the democracies further by securing revision of the Neutrality Act which would free the United States to act as an arsenal for the Western powers.

11 The Approach of War

In the summer of 1939 Roosevelt directed his main efforts towards securing neutrality revision, which he regarded as a vital American contribution to the European 'peace front' against further German expansion. It was hoped in Washington that modification of the Neutrality Act and an Anglo-French alliance with the Soviet Union would complete the establishment of a European security system and deter Hitler. Congress, however, rejected neutrality revision. Its action represented a revolt against increased executive power rather than an expression of unyielding isolationism, but the Senate had destroyed the main American contribution to the 'peace front' at a critical juncture. Moreover the Western powers proved unable to reach an agreement with Russia. Stalin opted instead for the Nazi-Soviet Pact, a choice which doomed Poland and undermined the entire guarantee system in Eastern Europe. In the ensuing crisis at the end of August, the President found himself powerless to counter further German aggression. All that the administration could do was to guard against a second Munich on the part of Chamberlain.

At the beginning of May there was a feeling of confidence in Europe that further axis moves had been averted because of the guarantees to Poland, Greece and Rumania.[1] Roosevelt was confident that weakened by their deteriorating economies and faced with the creation of a new balance of power, the dictators would hesitate to risk war.[2] The signature of the 'Pact of Steel' between Germany and Italy on 22 May did not alter the President's view. It was interpreted by the United States as an attempt to divert attention from the German diplomatic failures represented by the guarantee system and the Anglo-Soviet negotiations. Phillips, in Rome, predicted that the new alliance might even inhibit German action. Mussolini was unprepared for war and could use the consultative clauses in the treaty to restrain Hitler from further adventures.[3]

In this situation Roosevelt desired to secure neutrality revision in order to add to the deterrents against further German expansion. His determination was hardened by reports from Europe emphasising that any weakening of the 'peace front' would encourage Hitler to strike. Ribbentrop would use the continuing existence of the act to persuade Hitler that the democracies could be destroyed without danger of American intervention.[4] Roosevelt was 'especially anxious' to repeal the section of the act imposing an embargo on arms sales to belligerents.[5] Such a modification would prove to the axis that the industrial resources of the United States stood behind Britain and France in the event of war. Unfortunately neutrality revision was not proceeding smoothly. The administration had relied upon the parliamentary skills of Senator Pittman to introduce new legislation, but he was running into difficulties and was reluctant to make a fight for his bill.[6] Pittman had received little support from the State Department or the White House. Hull was unwilling to testify before the Senate Foreign Affairs Committee in favour of revision. Roosevelt, recognising that Congress was in a mood to reject Presidential leadership, preferred to stay in the background and relied upon public opinion to stimulate Congressional action.[7] Without executive leadership, however, public opinion failed to make any impact and on 12 May Pittman decided to abandon his effort.[8] His capitulation prompted greater Presidential involvement. Roosevelt decided that legislation should be transferred to the House of Representatives, which was more responsive than the Senate to public opinion. Leadership of the revision struggle was entrusted to Sol Bloom, chairman of the House Foreign Affairs Committee, and administration influence was placed behind his legislation.[9] On 19 May the President called a conference of congressional leaders at the White House. He argued that revision was essential to American security and would preserve peace. Failure to act would encourage Hitler and lead to the German conquest of Europe. This would be followed by a direct axis assault on the Western Hemisphere.[10] At a press conference on 30 May Roosevelt repeated the call for speedy congressional action. State Department officials were asked to talk to as many Congressmen as possible about the necessity for a new act and Hull himself sent an open letter to Bloom and Pittman calling for repeal of the arms embargo.[11]

At this stage the British, like the Americans, hoped that the creation of a balance of power against Germany would convince Hitler that further aggression was dangerous and preserve

European peace. The government was, therefore, anxious to secure some tangible gesture of support for the guarantee system from the two uncommitted great powers, the Soviet Union and the United States. In the case of the USSR this meant securing Soviet commitment to the 'peace front'. In the case of the United States it meant avoiding any action which might jeopardise the chances of neutrality revision. The decision to include the Russians was taken reluctantly. Both Chamberlain and Halifax distrusted Stalin and at first opposed any close connection with Moscow.[12] The French, however, insisted that some reciprocal assistance pact be concluded and on 16 May the Chiefs of Staff warned about the danger of a Nazi-Soviet rapproachment should Stalin be forced into isolation.[13] On 24 May, it was decided to accept Russian demands for a firm treaty with the West.[14] The new arrangement was to be linked to article 16 of the League of Nations covenant in order to give it a 'temporary character'.[15] Chamberlain had no intention of tying Britain to Russia indefinitely and hoped to abandon the unpalatable alliance once Hitler had been safely deterred.

Britain was eager to emphasise a second factor to convince Hitler of its strong position: American sympathy with the democracies. The government was anxious that neutrality revision succeed in order to disabuse the Nazis of the idea that the United States was isolationist. The Foreign Office was careful to avoid intervention in the political debate, recognising that any hint of outside pressure would only embarrass Roosevelt and give ammunition to his opponents.[16] It was believed, however, that American public opinion could be subtly cultivated in a sense favourable to Britain. In particular it was hoped that the Royal visit to the United States at the beginning of June had stimulated sympathy for the democracies and improved the chances of revision. Lindsay reported on 12 June that the visit had 'deepened and fixed already existing feelings of friendliness. Coming at a crucial moment it is of capital importance and its effects will not wear off'. While it was impossible to predict the impact of the Royal tour on the chances of revision it was 'quite certain' to have 'increased the pressure' against the opponents of new legislation.[17]

While establishing a position of diplomatic strength, the government was careful not to close the door on negotiations with Germany, provided Hitler first abandoned aggression. It was hoped that a firm line against military threats would discourage the Nazi 'extremists', while expressions of readiness to meet legitimate

German claims would encourage 'moderates' like Göring. Chamberlain also hoped to counter Goebbels' encirclement propaganda and make the German people unenthusiastic about war by proving that Britain was not 'about to fall on them'.[18] On 8 June Halifax informed the Lords that while the government would not tolerate aggression, 'any of Germany's claims' were 'open to consideration round a table', sentiments which he reiterated in a speech at Chatham House on 29 June.[19] This attempt to balance between deterrence and conciliation concealed the difficulties which Britain faced after Prague. On the one hand Chamberlain doubted the possibility of a lasting peace while Hitler ruled Germany.[20] On the other hand he did not believe in preventive war which meant that the door had to be left open to negotiations. The problem was to avoid sliding into renewed appeasement. In the case of Poland some formula had to be found which would solve the issues of Danzig and the Corridor without endangering Polish independence. This was the prerequisite for any general settlement. Yet how could Hitler be trusted after he had torn up the Munich agreement? What credible guarantees could be given to Warsaw and London? Chamberlain vaguely hoped that Mussolini might help here but a solution proved evasive.[21] Privately the Prime Minister hoped that the whole problem would be solved by the death of Hitler, either by assassination or from natural causes.[22] He was by no means convinced that there was any other way in which war could be avoided. As he informed Kennedy on 9 June, the Führer might be determined 'to take England on'.[23]

At the beginning of June Roosevelt, like Chamberlain, began to feel apprehensive. The optimism expressed at cabinet in May was replaced by concern in a letter to Phillips on 7 June. He informed the ambassador that if Hitler and Mussolini wanted peace they would reduce their rearmament programmes. Germany and Italy, however, were still spending 'enormous sums' on arms.[24] The President suspected that Hitler might risk war while Congress was debating revision, hoping to achieve victory before American aid could become effective. There was also concern about axis activity in the Far East. It was rumoured that Japan had designs on Shanghai and French Indo-China.[25] On 9 June Welles informed Moffat that 'he was becoming more and more concerned at developments in Europe and the Far East. He thought that a new crisis was brewing . . . All of this brought him to the conclusion that we should redouble our efforts to amend the neutrality act'.[26]

Welles' concern was not misplaced. On 14 June, the day after Bloom's bill passed out of committee, the Japanese began a blockade of the British concession at Tientsin.

Tokyo claimed that the concession was used as a base by Chinese guerrillas. It also demanded the silver bullion deposited at Tientsin by the Chinese government.[27] The blockade was embarrassing because of the European situation. Britain hoped for American support in the crisis, as it was perhaps entitled to do by virtue of the unwritten agreement of April 1939 under which the United States adopted the leading role in the Far East. The administration, however, felt unable to act because of the neutrality debate, fearing accusations of entanglement.[28] In the absence of American support, Britain had no choice but to negotiate with Japan. The danger was that surrender to threats in the Far East might encourage Hitler to risk aggression in Europe. The Berlin embassy warned the government that 'Our experiences at Tientsin are making a considerable impression in confirmation of the idea that we shall do nothing about Danzig.'[29] On 21 June, however, the Cabinet decided that Britain could not risk involvement in China.[30] Washington was informed on 27 June that Britain had to negotiate with Japan rather than divert scarce military resources from Europe.[31] Simultaneously the government took steps to deter parallel German action in Poland. On 10 July Chamberlain informed the Commons that Danzig was essential to the Polish economy. A threat to Danzig was, therefore, a threat to Polish independence which Warsaw would be justified in resisting.[32]

The Americans were more alarmed than the British by the Tientsin dispute and the ensuing scare over Danzig. Once again, alarmist reports from Paris conditioned Roosevelt's response. It was believed in Washington that far more was at stake in Tientsin than the British position in the Far East. It was feared that the Japanese blockade was part of a coordinated axis plot. As Berle noted on 17 June: 'All of us believe that the Japanese move is timed to synchronise with a German move in Central Europe and may be regarded therefore as a forerunner of a smashing crisis.'[33] German military movements seemed to point towards imminent action. Bullitt reported on 28 June that Bonnet 'felt certain that Germany would provoke a crisis of the most dangerous sort in the near future over the issue of Danzig'. Preparations would be completed 'about the first of August'.[34] The British decision to negotiate at Tientsin seemed an obvious stimulus to German action.[35] Roosevelt had refused to support Britain in the Far East in order to secure neutrality revision which he believed would deter further axis coups in Europe or Asia. On 30 June, however, at the very height of the crises in Tientsin and Danzig, the House of Representatives crippled Bloom's legislation. The bill was sent to the Senate but only with an amendment retaining the arms embargo.[36] Roosevelt was furious and felt that the House decision would encourage Hitler by depriving the guarantee system of American support. At an impromptu press conference on 4 July the President made it clear that the revision struggle would not be abandoned. The Senate would be kept in session until September in order to secure new legislation.[37] It was hoped that this would raise doubts in Berlin about American non-involvement and deter German action against Poland.

There was also concern in Washington about the failure of the Western powers to secure an alliance with the Soviet Union at such a critical juncture. As Berle noted on 30 June:

> The horrible thing about all this is that about all the Germans need to know to consider that their hour has arrived is a) that the Anglo-Russian alliance has failed b) that supplies cannot be had from here. They are pretty clear about a) already, and the Congress of the United States is doing its level best to demonstrate b).[38]

The negotiations with the Soviet Union were being delayed because of the Soviet demand that a list of East European states be guaranteed against 'indirect aggression', a condition which Britain found unpalatable because it seemed to open the way to widespread Soviet intervention in the affairs of Russia's neighbours.[39] The Americans were worried about the situation because they knew, through a secret source in the German embassy in Moscow, that tentative attempts were being made to improve Nazi-Soviet relations, although these had not gone far because Ribbentrop was reluctant to abandon Japan.[40] This was a major barrier since an undeclared Russo-Japanese war was raging at Nomohan over a disputed border. Roosevelt was nevertheless perturbed.

On 30 June he intervened unofficially with the Russians to avert the possibility of a Nazi-Soviet pact and to persuade them to stop raising difficulties in the negotiations with the West. The President informed Oumansky, the Soviet ambassador, that it was in the

Russian interest to conclude an alliance with Britain and France as quickly as possible, otherwise Hitler would destroy his enemies one by one.[41] The decision to continue the revision struggle and the appeal to Moscow show that Roosevelt had not yet abandoned hope that at the last moment 'a preponderant balance of military force' would emerge to deter further axis aggression.

Roosevelt had no success in either securing revision from the Senate or in convincing the Russians. Between 3 and 10 July the administration exerted all its influence on members of the Senate Foreign Affairs Committee in the hope of removing the arms embargo. The isolationists also began to organise, however, and with the support of anti-administration Democrats secured on 10 July a vote to postpone consideration of new legislation until January 1940.[42] Roosevelt at first wished to condemn the committee's action, but he was persuaded by Hull to adopt a more cautious approach. The committee decision had been reached by a majority of one and Hull hoped that it might be reversed by a reasoned appeal to the Senate.[43] Roosevelt, therefore, sent a message to Congress on 14 July which avoided polemic but stated that 'In the light of present world conditions' revision was 'highly advisable' before 1940. Hull made a similar statement, pointing out that since the arms embargo encouraged agressors its results were 'directly prejudicial to the highest interests and to the peace and security of the United States'.[44] When Roosevelt met Senate leaders at the White House on 18 July, however, it became evident that they would refuse to override the Foreign Affairs Committee. Senator Borah denied that a crisis in Europe was imminent and argued in favour of postponing new legislation until January. He was supported by the rest of the group and the administration had finally to concede defeat.[45]

The British government was disappointed with this outcome, particularly since the neutrality debate had inhibited American action in support of the Western position in China. Britain now had the worst of both worlds, no American support in the Far East and no neutrality reform. Halifax informed the Cabinet on 12 July that the decision of the Senate Foreign Affairs Committee was 'unfortunate especially in view of the fact that . . . [the Americans] had given as their reason for being unable to help us in several matters that it would prejudice the passage of the amending legislation'.[46] The Foreign Office found consolation in the argument that the Senate's decision did not affect general American sympathy with the democracies and that the dictators must be aware of the fact. *The Times* adopted a similar attitude, warning the dictators not to gamble on American neutrality whatever action Congress might take.[47]

If the Senate's decision deprived the guarantee system of American support, there seemed to be an increasing danger that Russia also would withdraw from the 'peace front'. On 1 July the American embassy in Moscow reported a meeting between Schulenburg and Molotov. Schulenburg had given the Russians an assurance that Germany 'entertained no aggressive designs against the Soviet Union'. He had asked if Moscow desired a non-aggression treaty with Germany along the lines of German treaties with the Baltic states. Molotov rejected this suggestion but 'had manifested a certain interest in a concrete offer of a political character from Germany'.[48] The dangerous possibility, therefore, arose that the Russians might be prepared to bargain with both sides. Once again Roosevelt hoped that American influence might persuade Moscow to conclude a firm agreement with Britain and France. On 18 July he dined with Joseph E. Davies, the ex-ambassador to Russia, and expressed concern about the world situation. He then asked Davies to use his influence with Stalin in favour of a Soviet agreement with the West rather than with Hitler.[49] Although there were no further political discussions between Schulenburg and Molotov, the American embassy remained concerned about the situation. Grummon reported on 19 July that German diplomats were 'openly confident that the Soviet Union will not align itself with England and France.'[50]

Britain was also worried about the continued delay in reaching a firm agreement with the USSR. Molotov was demanding not only Western acceptance of the Soviet definition of indirect aggression, which would give Moscow a free hand to intervene at will in Eastern Europe, but also that political and military agreements with the West enter into force simultaneously. Until a military protocol had been completed any political arrangement would be invalid.[51] London was unhappy about these demands and inclined to reject them. It was decided to enter staff talks on 21 July, however, to prevent Russia from 'entering the German camp'.[52] It was hoped to keep Moscow in play until 1 October when the weather would render a German attack on Poland impossible.[53] By 1940 Germany might be economically incapable of supporting a war.

At this point Roosevelt made a direct appeal to Moscow. On 4

August a message was sent to Steinhardt by special courier ordering him to request an urgent meeting with Molotov. The ambassador was to repeat Roosevelt's earlier warning to Oumansky about the Nazi threat to Soviet security and argue in favour of a Western alliance. The message contained an appeal to Russian self-interest, pointing out that the axis threatened the USSR not only in Europe but also in the Far East, where the Nomoham incident remained unsettled.[54] Roosevelt was attempting to exploit Ribbentrop's reluctance to abandon Tokyo, which was inhibiting German negotiations with Moscow. The American initiative represented a final effort to create a balance of power against Germany and was prompted by information which seemed to point towards an imminent German assault on Poland. On 3 August Bullitt reported that the Poles expected to be attacked around 15 August and there was news of intensive German troop movements.[55] If the Russians joined the 'peace front', however, Hitler might yet hesitate.

The force of Roosevelt's appeal was weakened by the failure of neutrality revision. The President was asking the Russians to support the guarantee system at a time when Congress had emphasised America's own isolation from Europe. Moreover, by the time Steinhardt saw Molotov on 15 August, the Germans had indicated their willingness to abandon Japan, destroying the axis conspiracy argument which was the basis of Roosevelt's message. On 5 August Schulenburg again saw Molotov and indicated that Germany had no designs on Russia and would respect Soviet interests in the Baltic. Molotov replied that the USSR distrusted Germany because of the Anti-Comintern Pact and Nazi encouragement of Japan. Schulenburg then denied that the pact was aimed against Russia. It was in fact an anti-British instrument. Germany was interested in good relations with the Soviet Union but only if Moscow remained outside the 'peace front'.[56] When Steinhardt saw Molotov, therefore, the Russians already knew that Germany was prepared to offer an agreement which would grant them security in both Europe and the Far East. By contrast the Western powers could offer only the prospect of war with Germany. Shortly after the Steinhardt interview a Nazi-Soviet agreement was concluded, defining spheres of influence in the Baltic and pledging Germany to abandon Japan.[57] The American embassy, informed of this development by its German contact, forwarded the bad news to Washington. There was little Roosevelt could do except warn the British. Welles saw Lindsay on 17 August and informed him that the

United States had learned from a reliable secret source that Germany and Russia were about to sign an agreement. The ambassador's telegram, however, was not decoded until 22 August, the day the Nazi-Soviet Pact was officially signed.[58]

There was some doubt in Washington about British determination to stand firm in this period as the Russian alliance slipped away and neutrality revision was defeated. Once again, as in June, events in Europe and the Far East interacted. Britain had hoped for American support in the talks on the Tientsin dispute which were to begin in Tokyo on 25 July. On 15 July, however, Welles rejected a request for cooperation. He informed Lindsay that the administration could not afford to give 'too much of a handle to the isolationists' since it was hoped that Congress 'might be influenced by the President's message' on neutrality revision.[59] Deprived of American support and worried by the situation in Europe, the government was forced to accede to Japanese demands that Britain recognise the 'special position' of Japan in China as a basis for discussion. This so-called Craigie-Arita formula subsequently proved meaningless.[60] The United States, however, was alarmed by such a departure from non-recognition. Roosevelt decided that something must be done to restrain Japan and warn the dictators against parallel action. The President had been considering some form of sanctions since the beginning of the Tientsin blockade[61] and the Senate's decision to postpone consideration of revised neutrality legislation on 18 July allowed him to adopt a stronger line in the Far East. It was decided to warn Japan against exploiting the European situation by denouncing the American-Japanese trade treaty of 1911.[62] On 28 July Lindsay informed London that although the American action was justified on commercial grounds, the real reason was concern about the situation in China. Roosevelt was alarmed 'by the profound disturbance of power in the Far East' which had been growing steadily for some time.[63]

Since the United States had taken action in the Far East, the President expected Britain to adopt a firmer line with Japan. At the beginning of August, however, it was rumoured that Chamberlain intended to appease Tokyo by closing the Burma Road. France would follow suit by suspending exports from Indo-China to the Chinese nationalists.[64] On 3 August Welles sent for Mallet and informed him that he had discussed these rumours with Roosevelt. The President had remarked 'If this is true the position of the United States would be that of a government which is trying to lend its moral support to a power which is deliberately intent on suicide.'[65] This warning was delivered against appeasement in Europe as well as in the Far East. Despite the collapse of the Dusseldorf agreements after Prague, the Americans continued to suspect that Chamberlain would welcome an economic deal with Germany. The emphasis in British speeches on the government's readiness to discuss legitimate economic grievances with Berlin kept this fear alive. On 24 May Morgenthau noted City gossip about Chamberlain's plans to build a 'golden bridge' to Berlin.[66] On 29 June Feis, the economic adviser to the State Department, drew attention to the emphasis in some of the Prime Minister's recent speeches on the Anglo-German payments agreement as a basis for further discussions.[67] The issue came to a head on 22 and 23 July when the *News Chronicle* and the *Daily Express* published details of a meeting between Hudson, of the Department of Overseas Trade, and Wohltat, a German official. According to these reports Hudson had offered Germany a huge loan to finance disarmament. Joint marketing arrangements and other economic matters were also discussed. It later emerged that Wohltat had also seen Sir Horace Wilson.[68] Wilson did not mention a loan but did talk about a general scheme of Anglo-German economic cooperation.[69] It was widely believed that the conversations prefigured a fresh attempt at appeasement. This, however, overstated the case. The discussions, like Chamberlain's previous speeches, were designed to prove that Britain had no desire to encircle and stifle Germany. It was hoped that Wohltat's chief, Göring, would use the conversations to influence Hitler in favour of 'moderation'.[70] Both Hudson and Wilson made it clear that Britain would assist Germany only if Hitler abandoned armaments and aggression. The press leaks did not emphasise this aspect of the discussions and thus gave an impression of unilateral appeasement. British credibility was seriously damaged. As Harvey noted on 23 July: 'The story is calculated to do infinite harm to Soviet negotiations and US opinion, where our bona fides are not so above suspicion as not to be easily called in doubt.'[71]

The revelations were certainly damaging. In conjunction with the Craigie-Arita formula they raised doubts about Chamberlain's determination to resist aggression. It was feared that Chamberlain would buy off Japan by sacrificing China and appease Hitler at the expense of Poland. Biddle reported from Warsaw on 26 July that Hudson 'could not have engaged in such discussions . . . without some degree of preliminary guidance from his government'. The Poles were 'perplexed' by talk of £100 million to finance German disarmament while Poland was experiencing difficulty in extracting a £5 million loan from London. Biddle had learned from 'a reliable source' that a group of appeasers, Chamberlain, Simon, Wilson and Hudson, hoped that Britain could 'buy off Hitler'. They were being encouraged by New York 'banking circles' which Hudson had contacted during a trip to the World's Fair. According to Biddle, Chamberlain desired to 'conciliate rather than to stand up to aggressors'.[72] On 28 July Cudahy reported from Dublin that American businessmen predicted an Anglo-German economic agreement by the end of September. Poland would be persuaded to accept a compromise in the cause of peace.[73] Bullitt had been suspicious of Wohltat's activities even before the press revelations and believed that Chamberlain would surrender to axis demands in both Europe and Asia.[74] On 3 August he warned Washington that circles close to Lord Beaverbrook expected the Prime Minister to abandon Poland at the last moment.[75] The American embassy in London noted similar rumours of a new Munich on 8 August and remarked that 'public opinion was . . . actively focused on this issue by the widely publicised conversations of R. H. Hudson and Herr Wohltat'.[76] The Foreign Office was sensitive to such stories. When Johnson raised the matter on 9 August, Cadogan 'spoke with some feeling' against those who accused Britain of appeasement. 'If these people do not want to wage a preventive war what do they expect the Government to do but to build up the country's defences . . . and to leave the door wide open to Germany for a peaceful settlement.'[77] It was emphasised that Britain would resist aggression and that there were no secret negotiations with Germany.[78] The State Department was now wholly convinced. Moffat noted on 14 August that rumours of a new Munich were widespread. It would be 'a mistake even to try and analyse [such rumours] until the sediment settles again and we can see what is the . . . reaction to what I suspect will be a renewed peace offensive'.[79]

The Nazi-Soviet Pact provided the basis for such a German 'peace offensive', designed to separate the Western powers from Poland. Hitler believed that once Britain and France realised that encirclement had failed and that Poland was now militarily indefensible, they would be reluctant to fulfil their obligations towards Warsaw. The Poles, like the Czechs, would be forced to accept German terms. In the event he was disappointed and the West stood firm. The Nazi-Soviet Pact, however, stimulated American fears first roused by the Craigie-Arita formula and the Hudson-Wohltat talks, that Chamberlain might yet make terms with Hitler. In the last days of peace, Anglo-German exchanges were anxiously scrutinised by Washington for any hint of a second Munich at the expense of Poland.

12 The Last Days of Peace

The Nazi-Soviet Pact improved the strategic position of Britain and France by destroying the Anti-Comintern grouping. It discredited the Japanese military 'extremists' who had been pressing for closer ties with Germany. The Hiranuma government which had been discussing Ribbentrop's tripartite alliance resigned and was replaced by a cabinet determined to pursue a policy of non-involvement in European affairs.[1] The Western powers were thus freed of the axis threat in the Far East. It was already clear that Mussolini was reluctant to support German designs on Poland[2] and the new pact did nothing to stimulate Italian enthusiasm for war. On the other hand it doomed Poland if Hitler chose to launch an attack. The main question faced in Washington was whether Chamberlain would defend Poland or whether he would respond to peace feelers from Berlin. If the Prime Minister stood firm Hitler might hesitate to risk war with only the unreliable Stalin as an ally. The main aim of Roosevelt's policy during the Polish crisis, therefore, was to keep Italy at a distance from its erstwhile axis partner while doing nothing to encourage a second Munich at the expense of Poland.

The British government reacted to the Nazi-Soviet Pact by again emphasising its determination to resist any German attack on Poland. On 22 August Chamberlain sent a letter to Hitler warning him that Britain would honour its obligations regardless of the new treaty.[3] This warning was lent weight by calling up the Auxiliary Air Force and 5000 naval reservists.[4] Simultaneously an attempt was made to exploit Italian reluctance to become involved in a war. On 23 August Mussolini sent a message to London expressing his interest in a peaceful solution of the Polish question. As a prerequisite, Warsaw must 'freely recognise' Danzig's right to return to the Reich.[5] It was decided to keep Italy in play. On 24 August Halifax informed the Italians that their 'helpful attitude' was greatly appreciated. At the same time, however, Mussolini was warned that a settlement at Danzig was only possible under international guarantee and with due attention to Polish rights in the city.[6] Harvey noted 'Distinct signs of wobble in Italy. We have asked Muss[olini] to use influence with Hitler, whilst assuring him of our determination to fight.'[7]

Roosevelt also hoped to isolate Germany by playing upon Italian reluctance to become involved in war. On 23 August he sent a peace appeal to King Victor Emmanuele. The President hoped by such tactics to bypass Mussolini and Ciano, who had signed the Pact of Steel, and to ensure that the Italian public learned of his message. The American note pointed out the danger that a war would destroy European civilisation. It went on to argue that if only adequate guarantees could be secured against aggression it would be possible to ease the burden of armaments and restore international trade. If the Italian government formulated proposals for a solution of the Polish crisis along such lines it was 'assured of the earnest sympathy of the United States'.[8] There was little expectation that Italian intervention would persuade Hitler to preserve peace. Roosevelt was merely interested in widening the division between Italy and its erstwhile axis partner.

If there was optimism about Italian neutrality, however, there were also continued doubts about British determination to stand firm. Although the government adopted a strong line with Hitler, ministers privately expressed concern about the situation created by the Nazi-Soviet Pact. On 23 August Kennedy saw both Chamberlain and Halifax. The Prime Minister was pessimistic. He informed Kennedy that to push the Poles to make concessions would be 'disastrous', but felt that the 'futility of it all . . . is frightful; after all [the British] cannot save the Poles; they can merely carry on a war of revenge that will mean the destruction of the whole of Europe'. Halifax was also concerned about the position but emphasised that Britain would 'definitely go to war if Poland starts to fight'. Kennedy, however, reported that the British did not wish 'to be more Polish than the Poles and . . . are praying the Poles will find some way of adjusting their differences with the Germans at once'.[9] This emphasis perhaps owed something to Kennedy's own belief that the Poles should be convinced of the 'profound difference' in their position created by the Nazi-Soviet Pact, an invitation to appeasement explicitly rejected by Halifax on 23 August.[10] Nevertheless it was clear that the government hoped some way might be found to bring Poland and Germany together before war broke out. The question was raised at cabinet on 24 August. It was agreed that the two powers should discuss minority problems. The difficulty was that Britain could not advise Warsaw to negotiate since such an intervention would 'involve some risk of loss of confidence in us by the Poles'.[11] After Cabinet Chamberlain thought of a way round this barrier. He requested the Americans to intervene in Warsaw on his behalf. Wilson informed Kennedy on 24 August that

> He saw no way of avoiding war unless the Poles were willing to negotiate with the Germans . . . As things now stand that is the place to apply the pressure. The British are in no position to press the Poles strongly but if anything is to be accomplished action must be taken at once, as the Prime Minister fears the blow is very near.[12]

Kennedy immediately relayed this message to Roosevelt. He also phoned Welles to say that Britain wanted one thing of the United States 'and one thing only, namely that we put pressure on the Poles'.[13] In Washington this approach was interpreted as an attempt to prepare a new Munich. Moffat noted 'As we saw it here, it merely meant that they wanted us to assume the responsibility for a new Munich and to do their dirty work for them. The idea received short shrift from the President, the Secretary and Sumner Welles down.'[14] American fears of an Anglo-German bargain at Polish expense were exaggerated. What London desired was that the Poles state their willingness to negotiate in order to put Hitler clearly in the wrong if he attacked and which, if he reciprocated, would tie Germany up in talks until the September rains made an invasion impossible. Kennedy's hysterical reporting, however, gave the impression that Britain wanted Poland forced into unilateral concessions, a solution which the ambassador himself would have welcomed. In fact the President's appeal to both sides on 24 August to settle their dispute by direct negotiation or arbitration and the positive Polish response met British requirements.[15]

Roosevelt, while imagining that he was avoiding a subtle British trap, launched an appeal of his own on 24 August, calling for a peaceful settlement of the German–Polish dispute.[16] The President had little hope that his message would prove effective in averting hostilities. He desired, however, to prove to both the American and the German people that responsibility for war rested with Hitler. This would damage German morale and make it easier for the administration to conduct a pro-allied policy. Roosevelt planned to call Congress into special session if war broke out to secure repeal of the arms embargo.[17] Germany did not reply to the American message, but Poland expressed its willingness to negotiate on 26 August, a result which suited the President's tactic of putting 'the bee on Germany, which no one did in 1914'.[18]

Despite widespread fears that an invasion of Poland was imminent, there was a pause on 25 August. Hitler postponed his attack because Britain showed no signs of abandoning Poland, despite the Nazi-Soviet Pact, while Italy showed every sign of deserting Germany. This impression was confirmed in the course of the day by the conclusion of an Anglo-Polish alliance and a message from Mussolini stating that Italy was unprepared for war. The order to commence military operations was suspended.[19] Hitler embarked upon a new course, designed to separate London and Warsaw by indicating his desire for a firm Anglo-German agreement once he had solved the Polish question on his own terms. He did not succeed, but German offers of a future settlement did ensure that suspicion of Chamberlain remained strong in Washington. Could the Prime Minister resist the temptation to make a deal at the expense of his ally?

On 25 August Hitler summoned Henderson and informed the ambassador that he desired a settlement with Britain. He was prepared to guarantee the British Empire and would approach London 'with an offer' once the Polish question had been settled.[20] The same day the Führer agreed that Göring should send an unofficial emissary, the Swedish businessman Birger Dahlerus, to London to express a similar desire for an Anglo-German rapprochement.[21] Between 26 and 28 August a series of Cabinet meetings was held to consider Hitler's message. The government attached great importance to his 'offer' since the invasion of Poland had clearly been postponed pending the British reply. There was a feeling that Hitler was backing down and might yet be persuaded to discuss his differences with Poland if only London maintained a stiff attitude. The main problem was to make Hitler state his terms for a settlement and to stimulate direct discussions between Berlin and Warsaw. The government had no intention of being lured by Hitler into negotiating on behalf of a third power and then imposing a solution as in 1938.

In order to keep Göring in play, Dahlerus was despatched back to Berlin on 26 August with a 'platitudinous' message expressing British interest in a. peaceful settlement.[22] The same day the Cabinet considered the official British reply. No definite text emerged but it was agreed that the note should be 'firm yet moderate'. It was thought that the minority question might provide the basis for German-Polish talks.[23] On 27 August Dahlerus returned from Germany with a summary of Hitler's terms for a general settlement. He desired a pact with Britain and was prepared to guarantee the Empire, but Chamberlain must 'help' Germany realise its claims on Poland and allow the return of Danzig and the Corridor to the Reich.[24] Dahlerus discussed this message with Chamberlain and Halifax that afternoon. The Prime Minister and his Foreign Secretary refused to be drawn into any scheme to impose German claims on Warsaw as Hitler suggested and stressed their determination to stand by the guarantee to Poland. At the same time, however, they emphasised that frontier and minority problems could be peacefully settled by direct negotiation between Berlin and Warsaw. Any German-Polish agreement which emerged must be internationally guaranteed. Dahlerus was asked to phone Göring to ascertain whether Henderson's return to Britain could be postponed until the Swede had expressed the British standpoint unofficially. Göring agreed.[25] As a result it was believed that Hitler was weakening and that the 'moderates' were regaining their influence.[26]

On 28 August Dahlerus met Göring who agreed that there must be direct German-Polish discussions. Hitler felt that Britain should persuade Poland to initiate negotiations immediately.[27] The Cabinet discussed this response at noon on 28 August. A reply to Hitler was drawn up along the lines of the unofficial message delivered by the Swede. It stated that Britain would welcome Anglo-German discussions once the Polish question had been settled but warned that Britain would not abandon Poland for the sake of an agreement with Berlin. It was felt, however, that a settlement which safeguarded Poland's 'essential interests' was not impossible. London had already received an assurance from Warsaw that the Polish government was prepared to enter into negotiations with Berlin. The British note went on to warn of the dangers of a resort to force, but concluded by extending an economic carrot to Germany. In the event of a peaceful settlement the Reich could expect economic assistance to smooth the transition from autarky to peaceful trade.[28] The message was designed to strike a balance between deterrence and provocation. It was intended to disabuse Hitler of the notion that he could divide Britain and Poland. At the same time he was given a clear alternative to war, direct discussions with Poland. The economic carrot was intended to encourage Göring and the 'moderates' who were thought to be pressing this solution on the Führer.

Henderson presented the British note to Hitler on the evening of 28 August. The Führer promised to give the contents careful consideration. He then asked Henderson 'whether England would be willing to accept an alliance with Germany'. The ambassador exceeded his instructions at this point and replied that 'speaking personally' he did not exclude such a possibility provided 'the development of events justified it'.[29] Hitler's moderate tone raised British hopes. It was felt that the Führer was weakening because of Germany's isolated position. Halifax believed that Hitler was 'in a fix'. It was 'very important to get into negotiation and then be very stiff and Hitler would be beat'.[30] The only cause for concern was Henderson's response to Hitler's offer of an alliance which it was felt might weaken the British position and arouse suspicions of a new Munich if it leaked out. Vansittart noted 'An alliance means a military alliance if it means anything. And against whom would we be allying ourselves with such a gang as the present regime in Germany? The merest suggestion of it would ruin us in the United States.'[31] Halifax agreed and Henderson was warned against making such personal statements in the future.[32]

The German reply to Britain was given to Henderson on the evening of 29 August. Hitler welcomed the idea of an Anglo-German pact and stated that he would enter into direct negotiation with Warsaw provided a Polish emissary arrived in Berlin by noon on 30 August. He denied that this amounted to an ultimatum.[33] Hitler had not abandoned hope of dividing Warsaw and London. If Chamberlain was tempted by the offer of an Anglo-German alliance into putting pressure on Beck, two possibilities might arise. The Poles might refuse to negotiate, in which case Chamberlain would feel justified in revoking the British guarantee. Alternatively, if an emissary arrived and talks collapsed because of Polish 'intransigence' Chamberlain might refuse to fight on the grounds that Poland had provoked a war. Chamberlain, however, had no intention of falling into such a trap. He informed the Cabinet on 30 August that the demand for a Polish emissary was unacceptable. 'This definitely represented part of the old technique. It was essential that we should make it clear that we were not going to yield on this point.'[34] The British reply was, therefore, stiff in tone and reflected the desire to tie Hitler up in discussions. It stated that the government was informing Warsaw that Germany was prepared to enter into discussions but that it was felt in London to be 'impracticable to establish contact as early as today'. Any Anglo-German agreement was conditional upon a just settlement with Poland under international guarantee.[35]

The British note was delivered to Ribbentrop at midnight on 30 August. Ribbentrop, however, was not interested in the document. Instead he read Henderson a sixteen point memorandum outlining the German terms for a settlement with Poland. He then claimed that the German 'offer' was out of date since no Polish emissary had arrived to discuss it.[36] It seems clear that by this stage Hitler had decided he could afford no further delay in commencing military operations. The last favourable date for an invasion of Poland was 1 September and he was forced, therefore, to abandon the scheme of splitting Warsaw and London.[37] He was not going to fall into a British trap and waste time negotiating while the weather deteriorated. In this sense Chamberlain's rejection of the time limit for the arrival of a Polish envoy was probably decisive. On 1 September Hitler risked British intervention and launched the German forces against Poland.

In the period 26–31 August Britain was anxious to reassure the United States that no attempt was being made to betray Poland. Such assurances, however, did not convince Washington. Chamberlain was distrusted because of Munich and the recent revelations concerning the Hudson–Wohltat talks. As a result the Americans formed a false impression of what was taking place in London. It was believed that Chamberlain and the 'City' group in his Cabinet hoped to evade British obligations towards Poland, if possible placing responsibility for the 'sell-out' on the United States. Kennedy was thought to be collaborating in this scheme. The object of American policy was to encourage the 'anti-appeasers' who, under the leadership of Halifax, were supposed to be arguing that Britain must stand firm.[38] American suspicions of a new Munich were immediately aroused by Hitler's offer to Henderson on 25 August. Kennedy sent a summary of the Führer's proposals to Washington the same day. He informed Roosevelt that Chamberlain's reply would warn Hitler that Britain could not allow the partition of Poland between Germany and Russia. It would also emphasise, however, British interest in a German-Polish settlement. If a 'fair deal' could be worked out it might open the way to a general economic conference.[39] Roosevelt suspected that the Prime Minister had not revealed the full text of Hitler's message to Kennedy and was concerned about Chamberlain's remarks on the subject of economic appeasement. The President telephoned Bullitt several times on 25 and 26 August to ask if the ambassador had any idea of 'what passed between Hitler and Henderson'.[40] Bullitt spoke to Léger on 26 August and asked the Frenchman if he did not fear that 'Henderson's conversation with Hitler was the prelude to British action designed to disintegrate Polish resistance'. Léger replied that Chamberlain was standing by Poland.[41] This message did not reassure Washington where it was suspected that the British were misleading the French. Moffat noted on 26 August 'I don't think the British have been entirely frank with the French or with us'.[42] It was believed that a struggle was raging in London over the British reply to Hitler. Chamberlain, Simon and Wilson were 'all for appeasement' and had only been prevented from sacrificing Poland by Halifax's threat to resign and bring down the government. The final version of the note to the Führer on 28 August represented a compromise between the two factions. Berle remarked that the message was 'a goulash' which 'began with some firm talk and wound up by offering to discuss a lot of things which really, under their alliance with Poland, are not open for discussion'.[43] Moffat noted that the decision to reply to Hitler

> struck us all as a mere play for time and completely unrealistic . . . The most charitable explanation was that Britain and Germany were playing to throw the actual blame for a breach on each other. The less charitable explanation was that the British were not above a dicker leaving Poland to pay the price.[44]

The Americans were haunted by memories of Munich and overlooked the fact that London had obtained Poland's permission before raising the question of direct talks between Berlin and Warsaw. The British note of 28 August was in no sense intended to undermine the Anglo-Polish alliance.

American suspicions reached a height on 30 August when it was learned that Hitler had agreed to German-Polish negotiations provided a Polish emissary 'with full powers' came immediately to Berlin. It was feared that Chamberlain would seize the opportunity to sacrifice Poland in the interests of an Anglo-German economic deal. Beck would be forced to go to Germany where he·would meet the fate of Schuschnigg and Hacha. On 31 August the President made plain American opposition to such an outcome. At an interview with Lothian, the new British ambassador, Roosevelt

> Expressed the view that the most serious danger from the standpoint of American public opinion would be if it formed the conclusion that Herr Hitler was entangling the British Government in negotiations leading to pressure on Poland . . . to abandon vital interests. What right had Germany to demand that a Polish representative should go to Berlin to be treated like Dr Schuschnigg or Hacha and not to some neutral capital or with proper security against such treatment.[45]

While attempting to discourage the 'appeasers' by expressing his opposition to appeasement, the President also attempted to strengthen the 'anti-appeasers' in London. At an interview with Lindsay on 26 August he indicated his willingness to interpret the neutrality act in favour of the allies[46] and on 31 August he confirmed the tacit Anglo-American strategic agreement under which the United States assumed the main responsibility for restraining Japan. The President informed Lothian that the Nazi-Soviet Pact 'would probably lead to a fundamental realignment of Japanese policy in the direction of coming to terms with China'. If Tokyo remained hostile, however, he had two methods of pressure 'in the locker'. One was to send bombers and aircraft carriers to the Aleutians where they could threaten the Home Islands. the second was to move the Pacific fleet from San Francisco to Hawaii.[47]

The German invasion of Poland on 1 September did not at first remove American doubts about Chamberlain. There was a delay in issuing a British declaration of war which ensured that suspicion lingered in Washington. The delay was due to the French who placed every obstacle in the way of delivering an ultimatum to Berlin. Bonnet spent two days procrastinating in the hope that the Polish question could be settled at an international conference proposed by Mussolini.[48] Chamberlain had wished to deliver an ultimatum to Berlin in concert with France but the suspicions roused by the delay both amongst the opposition and within the government itself finally forced him to act alone. On the night of 2 September Corbin was summoned to Downing Street and informed that a British ultimatum was being sent to Berlin timed to expire at 11 a.m. the next day. If France did not follow suit Britain would act independently.[49] Chamberlain had decided to risk the sacrifice of Anglo-French solidarity rather than allow fears of another Munich to flourish. News of the British decision reached the White House on 2 September during a late night poker game attended by Ickes. The Secretary of the Interior noted that everyone was pleased by the news,

> Not because any of us wanted war, but because, believing it to be inevitable in the end, we thought that it was better for England and France to get into it as quickly as possible. The President said that, up to the last, Cordell Hull had said that personally he was from Missouri. He had no faith that Chamberlain would not again turn his hand from the plow.[50]

The opprobium of Munich remained attached to the Prime Minister both at home and abroad until the end.

Despite the outbreak of war on 3 September, neither Chamberlain nor Roosevelt had completely abandoned hopes of a negotiated solution to the German problem. The Prime Minister believed that Germany, abandoned by Italy and Japan and squeezed by the British blockade, might yet be forced to come to terms with the allies. The Führer would be swept away by a collapse of the German home front and replaced by a more trustworthy regime.[51] Roosevelt also hoped for such a development. He informed Lothian on 14 December that he desired, before his term expired, to intervene as 'a kind of umpire [and] . . . lay down the conditions for an armistice'. The time, however, had 'not yet come for this'. Britain and France, supplied with American munitions following neutrality revision in November 1939, must first convince Germany that 'its attempt to break through the West, to undermine British seapower or to starve Britain out had definitely failed'. The President hoped to overcome German fears of a new Versailles by stressing four points to which 'all Germans will respond', namely that the democracies stood for the four basic freedoms – freedom of speech, freedom of religion, freedom from fear and freedom of trade and access to raw materials.[52] In February 1940 Sumner Welles was despatched to Europe to investigate the possibility of peace on such terms. Roosevelt had a vague plan to offer American mediation on the basis of Welles' enquiries. If Hitler accepted, he would be forced to disarm and accept stringent security guarantees. If he rejected the American initiative, German isolation would be emphasised and the German people convinced that Führer stood for aggression and not for legitimate rights of self-defence.[53] Such a revelation might topple the Nazi regime and avert a spring offensive.

The successful German invasion of France and the Low Countries in 1940 destroyed all hope of such a negotiated peace and led to the fall of Chamberlain. Moreover, the military victories of the summer ended Hitler's isolation and opened up the prospect of an ultimate German triumph. The axis 'conspiracy' which existed before the Nazi-Soviet Pact was rejuvenated. Italy declared war on Britain and France. Spain was hostile and threatened to follow suit. In the Far East, Japanese expansion was renewed and Tokyo signed the tripartite pact, a blatantly anti-American instrument. It was clear that Tokyo hoped for gains at the expense of Britain, France and Holland in Indo-China, Malaya and the Netherlands East Indies. The threat of American isolation in a totalitarian world forced Roosevelt to envisage a wider role for the United States than the mere supply of munitions to Britain. In sheer self-defence the President was forced to abandon a limited liability role and in 1940–1 to fight what amounted to an undeclared war against the axis.

Conclusions

Although his efforts ultimately produced a government crisis in London, Roosevelt was unable to exert a decisive influence on British policy in 1937–8. He failed to coordinate an appeasement plan with Chamberlain as he had originally hoped. Offner blames isolationism for this failure, arguing that the President was asking London to place vital British interest in the hands of a power which itself emphasised lack of interest in political questions.[1] This was certainly a major weakness in American peace plans. Although Britain would have to make the main sacrifices in any European settlement and had most to lose if appeasement failed, Chamberlain was being asked to accept American leadership and American timing. He was being offered little in return except an economic contribution to a peace settlement. Had Roosevelt been prepared to go further and underwrite a new European security system to replace Locarno, an initiative might have been more welcome in London. As matters stood the President was asking too much and offering too little. He hoped to achieve such ambitious goals as world peace and free trade through moral force rather than hard political bargaining. In retrospect his plans seem rather naive. In 1919 Wilson had recognised that the United States must guarantee a European settlement if its other aims were to be realised. Roosevelt was unable and probably unwilling to undertake such a commitment.

The feeling that the United States was asking Britain to risk vital interests remained a stumbling block to closer cooperation when Roosevelt began to advocate a stiffer line towards Germany. The purge of the German conservatives in February 1938 aroused the President's first doubts about the prospects of appeasement, doubts which were confirmed after Munich by Ribbentrop's attempts to strengthen the Anti-Comintern Pact. Roosevelt saw Germany as the driving force behind a totalitarian conspiracy to dominate Europe and Asia which, if allowed to succeed, would exclude the United States from world markets and undermine its position in

Latin America. Resistance to this threat, however, meant cooperation with Britain and just as before Munich London was expected to bear the major burdens of appeasement, it was now expected to take the leading role in containing Germany. It was assumed in Washington that Britain would act as America's first line of defence because Hitler menaced British vital interests as much as American. This, however, was not as obvious in London as it seemed in Washington.

Chamberlain had not abandoned hope of concluding an Anglo-German agreement. He certainly envisaged a larger role for the United States in British policy after *Kristallnacht*. The Prime Minister welcomed Roosevelt's attempts to lead the United States out of isolation and his publicly expressed hostility to the axis as factors likely to restrain the 'extremists' in Germany and Japan. He had no intention, however, of becoming a mere cipher in the hands of Roosevelt. He realised that although the Americans advocated a stiffer line towards Germany, Britain and not the United States would be the first to suffer if Hitler were provoked into war. Total reliance on the United States would mean German hostility in return for American moral support and some material assistance in the shape of equipment rather than men. Moreover the price of such aid would be American economic domination of the Empire. This was not an ideal bargain while the possibility of a European settlement still existed, however remotely. Britain pursued such a settlement in February 1939 despite American protests. This policy gave rise in Washington to the suspicion that Chamberlain would appease Hitler indefinitely and the feeling that Britain was no longer acting as a great power. The Americans never appear to have considered that Britain was being asked to risk its very existence in return for very little from Washington except good advice. If the United States had signified its readiness to intervene in Europe if necessary, a stiffer policy might have seemed more attractive to Chamberlain.

Only in March 1939 did British and American vital interests coincide. The seizure of Prague convinced Chamberlain that Hitler aimed at world domination and must be resisted. The failure of appeasement forced him to give more consideration to American wishes than he had in the past. American moral and material support for the guarantee system was required. American naval assistance in the Far East was vital. The failure of appeasement, therefore, marked the beginning of British dependence on the

United States, a dependence which became greater with the outbreak of war in September 1939 and total with the fall of France in 1940. As Chamberlain had always suspected, the ultimate price of Roosevelt's support was British acceptance of an American dominated world order which involved the modification of imperial preference and the opening up of the Empire to US trade and investment.[2]

Roosevelt found it equally difficult to influence German policy in the period 1936–9. 'Moderates' such as Schacht were prepared to encourage American appeasement schemes in the hope of persuading Washington to exert pressure on London in favour of German colonial claims but were no more willing than Chamberlain to allow the United States to dictate the timing and content of talks. Even had Schacht endorsed an American initiative it would have carried little weight with Hitler who was interested in securing 'living space' by conquest rather than by negotiation.[3] After Munich Roosevelt tried to deter further German expansion by raising doubts in Hitler's mind about American neutrality in the event of war. He succeeded in worrying the German Foreign Office and even Göring but there is no evidence that this concern was shared by Hitler or Ribbentrop. At most the Führer regarded the President as a nuisance. Until the last minute Hitler did not seriously believe that Britain would intervene in defence of Poland. It is, therefore, hardly surprising that he discounted as a political factor a power with weak armaments and a neutrality law. Hitler relied upon isolationist sentiment to restrain the President and dismissed his anti-axis policy after Munich as '*Bluffpolitik*'. Fundamentally the Führer believed that 'the United States was incapable of conducting war'.[4]

Isolationism, therefore, inhibited Roosevelt's attempts to play a larger role in world affairs. Controversy still exists as to whether the President could have done more to educate public opinion thus allowing himself more room to manoeuvre in foreign policy. Offner has condemned the administration for accepting the Neutrality Act and Divine has criticised Roosevelt for not moving quickly enough to secure revision.[5] The President was undoubtedly in a difficult position. Between 1937 and 1939 as international tension rose, his relations with Congress deteriorated and there was an understandable reluctance to stimulate controversy by initiating a debate on foreign affairs. Until 1939 Roosevelt preferred trial balloons such as the 'quarantine' speech to a sustained campaign of public education. The President was in a dilemma. It was difficult to persuade public opinion that an axis danger existed while Chamberlain continued to talk about an Anglo-German agreement. Yet Roosevelt could not persuade Britain to take a stiffer line with Germany without widespread support for an anti-axis policy which would convince London that American support would be quickly forthcoming in the event of war. The President was caught between the desire to play a larger part in world affairs and the necessity of preserving his political position at home. He never solved the problem of balancing these two factors. While public opinion increasingly supported an active anti-axis policy after September 1939, it never reached the point of endorsing American military intervention. It was an outside force, in the shape of the Japanese attack on Pearl Harbor in December 1941, which freed Roosevelt from domestic restraints and allowed the full deployment of American power against the axis.

Notes

NOTES TO INTRODUCTION

1. A. J. P. Taylor, *The Origins of the Second World War* (London, 1962); M. Gilbert, *The Roots of Appeasement* (London, 1966).
2. K. Robbins, *Munich 1938* (London, 1968).
3. W. R. Louis, *British Strategy in the Far East* (Oxford, 1971).
4. W. L. Langer and S. E. Gleason, *The Challenge to Isolation* (New York, 1952).
5. D. Borg, *The United States and the Far Eastern Crisis 1933–38* (Cambridge, Mass., 1964).
6. A. A. Offner, *American Appeasement* (Cambridge, Mass., 1969).

NOTES TO CHAPTER ONE

1. Cudahy to Roosevelt, 20 March 1936, President's Secretary's File: Poland. Franklin D. Roosevelt Library, Hyde Park, New York. (Hereafter PSF.)
2. *Ambassador Dodd's Diary 1933–1938*, W. E. Dodd Jr and M. Dodd (eds) (London, 1941) p. 370. (Hereafter *Dodd's Diary*.)
3. 'Joseph E. Davies Diary', 15 December 1936, Joseph Davies Papers, Chronological File, Box 3. Library of Congress, Manuscripts Division, Washington, D.C. (Hereafter 'Davies Diary'.)
4. Speech at Chautauqua, 14 August 1936. *Franklin D. Roosevelt and Foreign Affairs*, E. B. Nixon (ed.), 3 volumes (Cambridge, Mass., 1969) vol. 3, pp. 377–83. Runciman to Baldwin, 26 January 1937, Foreign Office Correspondence, A668/93/45, FO371/20656, Public Record Office, London.
5. R. E. Divine, *The Illusion of Neutrality* (Chicago, 1962) pp. 155–6.
6. Nixon, *FDR and Foreign Affairs*, vol. 3, pp. 377–83.
7. *New York Times*, 26 August 1936.
8. Ibid., 27 August 1936.
9. Department of Western European Affairs memorandum, 16 February 1937, Norman Davis Papers, Box 24, Library of Congress, Manuscripts Division, Washington, D.C.; F. B. Sayre, *The American Trade Agreements Program* (New York, 1939).
10. Bingham to Roosevelt, 15 April 1936, President's Personal File: Bingham. (Hereafter PPF.)
11. *Dodd's Diary*, p. 232.
12. Dodd to Hull, 28 November 1936, State Department Papers, 862.50/969, National Archives, Washington, D.C. (Hereafter SD.)
13. Cudahy to Roosevelt, 26 December 1935, PSF: Poland.

14. Roosevelt to Cudahy, 15 January 1937, *Foreign Relations of the United States, 1937*, vol. 1, General (Washington, D.C., 1954) pp. 26–7. (Hereafter *FRUS*.)
15. Department of Western European Affairs, 16 February 1937, Norman Davis Papers, Box 24.
16. *Dodd's Diary*, pp. 258, 266, 271.
17. Ibid., pp. 115, 320; Dodd to Roosevelt, 7 December 1936, PSF: Germany.
18. Dodd to Hull, 27 August 1936, SD 862.5151/1735.
19. Gilbert (Geneva) to Hull, 12 November 1936, SD 862.5151/1753.
20. Dodd to Roosevelt, 7 December 1936, PSF: Germany.
21. Messersmith to Phillips, 26 June 1933, Messersmith Papers, File 203, University of Delaware, Newark, Delaware.
22. Messersmith to Hull, 5 December 1936, Messersmith Papers, File 790; Messersmith to Hull, 16 December 1936, ibid., File 799. Messersmith to Hull, 2 March 1937, ibid., File 867.
23. *Dodd's Diary*, pp. 282, 372; Dodd to Hull, 28 November 1936, SD 862.50/969.
24. Roosevelt to Dodd, 5 August 1936, PSF: Germany.
25. Dodd to Hull, 18 August 1936, SD 711.62/116.
26. Dodd to Roosevelt, 19 October 1936, PSF: Germany.
27. R. Dallek, *Democrat and Diplomat* (New York, 1968) pp. 293–7.
28. Bullitt to Roosevelt, 8 November 1936, PSF: France.
29. Bullitt to Roosevelt, 20 December 1936, PSF: France; Bullitt to Roosevelt, 16 December 1936, ibid.; *The Diplomats 1919–1939*, G. A. Craig and F. Gilbert (eds), 2 volumes (New York, 1962) vol. 2, pp. 656–7.
30. Cudahy to Hull, 29 December 1936, SD 852.00/4378.
31. Cudahy to Roosevelt, 26 December 1936, PSF: Poland.
32. 'Davies Diary', 28 August 1936.
33. 'Morgenthau Diary', 4 January 1937, Book 51, pp. 15–17. Franklin D. Roosevelt Library, Hyde Park, New York. (Hereafter 'Morgenthau Diary'.)
34. Memorandum by Hull, 18 January 1937, Norman Davis Papers, Box 24.
35. Undated memorandum on economic recovery (1935). Hull Papers, Subject File 63 'Currency Stabilisation', Library of Congress, Manuscripts Division, Washington, D.C.
36. Hjalmar Schacht, 'Germany's Colonial Claims', *Foreign Affairs*, vol. 15, no. 2, (January 1937) pp. 222–34.
37. A. A. Offner, *American Appeasement* (Cambridge, Mass., 1969) p. 231.
38. Kirk (Rome) to Hull, 7 May 1937, SD 740.00/167.
39. Davies to Roosevelt, 20 January 1937, *FRUS, 1937*, vol. 1, pp. 19–31.
40. *Dodd's Diary*, p. 395.
41. Memorandum by Hull, 18 January 1937, op. cit.
42. Department of Western European Affairs memorandum, 20 February 1937, SD A/B641.11/3; R. N. Kottman, *Reciprocity and the North Atlantic Triangle* (New York, 1968), pp. 164–5.
43. Bullitt to Hull, 1 November 1936, SD 851.00/1602.
44. Cochran to Morgenthau, 15 January 1937, in Nixon, *FDR and Foreign Affairs*, vol. 3, pp. 586–8.
45. D. Borg, *The United States and the Far Eastern Crisis* (Cambridge, Mass., 1964) pp. 373–4.
46. Department of Western European Affairs memorandum, 16 February 1937, Norman Davis Papers, Box 24.

NOTES TO CHAPTER TWO

1. C. A. MacDonald, 'Economic Appeasement and the German Moderates', *Past and Present*, no. 56 (August 1972).
2. Ibid.
3. J. Harvey (ed.), *The Diplomatic Diaries of Oliver Harvey* (London, 1970) p. 85. Welles to Roosevelt, 8 March 1938, PSF: Great Britain.
4. Cabinet Committee on Foreign Policy, 10 May 1937, CAB27/622.
5. K. Middlemas, *The Diplomacy of Illusion* (London, 1972) pp. 112–15.
6. Memorandum by Eden, 4 May 1937, C3345/1533/62, FO371/10704.
7. Minute by Eden, 7 November 1936, A8860/103/45, FO371/19827.
8. Lord Avon, *Facing the Dictators* (London, 1962) p. 487.
9. M. Howard, *The Continental Commitment* (London, 1972) pp. 113–14.
10. Bingham to Hull, 11 March 1937, *FRUS, 1937*, vol.1, pp. 58–66.
11. D. C. Watt, *Personalities and Policies* (London, 1965) p. 42.
12. Viscount Templewood, *Nine Troubled Years* (London, 1954) p. 263.
13. C. Thorne, *The Limits of Foreign Policy* (London, 1972) p. 247; K. Middlemas and J. Barnes, *Baldwin* (London, 1969) p. 729.
14. Simon to MacDonald, 29 January 1932, *Documents on British Foreign Policy*, series 2, 13 volumes (London, 1946–70) vol. 9, pp. 215–17. (Hereafter *DBFP*.)
15. Lindsay to Simon, 3 March 1932, ibid., pp. 709–11.
16. Chamberlain to Simon, 1 September 1934, ibid., vol. 13, pp. 24–31.
17. W. N. Medlicott, *British Foreign Policy Since Versailles* (London, 1967) pp. 160–1.
18. Templewood, *Nine Troubled Years*, p. 264.
19. *From the Morgenthau Diaries*, J. M. Blum (ed.), 3 volumes (Boston, Mass., 1965) vol. 1, p. 457.
20. R. N. Gardner, *Sterling-Dollar Diplomacy* (London, 1969) pp. 31–2.
21. Middlemas and Barnes, *Baldwin*, p. 685.
22. Memorandum by the Economic Section, 1 April 1937, W6363/5/50, FO371/21215; Dirksen to Ribbentrop, 19 October 1938, *Documents on German Foreign Policy*, Series D, 7 volumes (London, 1949–56) vol. 4, pp. 314–17. (Hereafter *DGFP*.)
23. Kottman, *Reciprocity and the North Atlantic Triangle*, pp. 130, 227.
24. Gardner, *Sterling-Dollar Diplomacy*, pp. 30–3.
25. Johnson to Hull, 27 September 1937, *FRUS, 1937*, vol. 2, pp. 71–2.
26. Minute by Ashton-Gwatkin, 11 March 1937, A2847/228/45, FO371/20659.
27. Runciman to Baldwin, 26 January 1937, A668/93/45, FO371, 20656.
28. Minute by Troutbeck, 1 April 1937, A2378/38/45, FO371/20651.
29. Memorandum by Chamberlain, September 1934, NC8/19/1, Neville Chamberlain Papers, University of Birmingham.
30. 'Moffat Diary', 29 July 1937.
31. S. Aster, *Anthony Eden* (London, 1976) p. 46.
32. I. Colvin, *The Chamberlain Cabinet* (London, 1971) pp. 60–70; Avon, *Facing the Dictators*, pp. 490–8.
33. Lindsay to Eden, 22 March 1937, A2378/38/45, FO371/20651.
34. Minute by Ashton-Gwatkin, 5 April 1937, A2970/228/45, FO371/20659.
35. Davis to Hull, 29 April 1937, PSF Confidential: Great Britain.
36. Runciman to Baldwin, 26 January 1937, A668/93/45, FO371/20656.

37. Minute by Troutbeck, 1 April 1937, A2378/38/45, FO371/20651.
38. Kottman, *Reciprocity and the North Atlantic Triangle*, p. 147.
39. Davis to Hull, 10 April 1937, SD 740.00/143.
40. Davis to Roosevelt, 29 April 1937, PSF Confidential: Great Britain.
41. Cochran to Morgenthau, 15 January 1937 in Nixon, *FDR and Foreign Affairs*, vol. 3, pp. 586–8.
42. Dodd to Hull, 1 February 1937, SD 862.50 Four Year Plan/15.
43. Bullitt to Hull, 20 February 1937, PSF Confidential: France.
44. *Dodd's Diary*, pp. 392–4.
45. J. E. Davies, *Mission to Moscow* (London, 1942) pp. 99–100.
46. 'Davies Diary', 15 April 1937.
47. *Dodd's Diary*, pp. 400–14.
48. Bullitt to Hull, 12 May 1937, PSF Confidential: France.
49. E. Roosevelt (ed.), *FDR. His Personal Letters*, 3 volumes (New York, 1950) vol. 3, p. 209.
50. Davis to Chamberlain, 21 June 1937, A4412/228/45, FO371/20661.
51. Minute on Davis's message, ibid.
52. Ibid.
53. Memorandum on the Neutrality Act, 10 May 1937, A4581/228/45, FO371/20666.
54. Minute on Davis's message, op. cit.
55. Ibid.
56. Chamberlain to Eden, 2 July 1937, A4880/228/45, FO371/20661.
57. Borg, *The United States and the Far Eastern Crisis*, pp. 377–8.
58. Bingham to Hull, 13 July 1937, Norman Davis Papers, Box 27.
59. *New York Times*, 8 July 1937.
60. Roosevelt to Chamberlain, 28 July 1937, *FRUS, 1937*, vol. 1, p. 113.
61. Chamberlain to Roosevelt, 28 September 1937, ibid., pp. 131–2.
62. Roosevelt to Dodd, 30 August 1937, PPF Dodd; 'Moffat Diary', 30 July 1937.
63. Middlemas, *Diplomacy of Illusion*, p. 115; W. N. Medlicott, *British Foreign Policy since Versailles*, p. 154.

NOTES TO CHAPTER THREE

1. G. Barraclough, 'Watch out for Japan', *The New York Review of Books*, vol. xx, no. 9 (7 June 1973); T. Sommer, *Deutschland und Japan zwischen den Mächten* (Tübingen, 1962) pp. 1–16.
2. Cabinet, 8 December 1937, CAB 90/46(37).
3. T. R. Kittredge, 'Anglo-American Naval Cooperation', part 1, section D, pp. 48–9, unpublished manuscript, US Navy Yard, Washington, D.C.
4. Middlemas, *Diplomacy of Illusion*, p. 55.
5. Lord Avon, *Facing the Dictators*, p. 531.
6. 'Summary of Attempts to Secure Cooperation in the Far East', F5868/9/10, FO371/20954.
7. Borg, *The United States and the Far Eastern Crisis*, pp. 287–8.
8. Chamberlain to Hilda Chamberlain, 29 August 1937, Chamberlain Papers, NC18/1/10/9.

9. A. A. Berle and T. Jacobs (eds), *Navigating the Rapids 1918–1971* (New York, 1973) p. 137.
10. *New York Times*, 8 September 1937.
11. A. Bullock, *Hitler: A Study in Tyranny* (London, 1962) pp. 361–2.
12. Blum, *From the Morgenthau Diaries*, p. 462.
13. 'Davies Diary', 13 September 1937.
14. Ibid.
15. Memorandum by Moffat, 13 September 1937, SD 858.00/481; 'Moffat Diary', 16 September 1937; Gilbert to Hull, 27 September 1937, PSF Confidential: Germany.
16. 'Moffat Diary', 29 August 1937.
17. Borg, *The United States and the Far Eastern Crisis*, pp. 289–92; 'Moffat Diary', 27 August 1937.
18. Ibid.
19. Berle and Jacobs, *Navigating the Rapids*, pp. 137–8.
20. 'Moffat Diary', 15 September 1937.
21. Ibid., 28 September 1937.
22. H. Ickes (ed.), *The Secret Diary of Harold L. Ickes*, 3 volumes (London, 1955) vol. 2, pp. 211–13.
23. Borg, *The United States and the Far Eastern Crisis*, pp. 380–1.
24. *New York Times*, 6 October 1937.
25. Wickham-Steed to Vansittart, 13 October 1937, A7441/228/45, FO371/20663.
26. Borg, *The United States and the Far Eastern Crisis*, pp. 381–6.
27. 'Phillips Diary', 8 October 1937, William Phillips Papers, Houghton Library, Harvard.
28. W. L. Langer and S. E. Gleason, *The Challenge to Isolation* (London, 1964) p. 23.
29. Tweedsmuir to Chamberlain, 25 October 1937, Premier 1/229.
30. Sommer, *Deutschland und Japan*, pp. 56–82; N. R. Clifford, *The Retreat from China* (London, 1967) p. 28.
31. S. Welles, *The Time for Decision* (London, 1944) pp. 54–5.
32. Tweedsmuir to Chamberlain, 25 October 1937.
33. Memorandum by Welles, 26 October 1937, *FRUS, 1937*, vol. 1, pp. 667–8.
34. Chamberlain to Ida Chamberlain, 30 October 1937, Chamberlain Papers, NC18/1/1026.
35. Chamberlain to Hilda Chamberlain, 9 October 1937, Chamberlain Papers, NC18/1/1023; Cabinet, 6 October 1937, CAB 89/36(37).
36. Cabinet, 13 October 1937, CAB 89/37(37).
37. *The Times*, 16 October 1937.
38. Craigie to Eden, 29 October 1937, F8754/414/23, FO371/21040.
39. Avon, *Facing the Dictators*, pp. 506–8, 536.
40. Ibid., p. 492.
41. *The Times*, 10 November 1937.
42. Avon, *Facing the Dictators*, p. 509.
43. Neville Chamberlain to Ida Chamberlain, 26 November 1937, Chamberlain Papers, NC18/1/1630.
44. Borg, *The United States and the Far Eastern Crisis*, p. 406.
45. N. H. Hooker (ed.), *The Moffat Journals, Selections from the Diplomatic Journals of Jay Pierpont Moffat* (Cambridge, Mass., 1956) pp. 179–81. (Hereafter *The Moffat Journal*.)

46. Bullitt to Roosevelt, 24 November 1937, PSF: Bullitt.
47. Hooker, *The Moffat Journals*, pp. 162–5.
48. Harvey, *Diplomatic Diary*, pp. 56–7.
49. 'Moffat Diary', 24 September 1937; Hooker, *The Moffat Journals*, pp. 176–8.
50. Avon, *Facing the Dictators*, pp. 489, 539.
51. Harvey, *Diplomatic Diary*, p. 58.
52. Hooker, *The Moffat Journals*, pp. 176–8.
53. Harvey, *Diplomatic Diary*, p. 59.
54. Welles, *Time for Decision*, p. 55.
55. Berle and Jacobs, *Navigating the Rapids*, p. 150.
56. Hooker, *The Moffat Journals*, p. 183; Borg, *The United States and the Far Eastern Crisis*, pp. 433–4.
57. Welles, *Time for Decision*, p. 56.
58. Hooker, *The Moffat Journals*, pp. 181–3.
59. Borg, *The United States and the Far Eastern Crisis*, pp. 428–9.
60. Cabinet, 24 November 1937, CAB 90/43(37).
61. Chamberlain to Hilda Chamberlain, 17 December 1937, Chamberlain Papers, NC18/1/1032.
62. Cabinet, 24 November 1937.

NOTES TO CHAPTER FOUR

1. W. Phillips, *Ventures in Diplomacy* (London, 1965) pp. 108–9.
2. Dodd to Hull, 9 November 1937, PSF Confidential: Germany.
3. Ickes, *Secret Diary*, vol. 2, pp. 275–8.
4. Sommer, *Deutschland und Japan*, pp. 1–2.
5. 'Phillips Diary', 9 November 1937.
6. Chamberlain to Hilda Chamberlain, 21 November 1937, Chamberlain Papers, NC18/1/1029.
7. Lindsay to Eden, 16 November 1937, A8259/228/45, FO371/20664.
8. Sayre to Phillips, 19 November 1937, SD 711.652/119.
9. Ickes, *Secret Diary*, vol. 2, p. 269.
10. *Roosevelt's Foreign Policy. Unedited Speeches and Documents* (New York, 1942) p. 135.
11. 'Leahy Diary', 28 November 1937, Leahy Papers, Library of Congress, Manuscripts Division, Washington, D.C.
12. Kittredge, 'Anglo-American Naval Cooperation', unpublished manuscript study, US Navy Yard, Washington, D.C., pp. 48–9.
13. Cabinet, 24 November 1937, CAB90/43(37).
14. Cabinet, 8 December 1937, CAB90/46(37).
15. Chamberlain to Ida Chamberlain, 26 November 1937, Chamberlain Papers, NC18/1/1630.
16. MacDonald, 'Economic Appeasement', op. cit., p. 113.
17. Howard, *The Continental Commitment*, pp. 116–17; Colvin, *The Chamberlain Cabinet*, pp. 73–81.
18. Ibid.

19. Lindsay to Eden, 30 November 1937, F10285/9/10, FO371/20960.
20. Leahy to Roosevelt, 30 November 1937, PSF: Navy.
21. Ibid., 3 December 1937.
22. Bullitt to Roosevelt, 23 November 1937, PSF Confidential: France.
23. Memorandum for Hull and Welles, 29 November 1937, SD 741.62/206; Welles to Roosevelt, 16 December 1937, PSF: Germany.
24. Davies, *Mission to Moscow*, pp. 170–1.
25. Eden to Lindsay, 13 December 1937, F11086/10816/10, FO371/21021.
26. Lindsay to Eden, 13 December 1937, F10976/10816/10, FO371/21021.
27. Hull to Johnson, 13 December 1937, *FRUS, 1937*, vol. 4, p. 497.
28. Lindsay to Eden, 13 December 1937, F10976/10816/10, FO371/21021.
29. Lindsay to Eden, 14 December 1937, F11048/10816/10, FO371/21021.
30. Borg, *The United States and the Far Eastern Crisis*, p. 492.
31. Hull to Grew, 19 December 1937, *FRUS Japan*, vol. 1, pp. 523–4.
32. Blum, *From the Morgenthau Diaries*, p. 489.
33. 'Leahy Diary', 13 December 1937.
34. Cabinet, 15 December 1937, CAB90/47(37).
35. Eden to Lindsay, 15 December 1937, F10976/10816/10, FO371/21021.
36. Lindsay to Eden, 15 December 1937, F11072/10816/10, FO371/21021; ibid., 16 December 1937, F11116/9/10, FO371/20961.
37. Eden to Lindsay, 16 December 1937, F11116/9/10, FO371/20961.
38. Borg, *The United States and the Far Eastern Crisis*, p. 492.
39. Hull to Grew, 16 December 1937, *FRUS Japan*, vol. 1, p. 527.
40. Lindsay to Eden, 17 December 1937, F11215/10816/10, FO371/21021.
41. Blum, *From the Morgenthau Diaries*, pp. 490–1.
42. 'Morgenthau Diary', 18 December 1937, Book 103, pp. 88–90.
43. Ickes, *Secret Diary*, vol. 2, p. 278.
44. Lindsay to Eden, 17 December 1937, F11201/9/10, FO371/20961.
45. Blum, *From the Morgenthau Diaries*, pp. 490–1.
46. Lindsay to Eden, 17 December 1937.
47. Cabinet, 22 December 1937, CAB90/48(37).
48. Ibid.
49. Blum, *From the Morgenthau Diaries*, pp. 491–2.
50. 'Morgenthau Diary', 21 December 1937, Book 103, p. 248.
51. Borg, *The United States and the Far Eastern Crisis*, pp. 500–3.
52. Grew to Mrs Moffat, 4 January 1938, 'Grew Letters', vol. 92, Houghton Library, Harvard; 'Grew Diary', January 1938, Grew Papers, vol. 5.
53. Johnson to Hull, 29 December 1937, PSF: China.
54. Borg, *The United States and the Far Eastern Crisis*, p. 510.
55. Messersmith to Heinemann, 21 December 1937, Messersmith Papers, File 914.
56. Memorandum by Messersmith, 17 January 1938, *FRUS Soviet Union*, pp. 594–9.
57. Messersmith to Heinemann, 21 December 1937.
58. Kittredge, 'Anglo-American Naval Cooperation', pp. 48–9.
59. Davies to Roosevelt, 9 June 1938, *FRUS Soviet Union*, pp. 600–1.
60. J. Erickson, *The Soviet High Command* (London, 1968) pp. 475–6.
61. Davies to Roosevelt, 9 June 1938, *FRUS Soviet Union*, pp. 600–1.

NOTES TO CHAPTER FIVE

1. Memorandum by Welles, 10 January 1938, *FRUS, 1938*, vol. 1, pp. 115–17.
2. Berle and Jacobs, *Navigating the Rapids*, p. 163.
3. Borg, *The United States and the Far Eastern Crisis*, p. 510.
4. Berle and Jacobs, *Navigating the Rapids*, p. 163.
5. Lindsay to Foreign Office, 23 January 1938, A2127/64/45, FO371/21526.
6. Smith to War Department, 30 December 1937, Military Records Group 163, 2657-B-747, National Archives, Washington, D.C.
7. 'Moffat Diary', 5 January 1938.
8. *New York Times*, 11 January 1938.
9. Berle and Jacobs, *Navigating the Rapids*, p. 163.
10. Ibid.
11. Messersmith to Hull, 22 January 1938, Messersmith Papers, File 928.
12. *New York Times*, 4 January 1938.
13. Ibid., 29 January 1938.
14. C. Hull, *The Memoirs of Cordell Hull*, 2 volumes (London, 1948) vol. 1, p. 548.
15. Lindsay to Foreign Office, 11 January 1938, A2127/64/45, FO371/21526.
16. Ibid., 12 January 1938.
17. Cadogan to Chamberlain, 12 January 1938, ibid.
18. Speech by Simon, 28 November 1937, Johnson to Hull, SD 841. OOPR/519; MacDonald, 'Economic Appeasement', p. 113.
19. Speech by Simon, ibid.
20. Chamberlain to Hilda Chamberlain, 30 January 1938, Chamberlain Papers NC 18/1/1037.
21. Cabinet, 24 January 1938, CAB 92/1(38).
22. Templewood, *Nine Troubled Years*, pp. 270–1.
23. Ibid.
24. Chamberlain to Roosevelt, 14 January 1938, *FRUS, 1938*, vol. 1, pp. 118–20.
25. Harvey, *Diplomatic Diary*, pp. 67–8.
26. I. Macleod, *Neville Chamberlain* (London, 1961) p. 212.
27. Harvey, *Diplomatic Diary*, pp. 69–70.
28. Avon, *Facing the Dictators*, p. 550.
29. Harvey, *Diplomatic Diary*, p. 71.
30. Chamberlain to Ida Chamberlain, 23 January 1938, Chamberlain Papers, NC18/1/1036.
31. Roosevelt to Chamberlain, 17 January 1938, *FRUS, 1938*, vol. 1, pp. 120–2.
32. Hull, *Memoirs*, vol. 1, pp. 580–1.
33. Avon, *Facing the Dictators*, p. 557.
34. Harvey, *Diplomatic Diary*, p. 70.
35. Eden to Chamberlain, 18 January 1938, A2127/64/45, FO371/21526.
36. Harvey, *Diplomatic Diary*, pp. 76–7.
37. D. Dilks (ed.), *The Diaries of Sir Alexander Cadogan 1938–45* (London, 1971) p. 40.
38. Chamberlain to Hilda Chamberlain, 30 January 1938, Chamberlain Papers, NC18/1/1037.
39. Lindsay to Chamberlain, 22 January 1938, A2127/64/45, FO371/21526.
40. Ickes, *Secret Diary*, vol. 2, p. 315.
41. Messersmith to McIntyre, 2 February 1938, SD FW740.00/295.

42. Wiley to Hull, 15 February 1938, *FRUS, 1938*, vol. 1, pp. 393-4.
43. Harvey, *Diplomatic Diary*, p. 85.
44. Ibid., p. 83.
45. Middlemas, *Diplomacy of Illusion*, p. 150.
46. Avon, *Facing the Dictators*, pp. 578-83.
47. Middlemas, *Diplomacy of Illusion*, p. 148.
48. Memorandum by Moffat, 1 February 1938, SD 741.62/228; Messersmith to McIntyre, 2 February 1938, SD FW740.00/295.
49. Memorandum by Cadogan, 21 February 1938, A1410/1409/45, FO371/20547.
50. Hooker, *The Moffat Journals*, pp. 190-1; 'Moffat Diary', 23 February 1938; 'Moffat Diary', 25 February 1938.
51. Roosevelt to Cudahy, 16 April 1938, E. Roosevelt (ed.), *FDR. His Personal Letters*, 3 volumes, vol. 3, pp. 233-4.
52. Memorandum by Messersmith, 18 February 1938, *FRUS, 1938*, vol. 1, pp. 17-24; Messersmith to Geist, 7 February 1938, Messersmith Papers, File 941.
53. Roosevelt to Cudahy, 9 March 1938, E. Roosevelt (ed.), *FDR. His Personal Letters*, vol. 3, p. 232.
54. Kennedy to Hull, 4 March 1938, SD 711.41/389.
55. Welles to Roosevelt, 8 March 1938, PSF: Great Britain.
56. Kennedy to Hull, 11 April 1938, PSF Confidential: Great Britain.

NOTES TO CHAPTER SIX

1. S. Quentin to Bonnet, 11 March 1938, *Documents Diplomatiques Français*, 2nd Series (Paris, 1973) vol. 8, p. 729. (Hereafter *DDF*.)
2. E. L. Henson, 'Britain, America and the Month of Munich', *International Relations*, vol. 2, no. 5, pp. 298-300.
3. Malcolm Muggeridge (ed.), *Ciano's Diary 1937-38* (London, 1954) pp. 94-5.
4. Foreign Policy Committee, 29 March 1938, CAB27/623.
5. Kennedy to Hull, 6 April 1938, PSF Confidential: Great Britain.
6. *House of Commons Debates*, vol. 335, col. 545.
7. 'Moffat Diary', 18 April 1938; Hull, *Memoirs*, vol. 1, p. 581; Ickes, *Secret Diary*, vol. 2, p. 352.
8. Kennedy to Hull, 28, March 1938, SD 741.65/521; 'Phillips' Diary', 4 April 1938.
9. Memorandum, 7 February 1938, Hull Papers, Conversations File 57: China; 'Grew Diary', April 1938.
10. 'Moffat Diary', 16 March 1938.
11. Ibid., 18 April 1938.
12. *New York Times*, 12 May 1938; Hull, *Memoirs*, vol. 1, p. 582.
13. Ickes, *Secret Diary*, vol. 2, p. 348.
14. Colvin, *The Chamberlain Cabinet*, p. 115.
15. MacDonald, 'Economic Appeasement', p. 114; Harvey, *Diplomatic Diary*, p. 121.
16. Kennedy to Hull, 26 July 1938, SD 741.65/620.
17. Colvin, *The Chamberlain Cabinet*, pp. 108-11.
18. 'Morgenthau Diary', 18 February 1938, book III, pp. 259-63; Butterworth to Morgenthau, 30 March 1938, SD 841.5151/848.

19. Memorandum by Hudson, 8 July 1938, C7858/30318, FO371/21674; minute by Ashton-Gwatkin, ibid.
20. Sir Nevile Henderson, *Failure of a Mission* (London, 1940) pp. 80–95; MacDonald, 'Economic Appeasement', pp. 112–14.
21. Minute by Ashton-Gwatkin, C7858/30/18, FO371/21647.
22. Dallek, *Democrat and Diplomat*, pp. 237, 288.
23. Colvin, *The Chamberlain Cabinet*, pp. 108–11.
24. Lord Strang, *Home and Abroad* (London, 1956) pp. 132–3.
25. Middlemas, *Diplomacy of Illusion*, pp. 224–5.
26. *DBFP*, series 3, vol. 1 (London, 1949) pp. 198–233.
27. Wilson to Hull, 12 March 1938, SD 863.00/1425.
28. Halifax to Lindsay, 23 March 1938, C1933/132/18, FO371/21674.
29. Harvey, *Diplomatic Diary*, p. 151.
30. Memorandum by Moffat, 3 May 1938, SD 741.51/282.
31. 'Moffat Diary', 17 May 1938.
32. Ibid., 22 March 1938.
33. Morgenthau to Roosevelt, 1 March 1938, PSF: Treasury.
34. Davies to McIntyre, 4 April 1938, Davies Papers, Chronological File 6.
35. Memorandum by Messersmith, 18 February 1938, *FRUS, 1938*, vol. 1, pp. 17–24.
36. Hull, *Memoirs*, vol. 1, p. 601.
37. Ickes, *Secret Diary*, vol. 2, p. 474.
38. Thomsen to Ribbentrop, 12 September 1938, *DGFP*, series D, vol. 1, pp. 726–32.
39. Hull, *Memoirs*, vol. 1, p. 577.
40. Dieckhoff to Ribbentrop, 22 March 1938, *DGFP*, series D, vol. 1, p. 699.
41. *New York Times*, 14 April 1938.
42. Hull, *Memoirs*, vol. 1, p. 583.
43. *New York Times*, 18 June 1938.
44. Hull, *Memoirs*, vol. 1, p. 585.
45. *New York Times*, 18 June 1938.
46. Ibid., 15 July 1938.
47. Kottman, *Reciprocity and the North Atlantic Triangle*, pp. 250–1.
48. Hull, *Memoirs*, vol. 1, p. 575.
49. Kottman, *Reciprocity and the North Atlantic Triangle*, pp. 250–1.
50. Memorandum by Feis, 25 July 1938, Papers of the Adviser on International Economic Affairs, 836.51 Relief Credits/476, National Archives, Washington, D.C.
51. Dieckhoff to Weizäcker, 22 March 1938, *DGFP*, series D, vol. 1, pp. 696–7; Dieckhoff to Ribbentrop, 22 March 1938, ibid., p. 699.
52. Memorandum by Green, 18 January 1938, *FRUS, 1938*, vol. 2, pp. 297–300; John McVickar Haight, *American Aid to France* (New York, 1970) pp. 6–8.
53. Dieckhoff to Weizäcker, 30 March 1938, *DGFP*, series D, vol. 2, pp. 699–701.
54. Bullitt to Hull, 17 May 1938, *FRUS, 1938*, vol. 2, p. 307.
55. Colvin, *The Chamberlain Cabinet*, p. 110.
56. George Bonnet, *De Washington Au Quai d'orsay* (Paris, 1946) pp. 341–2.
57. Dieckhoff to Weizäcker, 31 May 1938, *DGFP*, series D, vol. 2, pp. 369–71.
58. *New York Times*, 19 June 1938.
59. Bullitt to Roosevelt, 20 May 1938, PSF: France.

60. Dirksen to Weizäcker, 20 July 1938, *DGFP*, series D, vol. 2, pp. 718–23.
61. Craig and Gilbert, *The Diplomats*, vol. 2, pp. 658–9.
62. 'Berle Diary', 19 March 1938, Berle Papers, Box 210, Franklin D. Roosevelt Library, Hyde Park, New York. (Hereafter 'Berle Diary'.)
63. Ibid., 18 February 1938.
64. Ibid., 19 September 1938.
65. Roosevelt to O'Laughlin, 14 June 1938, *Public Papers and Addresses*, p. 378; speech at Treasure Island, 14 July 1938, ibid., p. 456.
66. Offner, *American Appeasement*, p. 246.
67. Halifax to Phipps, 17 June 1938, *DBFP*, series 3, vol. 1, p. 477.
68. Colvin, *The Chamberlain Cabinet*, p. 134.
69. Harvey, *Diplomatic Diary*, p. 164.
70. Ibid., pp. 163–4.
71. Ibid.
72. Colvin, *The Chamberlain Cabinet*, p. 137.
73. Middlemas, *Diplomacy of Illusion*, p. 267.
74. Minute by Sargent, 2 August 1938, C7757/1941/18, FO371/21730.
75. Runciman to Roosevelt, 28 July 1938, PSF: Great Britain.
76. 'Moffat Diary', 12 May 1938; Hull to Roosevelt, 29 July 1938, President's Official File 20. (Hereafter OF.)
77. 'Moffat Diary', 6 August 1938.

NOTES TO CHAPTER SEVEN

1. Middlemas, *Diplomacy of Illusion*, pp. 270–1.
2. Keith Robbins, *Munich 1938* (London, 1968) p. 248.
3. A. P. Young, *The X Documents* (London, 1974) pp. 25, 50–9.
4. Robbins, *Munich 1938*, pp. 245–6.
5. Colvin, *The Chamberlain Cabinet*, pp. 140–2.
6. Ibid., pp. 148–9; Middlemas, *Diplomacy of Illusion*, p. 320.
7. Colvin, *The Chamberlain Cabinet*, p. 147; Middlemas, *Diplomacy of Illusion*, p. 320.
8. Robbins, *Munich 1938*, pp. 262–4.
9. Halifax to Phipps, 14 September 1938, *DBFP*, series 3, vol. 2, pp. 306–8; Harvey, *Diplomatic Diary*, p. 178.
10. Colvin, *The Chamberlain Cabinet*, pp. 153–4.
11. Middlemas, *Diplomacy of Illusion*, pp. 340–2.
12. Harvey, *Diplomatic Diary*, pp. 187–8.
13. Colvin, *The Chamberlain Cabinet*, p. 159.
14. Hull, *Memoirs*, vol. 1, p. 587.
15. Ibid.
16. Young, *The X Documents*, pp. 71–2.
17. Roosevelt to Bowers, 31 August 1938, PSF: Spain.
18. Young, *The X Documents*, p. 73; Feis to Bullitt, 6 September 1938, Herbert Feis Papers, General Correspondence, Box 12, Bullitt Folder, National Archives, Washington, D.C.
19. Glen Barclay, *Struggle for a Continent* (London, 1971) pp. 82–3.

20. Harvey, *Diplomatic Diary*, p. 176.
21. Halifax to Lindsay, 10 September 1938, *DBFP*, series 3, vol. 2, pp. 284–5.
22. Blum, *From the Morgenthau Diaries*, vol. 1, pp. 514–15.
23. Lindsay to Halifax, 12 September 1938, *DBFP*, series 3, vol. 2, p. 301.
24. Duff Cooper, *Old Men Forget* (London, 1953) p. 222; Middlemas, *Diplomacy of Illusion*, p. 333.
25. Bullitt to Roosevelt, 17 August 1938, PSF: France.
26. Kennedy to Roosevelt, 31 August 1938, PSF: Kennedy.
27. Jacobs and Berle, *Navigating the Rapids*, pp. 183–5.
28. 'Moffat Diary', 31 August 1938.
29. Kennedy to Hull, 31 August 1938, *FRUS, 1938*, vol. 1, pp. 560–1.
30. 'Morgenthau Diary', 1 September 1938, Book 138, pp. 33–5.
31. 'Moffat Diary', 1 September 1938.
32. Bullitt to Roosevelt, 7 September 1938, PSF: France.
33. *New York Times*, 10 September 1938.
34. 'Morgenthau Diary', 14 September 1938, Book 139, pp. 220–4.
35. Ibid., 13 September 1938.
36. Robert E. Sherwood, *The White House Papers of Harry L. Hopkins*, 2 volumes (London, 1948) vol. 1, p. 97.
37. Roosevelt to Phillips, 15 September 1938, E. Roosevelt (ed.), *FDR. His Personal Letters*, vol. 3, p. 241.
38. Bullitt to Roosevelt, 14 September 1938, PSF Confidential: France.
39. 'Morgenthau Diary', 18 September 1938, Book 141, pp. 112–14; 'Moffat Diary', 17 September 1938.
40. Ickes, *Secret Diary*, pp. 467–70.
41. Ibid., p. 474; Hull, *Memoirs*, vol. 1, pp. 589–90.
42. 'Morgenthau Diary', 19 September 1938, Book 141, p. 115.
43. Ickes, *Secret Diary*, p. 474.
44. Lindsay to Halifax, 20 September 1938, *DBFP*, series 3, vol. 7, pp. 627–9.
45. J. Wheeler-Benett, *Munich: Prologue to Tragedy* (London, 1948) pp. 123–8.
46. Colvin, *The Chamberlain Cabinet*, pp. 162–3.
47. Ibid., p. 164.
48. Robbins, *Munich*, pp. 297–8.
49. Conversation between Hitler and Wilson, 26 September 1938, *DBFP*, series 3, vol. 2, pp. 554–6.
50. Cooper, *Old Men Forget*, p. 239; Harvey, *Diplomatic Diary*, p. 202.
51. Hilter to Chamberlain, 27 September 1938, *DBFP*, series 3, vol. 2, pp. 576–8.
52. Feiling, *Neville Chamberlain*, p. 372.
53. Colvin, *The Chamberlain Cabinet*, p. 171; Middlemas, *Diplomacy of Illusion*, p. 405.
54. Kennedy to Hull, 25 September 1938, *FRUS, 1938*, vol. 1, p. 652.
55. Charles A. Lindbergh (ed.), *The Wartime Journals of Charles A. Lindbergh* (New York, 1970) p. 73.
56. Hooker, *The Moffat Journals*, pp. 212–13.
57. Hull, *Memoirs*, vol. 1, pp. 590–1.
58. Ibid.
59. Jacobs and Berle, *Navigating the Rapids*, pp. 186–7; Offner, *American Appeasement*, p. 262.
60. Welles, *The Time for Decision*, p. 58.
61. Ickes, *Secret Diary*, vol. 2, p. 479.

62. Offner, *American Appeasement*, p. 264.
63. Roosevelt to Hitler, 27 September 1938, *DGFP*, series D, vol. 2, pp. 963–5.
64. Welles, *Time for Decision*, p. 59.
65. Hull, *Memoirs*, vol. 1, p. 594.
66. Jean Baptiste-Duroselle, *From Wilson to Roosevelt* (London, 1964) p. 256.

NOTES TO CHAPTER EIGHT

1. St Quentin to Bonnet, 1 October 1938, *DDF*, 2nd series, vol. II, pp. 753–4; *New York Times*, 4 October 1938.
2. Jacobs and Berle, *Navigating the Rapids*, p. 189.
3. Richard J. Whalen, *The Founding Father* (New York, 1968) p. 248.
4. Hooker, *The Moffat Journals*, pp. 220–1.
5. Memorandum by Messersmith, 29 September 1938, *FRUS, 1938*, vol. 1 (1938) pp. 704–7.
6. Messersmith to Heinemann, 7 November 1938, Messersmith Papers, File 1067.
7. 'Morgenthau Diary', 11 and 20 October 1938, Book 145, pp. 254–5, 259–63.
8. Ibid.
9. Duroselle, *From Wilson to Roosevelt*, p. 256.
10. Mark S. Watson, *Chief of Staff: Prewar Plans and Preparations* (Washington, 1960) p. 132.
11. Dirksen to Ribbentrop, 19 October 1938, *DGFP*, series D, vol. 4, pp. 314–17.
12. Gott and Gilbert, *The Appeasers*, p. 200.
13. Berndt Jürgen-Wendt, *Economic Appeasement. Handel und Finanz in der Britischen Deutschland Politik* (Düsseldorf, 1971) p. 256.
14. Dirksen's political report, 3 January 1939, *DGFP*, series D, vol. 4, pp. 357–64.
15. Bowers to Roosevelt, 24 October 1938, PSF: Spain; Pell to Roosevelt, 21 October 1938, PSF: Spain.
16. Kennedy to Hull, 12 October 1938, *FRUS, 1938*, vol. 1, pp. 85–6; minute by Cadogan, 14 October 1938, C14447/42/18, FO371/21659.
17. Kennedy to Hull, 12 October 1938, 741.00/202.
18. Memorandum by Stanley, 10 October 1938, A7789/1/45, FO371/21506;/ Cabinet meeting, 15 October 1938, CAB23/90/49(38).
19. Memorandum by Halifax, 11 October 1938, A7789/1/45, FO371/21506.
20. Minute by Balfour, 12 October 1938, A7789/1/45, FO371/21506.
21. A. Bullock, *Hitler: A Study in Tyranny* (London, 1967) p. 473.
22. Foreign Office minute, 26 October 1938, A809/64/45, FO371/21527.
23. *Documents and Materials Relating to The Eve of the Second World War*, Ministry of Foreign Affairs of the USSR, 2 volumes (Moscow, 1948) vol. 2, *The Dirksen Papers*, pp. 54–7; Gott and Gilbert, *The Appeasers*, pp. 200–1.
24. State Department memorandum, 9 October 1938, SD 760F.62/1617.
25. Grew to Hull, 12 October 1938, *FRUS, 1938*, vol. 3, p. 316.
26. Scotten to Hull, 2 November 1938, *FRUS, 1938*, vol. 5, pp. 419–20; Long to Roosevelt, 18 November 1938, PSF: State Department.
27. Radio Address, *Public Papers and Addresses 1938*, pp. 563–6.
28. *New York Times*, 3 November, 7 November, 16 November 1938.

29. Ibid., 29 October 1938.
30. Conversation with Colonel Murray, 21 October 1938, Elibank Papers, File 8809, National Library of Scotland, Edinburgh.
31. 'Moffat Diary' 22 December 1938.
32. Craig and Gilbert, *The Diplomats*, p. 664.
33. 'Moffat Diary', 22 November 1938.
34. Hull, *Memoirs*, vol. 1, p. 599.
35. *New York Times*, 15 and 16 November 1938.
36. Harvey, *Diplomatic Diary*, p. 219.
37. Roosevelt to Pell, 12 November 1938, PSF: Spain.
38. *The Times*, 25 November 1948.
39. Ibid., 14 December 1938.
40. *House of Commons Debates*, vol. 342, col. 2519.
41. Chamberlain to Ida Chamberlain, 28 January 1939, Chamberlain Papers, NC/18/1/1583.
42. Dirksen to Ribbentrop, 3 January 1939, *DGFP*, series D, vol. 4, pp. 357–64.
43. Murray to Roosevelt, 13 December 1938, Elibank Papers, File 8809.
44. Memorandum by Murray, Premier 1/367, Public Record Office, London.
45. Harvey, *Diplomatic Diary*, p. 232.
46. Chamberlain to Hilda Chamberlain, 11 December 1938, Chamberlain Papers, NC18/1/1079.
47. Messersmith to Heinemann, 28 November 1938, Messersmith Papers, File 1083.
48. Gott and Gilbert, *The Appeasers*, pp. 199–200.
49. Messersmith to Geist, 8 December 1938, Messersmith Papers, File 1093.
50. Samuel I. Rosenman, *Working With Roosevelt* (New York, 1952) p. 182.
51. Blum, *From the Morgenthau Diaries*, vol. 2, pp. 79, 527–9.
52. Memorandum by the Economic Policy Department, 19 December 1938, *DGFP*, series D, vol. 4, pp. 659–62; Wilson to Hull, 5 January 1939, 711.62/194.
53. 'Morgenthau Diary', 19 November 1938, Book 151, pp. 318–21.
54. Blum, *From the Morgenthau Diaries*, vol. 2, p. 81.
55. Memorandum by Feis, 17 January 1939, SD 862.51/4702.
56. MacDonald, 'Economic Appeasement', pp. 115–16.
57. Magowan to the Foreign Office, 6 December 1938, C15187/30/18, FO371/21648.
58. Gilbert to Hull, 8 February 1939, SD 641.6231/165.
59. MacDonald, 'Economic Appeasement', p. 127.
60. *House of Commons Debates*, vol. 342, col. 502.
61. State Department memorandum, 5 December 1938, *FRUS, 1938*, vol. 3, pp. 406–9; Halifax to Mallet, 23 January 1939, *DBFP*, series 3, vol. 8, pp. 411–14.
62. Craigie to Halifax, 8 February 1939, F1285/44/10, FO317/23436.
63. Blum, *From the Morgenthau Diaries*, vol. 2, p. 61; Cabinet meeting, 18 January 1939, CAB23/97/1(39).
64. Chamberlain to Ida Chamberlain, 8 January 1939, Chamberlain Papers, NC18/1/1091; Rogers to Messersmith, 1 December 1938, Messersmith Papers, File 1085.
65. Harvey, *Diplomatic Diary*, pp. 209–10.

66. Cabinet meeting, 30 November 1938, CAB23/96(38).
67. 'Moffat Diary', 5 December 1938; Ickes, *Secret Diary*, vol. 2, p. 548.
68. Christopher Hibbert, *Benito Mussolini* (London, 1962) p. 186; Malcolm Muggeridge (ed.), *Ciano's Diary* (London, 1962) p. 4.
69. Blum, *From the Morgenthau Diaries*, vol. 2, pp. 48–9.
70. Haight, *American Aid to France*, pp. 60–3.
71. Watson, *Chief of Staff*, pp. 142–3.
72. Blum, *From the Morgenthau Diaries*, vol. 2, p. 147.
73. Embassy in Washington to Foreign Ministry, 13 January 1939, *DGFP*, series D, vol. 4, pp. 672–3.
74. Blum, *From the Morgenthau Diaries*, vol. 2, pp. 68–9.
75. Divine, *The Illusion of Neutrality*, p. 233.
76. Message to Congress, 4 January 1939, *Public Papers and Addresses 1939*, pp. 1–12.

NOTES TO CHAPTER NINE

1. Ickes, *Secret Diary*, vol. 2, p. 558.
2. Biddle to Hull, 10 January 1939, *FRUS, 1939*, vol. 1, p. 1; Jean Szembek, *Journal* (Paris, 1952) p. 408.
3. Gilbert to Hull, 24 December 1938, SD 711.62/178.
4. Rublee to Hull, 21 January 1939, SD 840.48 Refugees/1328.
5. Memorandum by Messersmith, 23 January 1939, SD 711.62/220 1/2.
6. *The Times*, 6 January 1939.
7. Ibid., 5 January 1939.
8. Dirksen to the Foreign Ministry, 9 January 1939, *DGFP*, series D, vol. 4, pp. 379–82.
9. Duroselle, *From Wilson to Roosevelt*, p. 257.
10. Summary of information from Goerdeler, 21 January 1939, C864/15/18, FO371/22961.
11. Cabinet committee on foreign policy, 23 January 1939, CAB27/624.
12. Halifax to Mallet, 24 January 1939, *DBFP*, series 3, vol. 4, pp. 4–6.
13. MacDonald, 'Economic Appeasement', p. 122.
14. Harvey, *Diplomatic Diary*, p. 248.
15. *The Times*, 30 January 1939.
16. Ickes, *Secret Diary*, vol. 2, pp. 569–70.
17. Mallet to Halifax, 30 January 1939, *DBFP*, series 3, vol. 4, p. 52.
18. Hull, *Memoirs*, vol. 1, pp. 613–14.
19. Mallet to Halifax, 27 January 1939, *DBFP*, series 3, vol. 4, pp. 27–9.
20. Ickes, *Secret Diary*, vol. 2, pp. 571–2.
21. Roosevelt to Merriman, 15 February 1939, PSF: Great Britain.
22. Ickes, *Secret Diary*, vol. 2, p. 571.
23. Roosevelt to Merriman, 15 February 1939, PSF: Great Britain.
24. Norman H. Baynes (ed.), *The Speeches of Adolf Hitler*, 2 volumes (London, 1942) vol. 2, pp. 1567–78.
25. Chamberlain to Ida Chamberlain, 12 February 1939, Chamberlain Papers, NC18/1/1085.
26. Messersmith to Hull, 12 February 1939, Messersmith Papers, File 1150;

Nicholas Murray Butler to Hull, 10 February 1939, Hull Papers, Box 44, File 114.

27. Messersmith to Geist, 4 February 1939, Messersmith Papers, File 1152.
28. *House of Commons Debates*, vol. 343, cols 80–1.
29. MacDonald, 'Economic Appeasement', pp. 123–4.
30. Chamberlain to Ida Chamberlain, 28 January 1939, Chamberlain Papers, NC18/1/1583; Chamberlain to Hilda Chamberlain, 5 February 1939, Chamberlain Papers, NC18/1/1089.
31. Halifax to Henderson, 22 February 1939, *DBFP*, series 3, vol. 4, pp. 138–41.
32. MacDonald, 'Economic Appeasement', pp. 123–4.
33. *The Times*, 23 February 1939.
34. Report of Ashton-Gwatkin, 5 March 1939, *DBFP*, series 3, vol. 4, pp. 597–608.
35. MacDonald, 'Economic Appeasement', pp. 125–6.
36. Ibid.
37. Ibid., pp. 126–7.
38. Messersmith to Geist, 3 February 1939, Messersmith Papers, File 1151.
39. 'Moffat Diary', 9 February 1939.
40. Kennedy to Hull, 17 February 1939, *FRUS, 1939*, vol. 1, pp. 14–17.
41. Mallet to Halifax, 7 February 1939, *DBFP*, series 3, vol. 8, pp. 456–7; Ronald to Mallet, 16 February 1939, ibid.
42. 'Berle Diary', 7 March 1939, vol. 210.
43. Bullitt to Roosevelt, 16 February 1939, PSF Confidential: France.
44. Hull to the Adjutant General, 17 February 1939, Military Records Group, 189, 2657–E–361/5, National Archives, Washington, D.C.
45. Attaché in Berlin to War Department, 18 February 1939, 2657–E–361/7; Attaché in Rome to War Department, 24 February 1939, 2062–716–38; Attaché in Paris to War Department, 18 February 1939, 2657–E–361/6.
46. 'Phillips Diary', 18 February 1939.
47. Bullitt to Hull, 11 February 1939, *FRUS, 1939*, vol. 3, pp. 104–5.
48. 'Moffat Diary', 17 February 1939.
49. Memorandum by Welles, 20 February 1939, *FRUS, 1939*, vol. 1, pp. 18–20; Lindsay to Halifax, 20 February 1939, *DBFP*, series 3, vol. 4, pp. 124–5.
50. Davies to Hull and Welles, 21 February 1939, Davies Papers, Chronological File 9.
51. 'Berle Diary', 20 February 1939.
52. Welles to Kennedy, 7 March 1939, SD 641.6231/167.
53. Foreign Office minute, 20 February 1939, C2431/15/18, FO371/22965.
54. Halifax to Lindsay, 27 February 1939, *DBFP*, series 3, vol. 4, pp. 159–61.
55. Foreign Office memorandum, 17 February 1939, C2622/15/18, FO371/22966.
56. Chamberlain to Hilda Chamberlain, 19 February 1939, Chamberlain Papers, NC18/1/1086.
57. Bullitt to Hull, 28 February 1939, SD 852.01/494.
58. Davies to Hull and Welles, 2 March 1939, Davies Papers, Chronological File 9.
59. 'Moffat Diary', 2 March 1939.
60. Johnson to Hull, 2 March 1939, SD 631.6231/172.
61. Kennedy to Hull, 3 March 1939, SD 641.6231/167.
62. Welles to Kennedy, 20 March 1939, SD 641.6231/178.
63. Roosevelt to Cudahy, 4 March 1939, PSF: Ireland.
64. *New York Times*, 19 February 1939.

65. Ibid.
66. Ibid.
67. 'Morgenthau Diary', 12 March 1939, Book 200, pp. 146–8.
68. Cecil Roberts, *And So to America* (London, 1946) pp. 258–9.
69. Harvey, *Diplomatic Diary*, p. 260.
70. Leonard Mosley, *On Borrowed Time* (London, 1971) p. 148.
71. Halifax to Henderson, 13 March 1939, FO800/294.
72. Grew to Hull, 10 March 1939, SD 740.00/608.
73. Blum, *From the Morgenthau Diaries*, vol. 2, p. 81.
74. Ibid., p. 82.
75. Ickes, *Secret Diary*, vol. 2, pp. 597–8.
76. *New York Times*, 18 March 1939.
77. Welles to Bullitt, 15 March 1939, *FRUS, 1939*, vol. 1, p. 41.
78. *New York Times*, 18 March 1939.
79. Ibid., 12 March 1939.

NOTES TO CHAPTER TEN

1. *House of Commons Debates*, vol. 345, cols 435–40.
2. Moseley, *On Borrowed Time*, p. 170.
3. Halifax to Henderson, 15 March 1939, *DBFP*, series 3, vol. 4, pp. 270–2.
4. Halifax to Seeds, 17 March 1939, ibid., pp. 360–1.
5. Harvey, *Diplomatic Diary*, p. 259.
6. Moseley, *On Borrowed Time*, p. 172.
7. Minutes by Sargent and Cadogan, 17 March 1939, C3313/19/18, FO371/22993.
8. *The Times*, 18 March 1939.
9. Harvey, *Diplomatic Diary*, p. 259.
10. Kennedy to Hull, 17 March 1939, SD 740.00/628.
11. Kennedy to Hull, 18 March 1939, SD 740.00/630.
12. Halifax to Lindsay, 18 March 1939, *DBFP*, series 3, vol. 4, p. 380.
13. Sidney Aster, *1939: The Making of the Second World War* (London, 1973) p. 82; Kennedy to Hull, 22 March 1939, *FRUS, 1939*, vol. 1, p. 88.
14. Cabinet meeting, 18 March 1939, CAB98/12(39).
15. Halifax to Seeds, Kennard and Phipps, 20 March 1939, *DBFP*, series 3, vol. 4, p. 400.
16. Kennedy to Hull, 20 March 1939, PSF Confidential: Great Britain.
17. Halifax to Lindsay, 19 March 1939, F2879/456/23, FO371/23560; Kennedy to Hull, 22 March 1939, *FRUS, 1939*, vol. 1, p. 88.
18. Lindsay to Halifax, 21 March 1939, F2880/456/23, FO371/23560.
19. Lindsay to Halifax, 24 March 1939, F2942/456/23, FO371/23560.
20. Cabinet meeting, 20 March 1939, CAB98/13(39).
21. Chamberlain to Mussolini, 20 March 1939, *DBFP*, series 3, vol. 4, pp. 402–3.
22. Kennedy to Hull, 20 March 1939, PSF Confidential: Great Britain.
23. Phillips to Roosevelt, 17 March 1939, PSF: Italy.
24. Roosevelt to Welles, PSF: State Department.
25. 'Moffat Diary', 26 March 1939.

26. Young, *The X Documents*, pp. 185–6.
27. Hooker, *The Moffat Journals*, pp. 234–5.
28. Memorandum by Willert, A2907/1292/45, FO371/22829.
29. Bullitt to Hull, 25 March 1939, SD 740.00/688.
30. Halifax to Campbell, 23 March 1939, *DBFP*, series 3, vol. 4, pp. 487–8.
31. Kennedy to Hull, 20 March 1939, PSF Confidential: Great Britain.
32. Harvey, *Diplomatic Diary*, pp. 267–8.
33. Cabinet committee on foreign policy, 27 March 1939, CAB27/624.
34. Bullitt to Hull, 28 March 1939, SD 740.00/697.
35. Minute by Sargent, C4505/54/18, FO371/23015.
36. Halifax to Kennard, 31 March 1939, C4511/54/18, FO371/23015.
37. Harvey, *Diplomatic Diary*, p. 271.
38. Aster, *1939*, p. 103.
39. Cabinet meeting, 30 March 1939, CAB98/16(39).
40. *House of Commons Debates*, vol. 345, cols 2415–16.
41. Hooker, *The Moffat Journals*, p. 237.
42. Minute by Harvey, C4529/54/18, FO371/23015.
43. *The Times*, 5 April 1939.
44. Callum A. MacDonald, 'Britain, France and the April Crisis of 1939', *European Studies Review*, April 1972.
45. Cabinet meeting, 10 April 1939, CAB98/19(39).
46. Halifax to Lindsay, 11 April 1939, *DBFP*, series 3, vol. 5, p. 169.
47. Bullitt to Roosevelt, 11 April 1939, SD 740.00/770.
48. *New York Times*, 10 April 1939.
49. Ibid., 14 April 1939.
50. Ibid.
51. Bullitt to Roosevelt, 10 April 1939, *FRUS, 1939*, vol. 1, p. 123.
52. Bullitt to Roosevelt, 10 April 1939, SD 740.00/758.
53. Bullitt to Roosevelt, 11 April 1939, SD 740.00/770.
54. 'Leahy Diary', 11 April 1939.
55. Ibid., 15 April 1939.
56. Grew, *Ten Years in Japan*, p. 247.
57. Memorandum by Young, 20 August 1945, A. P. Young Papers; Messersmith to Hull, 25 March 1939, Messersmith Papers, File 1178.
58. Memorandum by Goerdeler, 16 March 1939, Messersmith Papers, File 1172.
59. Rev. Leiper (Federal Council of Churches) to Messersmith, 24 March 1939, ibid., file 1177.
60. Messersmith to Hull, 25 March 1939, ibid., file 1178.
61. Nicholas Murray Butler to Hull, 28 March 1939, Hull Papers, Box 44, File 114; Hull to Nicholas Murray Butler, 3 April 1939, Nicholas Murray Butler Papers, University of Columbia Library, New York.
62. *New York Times*, 15 April 1939.
63. Jacobs and Berle, *Navigating the Rapids*, p. 213.
64. Lindsay to Halifax, 17 April 1939, C5468/15/18, FO371/22969.
65. Ickes, *Secret Diary*, pp. 619–21.
66. 'Morgenthau Presidential Diary', 11 April 1939, vol. 1, p. 0059.
67. Chamberlain to Hilda Chamberlain, 15 April 1939, Chamberlain Papers, NC18/1/1094.
68. Phipps to Halifax, 20 April 1939, *DBFP*, series 3, vol. 5, pp. 251–2.

69. Hugh Dalton, *The Fateful Years* (London, 1957) p. 252.
70. Robert J. Minney, *The Private Papers of Hore-Belisha* (London, 1960) p. 199.
71. Cabinet meeting, 22 April 1939, CAB99/22(39)
72. Ibid.
73. *New York Times*, 29 April 1939.
74. Foreign Office minute, 6 June 1939, C8027/53/18, FO371/23008.
75. Phipps to Halifax, 28 April 1939, *DBFP*, series 3, vol. 5, p. 356.

NOTES TO CHAPTER ELEVEN

1. Bullitt to Hull, 10 May 1939, *FRUS, 1939*, vol. 1, pp. 184–5.
2. Ickes, *Secret Diary*, vol. 2, pp. 634–5.
3. Military attaché (Berlin) to War Department, 26 May 1939, 2657-B-804, Military Records Group 189; 'Phillips Diary', 22 and 26 May 1939.
4. Bullitt to Hull, 10 May 1939, *FRUS, 1939*, vol. 1, pp. 184–5.
5. Ickes, *Secret Diary*, vol. 2, p. 637.
6. Divine, *Illusion of Neutrality*, p. 261.
7. Ibid., pp. 260–6.
8. Moore to Roosevelt, 12 May 1939, PSF: Neutrality.
9. Divine, *Illusion of Neutrality*, pp. 261–2.
10. Langer and Gleason, *Challenge to Isolation*, vol. 1, pp. 138–9.
11. Divine, *Illusion of Neutrality*, pp. 265–7.
12. MacDonald, 'Britain, France and the April Crisis', pp. 165–6.
13. Cabinet committee on foreign policy, 16 May 1939, CAB27/625.
14. Cabinet meeting, 24 May 1939, CAB99/30(39).
15. Aster, *1939*, pp. 186–7.
16. Minute by Balfour, 3 May 1939, A3311/98/45, FO371/22814.
17. Lindsay to Halifax, 12 June 1939, A4139/27/45, FO371/22800.
18. Chamberlain to Ida Chamberlain, 10 June 1939, Chamberlain Papers, NC18/1/1102.
19. *House of Lords Debates*, vol. 113, cols 360–1; speech at Chatham House, 30 June 1939, *Documents Concerning German-Polish Relations and the Outbreak of Hostilities Between Great Britain and Germany* (HMSO: London, 1939) pp. 58–66.
20. Chamberlain to Hilda Chamberlain, 28 May 1939, Chamberlain Papers, NC18/1/1101; ibid., 30 July 1939, NC18/1/1110.
21. Ibid., 2 July 1939, NC18/1/1105; ibid., 15 July 1939, NC18/1/1107.
22. Ibid., 28 May 1939, NC18/1/1101; ibid., 30 July 1939, NC18/1/1110.
23. Kennedy to Hull, 9 June 1939, PSF Confidential: Great Britain. Chamberlain to Ida Chamberlain, 17 June 1939, Chamberlain Papers, NC18/1/1103.
24. Roosevelt to Phillips, 7 June 1939, E. Roosevelt (ed.), *FDR. His Personal Letters*, vol. 3, p. 265.
25. Craigie to Halifax, 15 May 1939, *DBFP*, series 3, vol. 8, p. 69; Bullitt to Hull, 15 May 1939, *FRUS, 1939*, vol. 3, p. 118.
26. 'Moffat Diary', 9 June 1939.
27. Medlicott, *Foreign Policy Since Versailles*, pp. 166–7.
28. Lindsay to Halifax, 20 June 1939, A4279/98/45, FO371/22814.
29. Holman to Kirkpatrick, 29 June 1939, *DBFP*, series 3, vol. 7, p. 208.
30. Cabinet meeting, 21 June 1939, CAB100/33(39).

31. Kennedy to Hull, 27 June 1939, SD 893.102 Tientsin/107.
32. *House of Commons Debates*, vol. 349, cols 1788–9.
33. 'Berle Diary', 17 June 1939.
34. Bullitt to Hull, 28 June 1939, *FRUS, 1939*, vol. 1, pp. 194–5.
35. Christopher Thorne, *The Approach of War* (London, 1968) p. 156.
36. Divine, *Illusion of Neutrality*, p. 272.
37. *New York Times*, 5 July 1939.
38. 'Berle Diary', 30 June 1939.
39. Aster, *1939*, pp. 271–2.
40. Charles E. Bohlen, *Witness to History 1929–69* (New York, 1973) pp. 74–5.
41. Davies, *Mission to Moscow*, pp. 286–7.
42. Divine, *Illusion of Neutrality*, p. 278.
43. Ibid., pp. 278–9.
44. Ibid., pp. 278–9.
45. Ibid., p. 280.
46. Cabinet meeting, 12 July 1939, CAB100/37(39).
47. Minute by Balfour, 21 July 1939, A4979/98/45, FO371/22815; *The Times*, 17 July 1939.
48. Grummon to Hull, 1 July 1939, *FRUS, 1939*, vol. 1, pp. 327–9.
49. Davies, *Mission to Moscow*, pp. 286–7.
50. Grummon to Hull, 19 July 1939, *FRUS, 1939*, vol. 1, pp. 286–7.
51. Aster, *1939*, p. 280.
52. Ibid., p. 282.
53. Johnson to Hull, 8 August 1939, *FRUS, 1939*, vol. 1, p. 294.
54. Roosevelt to Steinhardt, 4 August 1939, *FRUS, 1939*, vol. 1, pp. 293–4.
55. Bullitt to Hull, 3 August 1939, *FRUS, 1939*, vol. 1, pp. 203–4; 'Moffat Diary', 4 August 1939.
56. Bohlen, *Witness to History*, pp. 78–9.
57. Ibid., pp. 80–1.
58. Lindsay to Halifax, 17 August 1939, C11723/15/18, FO371/22967.
59. Lindsay to Halifax, 15 July 1939, F7394/6451/10, FO371/23527.
60. Medlicott, *Foreign Policy since Versailles*, p. 167.
61. 'Morgenthau Presidential Diary', 19 June 1939, vol. 1, p. 0126.
62. 'Moffat Diary', 26 July 1939.
63. Lindsay to Halifax, 28 July 1939, *DBFP*, series 3, vol. 9, pp. 348–9.
64. Ibid., 3 August 1939, pp. 395–6.
65. Ibid.
66. 'Morgenthau Diary', 24 May 1939, Book 191, pp. 335–6.
67. Feis to Hull, 29 June 1939, SD 740.00/1883.
68. Aster, *1939*, p. 248; memorandum by Hudson, 20 July 1939, C10371/16/18, FO371/22990.
69. Wilson to the Foreign Office, 1 October 1950, C10521/16/18, FO371/22990; memorandum by Dirksen, *Documents and Materials Relating to the Eve of the Second World War*, vol. 2, pp. 67–72.
70. Wilson to Foreign Office, ibid.
71. Harvey, *Diplomatic Diary*, p. 303.
72. Biddle to Hull, 26 July 1939, SD 741.62/383; Biddle to Roosevelt, 27 July 1939, PSF: Poland.
73. Cudahy to Roosevelt, 28 July 1939, PSF: Ireland.

74. Bullitt to Hull, 21 July 1939, SD 893.102 Tientsin/380.
75. Bullitt to Hull, 3 August 1939, *FRUS, 1939*, vol. 1, pp. 203–4.
76. Johnson to Hull, 8 August 1939, PSF Confidential: Great Britain.
77. Kennedy to Hull, 9 August 1939, ibid.
78. Johnson to Hull, 8 August 1939, ibid.
79. 'Moffat Diary', 14 August 1939.

NOTES TO CHAPTER TWELVE

1. Storry, *History of Japan*, p. 207.
2. Kirk to Hull, 19 August 1939, PSF Confidential: Germany.
3. Halifax to Henderson, 22 August 1939, *DBFP*, series 3, vol. 7, pp. 127–8.
4. Cabinet meeting, 22 August 1939, CAB100/41(39).
5. Loraine to Halifax, 23 August 1939, *DBFP*, series 3, vol. 7, pp. 157–8.
6. Halifax to Loraine, 24 August 1939, ibid., p. 186.
7. Harvey, *Diplomatic Diary*, p. 304.
8. Welles to Phillips, 23 August 1939, *FRUS, 1939*, vol. 1, pp. 351–2.
9. Kennedy to Hull, 23 August 1939, ibid., pp. 341–2, 355–6.
10. Memorandum by Halifax, 24 August 1939, C11836/15/18, FO371/22977.
11. Cabinet meeting, 24 August 1939, CAB100/42(39).
12. Kennedy to Hull and Roosevelt, 24 August 1939, PSF Confidential: Great Britain.
13. Hooker, *The Moffat Journals*, p. 253.
14. Ibid.
15. Harvey, *Diplomatic Diary*, p. 305.
16. Langer and Gleason, *Challenge to Isolation*, vol. 1, p. 190.
17. Lindsay to Halifax, 26 August 1939, *DBFP*, series 3, vol. 7, p. 262.
18. Ibid.
19. Esmonde M. Robertson, *Hitler's Pre-War Policy and Military Plans* (London, 1963) pp. 181–2.
20. Henderson to Halifax, 25 August 1939, *DBFP*, series 3, vol. 7, pp. 227–9.
21. Memorandum by Dahlerus, 25 August 1939, ibid.
22. Colvin, *The Chamberlain Cabinet*, p. 241.
23. Cabinet meeting, 26 August 1939, CAB100/43(39).
24. Memorandum by Dahlerus, 27 August 1939, *DBFP*, series 3, vol. 7, pp. 283–6.
25. Aster, *1939*, pp. 343–4.
26. Harvey, *Diplomatic Diary*, p. 307.
27. Ibid.
28. Halifax to Forbes, 28 August 1939, *DBFP*, series 3, vol. 7, pp. 330–2.
29. Henderson to Halifax, 28 August 1939, ibid., pp. 351–4.
30. Harvey, *Diplomatic Diary*, p. 309.
31. Minute by Vansittart, 29 August 1939, *DBFP*, series 3, vol. 7, p. 355.
32. Ibid.
33. Henderson to Halifax, 29 August 1939, ibid., pp. 374, 388–90.
34. Cabinet meeting, 30 August 1939, CAB100/46(39).
35. Halifax to Henderson, 30 August 1939, *DBFP*, series 3, vol. 7, pp. 413–14.
36. Henderson, *Failure of a Mission*, pp. 270–1.

37. Robertson, *Hitler's Pre-war Policy*, p. 191.
38. 'Berle Diary', 28 August 1939.
39. Kennedy to Hull, 25 August 1939, *FRUS, 1939*, vol. I, pp. 369–70.
40. Phipps to Cadogan, 26 August 1939, C12629/15/18, FO371/22980.
41. Bullitt to Hull, 26 August 1939, *FRUS, 1939*, vol. I, p. 373.
42. Hooker, *The Moffat Papers*, p. 255.
43. 'Berle Diary', 28 August 1939.
44. Hooker, *The Moffat Papers*, p. 256.
45. Lothian to Halifax, 31 August 1939, *DBFP*, series 3, vol. 7, pp. 428–9.
46. Lindsay to Halifax, 26 August 1939, ibid., p. 282.
47. Lothian to Halifax, 31 August 1939, ibid., pp. 428–9.
48. Aster, *1939*, pp. 375–83.
49. Ibid.
50. Ickes, *Secret Diary*, vol. 2, p. 713.
51. Feiling, *Chamberlain*, pp. 417–18.
52. Lothian to Halifax, 14 December 1939, FO800/397.
53. Lothian to Halifax, 2 February 1940, C1839/285/18, FO371/24417. Lothian to Halifax, 3 April 1940, C5073/89/18, FO371/24407.

NOTES TO CONCLUSIONS

1. Offner, *American Appeasement*, p. 231.
2. Gardner, *Sterling-Dollar Diplomacy*.
3. MacDonald, 'Economic Appeasement', pp. 128–30.
4. James V. Compton, *The Swastika and the Eagle* (London, 1968) p. 32.
5. Offner, *American Appeasement*; Divine, *Illusion of Neutrality*, p. 285.

General Bibliography

Primary Sources

I. THE UNITED STATES

(a) Unpublished documents
The Franklin D. Roosevelt Library, Hyde Park, New York
    The President's Confidential File
    The President's Official File
    The President's Personal File
    The President's Safe File
    The President's Secretary's File
    The Berle Papers
    The Hopkins Papers
    The Morgenthau Diaries
    The Morgenthau Presidential Diaries

The University of Delaware Library, Newark, Delaware
    The George S. Messersmith Papers

The Houghton Library, Harvard
    The Joseph C. Grew Papers
    The Jay Pierrepont Moffat Papers
    The William L. Phillips Papers

The University of Columbia Library, New York
    The Nicholas Murray Butler Papers

The Library of Congress, Manuscripts Section, Washington, D.C.
    The Joseph E. Davies Papers
    The Norman Davis Papers
    The Herbert Feis Papers
    The Cordell Hull Papers
    The William Leahy Papers
    The Leo Pasvolsky Papers
    The Laurence Steinhardt Papers

The National Archives, Washington, D.C.
The Papers of the Office of the Economic Adviser
The Military Records Group
The Papers of the US State Department

The US Navy Yard, Washington, D.C.
The Papers of the American Information Center
US Naval Attaché Reports
The Tracy S. Kittredge Manuscript Study on Anglo-American Naval Cooperation

(b) Published documents
Beatrice B. Berle and Travis B. Jacobs (eds), *Navigating the Rapids 1918–71. From the Papers of Adolf A. Berle* (New York, 1973).
Bullitt, Orville H. (ed.), *For the President. Personal and Secret Correspondence between Franklin D. Roosevelt and William C. Bullitt* (London, 1973).
Cannistraro, P. V. and Wynot, E. D. (eds), *Poland and the Coming of the Second World War. The Diplomatic Papers of A. J. Drexel Biddle Jnr* (Columbus, Ohio, 1976).
Hooker, Nancy H. (ed.), *The Moffat Papers. Selections from the Diplomatic Journals of Jay Pierrepont Moffat* (Cambridge, Mass., 1956).
Nixon, Edgar B. (ed.), *Franklin D. Roosevelt and Foreign Affairs*, 3 volumes (Cambridge, Mass., 1969).
Roosevelt, Elliot (ed.), *FDR. His Personal Letters*, 3 volumes (London, 1949–52).
Rosenman, Samuel I. (ed.), *The Public Papers and Addresses of Franklin D. Roosevelt*, 13 volumes (New York, 1938–50).
Department of State, *The Foreign Relations of the United States*, numerous volumes (Washington, D.C., 1952–6).

(c) Diaries, memoirs, etc.
Blum, John M. (ed.), *From the Morgenthau Diaries*, 3 volumes (Cambridge, Mass., 1959–67).
Bohlen, Charles E., *Witness to History 1929–69* (New York, 1973).
Davies, Joseph E., *Mission to Moscow* (London, 1942).
Dodd, William E. and Martha Dodd (eds), *Ambassador Dodd's Diary 1933–38* (London, 1941).
Grew, Joseph C., *Ten Years in Japan* (London, 1945).

Hull, Cordell, *The Memoirs of Cordell Hull*, 2 volumes (London, 1948).

Ickes, Harold L., *The Secret Diary of Harold L. Ickes*, 3 volumes (London, 1955).

Krock, Arthur, *Memoirs* (New York, 1968).

Lindbergh, Charles A. (ed.), *The Wartime Journals of Charles A. Lindbergh* (New York, 1970).

Phillips, William, *Ventures in Diplomacy* (London, 1955).

Rosenman, Samuel I., *Working with Roosevelt* (New York, 1958).

Welles, Sumner, *The Time for Decision* (London, 1944).

(d) Newspapers
New York Times
Washington Post

2. BRITAIN

(a) Unpublished documents
The University of Birmingham Library
   The Neville Chamberlain Papers

The Public Record Office, London
   The Cabinet Minutes, CAB23
   The Cabinet Papers, CAB24
   The Cabinet Committee on Foreign Policy, CAB27
   The Papers of the Foreign Office, Political Reports, FO371
   The Cadogan Papers, Fo800/294
   The Halifax Papers, Fo800/309–328
   The Nevile Henderson Papers, Fo800/270–71
   Papers of the Prime Minister's Office, PREM1

The Scottish Record Office, Edinburgh
   The Lothian Papers

The National Library of Scotland
   The Elibank Papers

Leamington Spa, Warwickshire
   The Arthur P. Young Papers (in the possession of his son)

(b) Published documents
Documents on British Foreign Policy, second series, 11 volumes (London, 1946–70).

Documents on British Foreign Policy, third series, 9 volumes (London, 1949–55).

Documents Concerning German–Polish Relations and the Outbreak of Hostilities Between Great Britain and Germany on September 3, 1939 (London, 1939).

Parliamentary Debates, fifth series.

(c) Diaries, memoirs, etc.

Avon, The Earl of, *The Eden Memoirs. Facing the Dictators* (London, 1962).

Dalton, Hugh, *The Fateful Years* (London, 1957).

Dilks, David (ed.), *The Diaries of Sir Alexander Cadogan 1938–45* (London, 1971).

Halifax, The Earl of, *Fullness of Days* (London, 1957).

Harvey, John (ed.), *The Diplomatic Diaries of Oliver Harvey* (London, 1970).

Henderson, Sir Nevile, *Failure of a Mission. Berlin 1937–39* (London, 1940).

Simon, Viscount, *Retrospect* (London, 1952).

Strang, Lord, *Home and Abroad* (London, 1956).

Templewood, Viscount, *Nine Troubled Years* (London, 1954).

Vansittart, Lord, *The Mist Procession* (London, 1958).

Young, Arthur P., *Across the Years* (London, 1971).

(d) Newspapers
The Times

3. FRANCE

(a) Published documents
Ministère des Affaires Étrangères, *Documents Diplomatiques Français* 2nd series (Paris, 1973).
——, *Le Livre Jaune Français, Documents Diplomatiques 1938–39* (Paris, 1939)

(b) Memoirs
Bonnet, Georges, *De Washington au Quai d'Orsay* (Paris, 1946).
Gamelin, Maurice G., *Servir*, 2 volumes (Paris, 1946).

4. GERMANY

(a) Published documents
Documents on German Foreign Policy, series D, 7 volumes (London, 1949–56).
Norman H. Baynes (ed.), *The Speeches of Adolf Hitler*, 2 volumes (London, 1942).

(b) Memoirs
Dirksen, Herbert von, *Moscow, Tokyo, London* (London, 1951).
Kordt, Erich, *Nicht aus den Akten* (Stuttgart, 1950).
Weizäcker, Ernst von, *Memoirs* (London, 1951).

5. ITALY

(a) Diaries
Muggeridge, Malcolm (ed.), *Ciano's Diary 1939–43* (London, 1947).

6. USSR

(a) Published documents
Ministry of Foreign Affairs of the USSR, *Documents and Materials Relating to the Eve of the Second World War*, 2 volumes (Moscow, 1948).

Secondary Sources

Adler, Selig, *The Isolationist Impulse. Its Twentieth Century Reaction* (New York, 1966)
Allen, H. C., *Great Britain and the United States* (London, 1954)
American Council on Public Affairs, *Economic Defence of the Western Hemisphere* (Washington, D.C., 1941)
Aster, Sidney, *1939: The Making of the Second World War* (London, 1973)
Barclay, Glenn, *Struggle for a Continent. The Diplomatic History of South America* (London, 1971)
Birkenhead, Earl of, *Halifax* (London, 1965)

Bisson, T. A., *American Policy in the Far East 1931–1940* (New York, 1940)

Bohlen, Charles E., *Witness to History 1929–1969* (New York, 1973)

Borg, Dorothy, *The United States and the Far Eastern Crisis 1933–1938* (Cambridge, Mass., 1964)

Bullock, Alan, *Hitler: A Study in Tyranny* (London, 1967)

Carr, William, *Arms, Autarky and Aggression* (London, 1972)

Clubb, O. Edmund, *Twentieth Century China* (New York and London, 1965)

Colvin, Ian, *The Chamberlain Cabinet* (London, 1971)

——, *Vansittart in Office* (London, 1965)

Compton, James V., *The Swastika and the Eagle. Hitler, the United States and the Origins of the Second World War* (London, 1968)

Conn, Stetson, and Fairchild, Byron, *The Framework of Hemisphere Defense* (Washington, D.C., 1960)

Craig, Gordon A., *The Politics of the Prussian Army 1660–1945* (Oxford, 1964)

Craig, Gordon A. and Felix, Gilbert, *The Diplomats* (Princeton, New Jersey, 1953)

Crane, Katherine, *Mr Carr of State* (New York, 1960)

Craven, Wesley Frank and Cate, James Lee (eds), *The Army Air Forces in World War II*, 7 volumes (Chicago, 1948)

Dallek, Robert, *Democrat and Diplomat: The Life of William E. Dodd* (New York, 1968)

Dietrich, Ethel B., *Far Eastern Trade of the United States* (New York, 1940)

Divine, Robert A., *The Illusion of Neutrality* (Chicago, 1968)

Drummond, Donald F., *The Passing of American Neutrality* (Ann Arbor, Mich., 1955)

Duroselle, Jean-Baptiste, *From Wilson to Roosevelt. Foreign Policy of the United States 1913–1945* (London, 1964)

Feiling, Keith, *The Life of Neville Chamberlain* (London, 1947)

Friedländer, Saul, *Prelude to Downfall: Hitler and the United States 1939–1941* (London, 1967)

Gardner, Lloyd C., *Economic Aspects of New Deal Diplomacy* (Madison, Wisconsin, 1974)

Gardner, Richard N., *Sterling-Dollar Diplomacy* (New York, 1969)

George, Margaret, *The Hollow Men* (London, 1965)

Gilbert, Martin, *The Roots of Appeasement* (London, 1966)

——, and Gott, Richard, *The Appeasers* (London, 1967)

Gramml, Hermann *et al.*, *The German Resistance to Hitler* (London, 1970)

Haight, John McVickar, *American Aid to France* (New York, 1970)

Herwig, Holger, H., *Politics of Frustration: The United States in German Naval Planning 1889–1941* (Boston, Mass., 1976)

Hibbert, Christopher, *Benito Mussolini* (London, 1962)

Howard, Michael, *The Continental Commitment: The Dilemma of British Defence Policy in the Era of the Two World Wars* (London, 1972)

Huntington, Samuel P., *The Soldier and the State* (New York, 1964)

Irving, David, *Breach of Security* (London, 1968)

Ishmaru, Tota, *Japan Must Fight Britain* (London, 1937)

Johnstone, William C., *The United States and Japan's New Order* (London, 1941)

Jones, F. C., *Japan's New Order in East Asia. Its Rise and Fall* (London, 1954)

Kottman, Richard N., *Reciprocity and the North Atlantic Triangle* (Ithaca, New York, 1968)

Kreider, C., *The Anglo-American Trade Agreement* (Princeton, New Jersey, 1943)

Langer, William L. and Gleason, S. Everett, *The Challenge to Isolation*, 2 volumes (New York, 1952)

Leutze, James R., *Bargaining for Supremacy: Anglo-American Naval Collaboration, 1937–1941* (North Carolina, 1977)

Lombard, Helen, *Washington Waltz* (London, 1942)

Louis, Wm. Roger, *British Strategy in the Far East 1919–1939* (Oxford, 1971)

MacLeod, Iain, *Neville Chamberlain* (London, 1961)

Manvell, Roger and Frankael, Heinrich, *Göring* (London, 1968)

Medlicott, William N., *British Foreign Policy Since Versailles 1919–1963* (London, 1968)

Middlemas, Keith, *Diplomacy of Illusion: The British Government and Germany 1937–1939* (London, 1972)

——, and Barnes, J., *Baldwin* (London, 1969)

Millis, Walter, *Arms and Men: A Study of American Military History* (New York, 1963)

Morison, Samuel E., *History of United States Naval Operations in World War II*, 15 volumes (London, 1948)

Mosley, Leonard, *On Borrowed Time* (London, 1969)

Namier, L. B., *Diplomatic Prelude 1938–1939* (London, 1948)

Neumann, Franz, *Behemoth: The Structure and Practice of National Socialism 1933–1944* (London, 1967)

Neumann, William L., *America Encounters Japan: From Perry to MacArthur* (New York, 1965)

Northedge, F. S., *The Troubled Giant: Britain Among the Great Powers 1916–1945* (London, 1966)

Offner, Arnold A., *American Appeasement. United States Foreign Policy and Germany 1933–1938* (Cambridge, Mass., 1969)

O'Neill, Robert J., *The German Army and the Nazi Party 1933–1939* (London, 1966)

Parkinson, Roger, *Peace for Our Time* (London, 1971)

Pratt, Julius, *Cordell Hull*, 2 volumes (New York, 1964)

Presseisen, Ernst L., *Germany and Japan: A Study in Totalitarian Diplomacy* (New York, 1969)

Rauch, Basil, *Roosevelt from Munich to Pearl Harbor* (New York, 1950)

Rauschning, Hermann, *Makers of Destruction* (London, 1942)

Ritter, Gerhardt, *The German Resistance: Carl Goerdeler's Struggle Against Tyranny* (London, 1958)

Robertson, Esmonde M., *Hitler's Pre-War Policy and Military Plans 1933–1939* (London, 1963)

——, (ed.), *The Origins of the Second World War* (London, 1971)

Russett, Bruce M., *No Clear and Present Danger. A Skeptical View of the U.S. Entry into World War II* (New York, 1972)

Sayre, Francis B., *The Way Forward: The American Trade Agreements Program* (New York, 1939)

Seabury, Paul, *The Wilhelmstrasse* (Berkeley and Los Angeles, 1954)

Sherwood, Robert E., *Roosevelt and Hopkins: An Intimate History* (New York, 1948)

Shirer, William L., *Berlin Diary 1934–1941* (London, 1970)

——, *The Rise and Fall of the Third Reich* (London, 1967)

Sommer, Theo, *Deutschland und Japan zwischen der Mächten* (Tübingen, 1962)

Storry, Richard, *A History of Modern Japan* (London, 1967)

Taylor, A. J. P., *The Origins of the Second World War* (London, 1961)

Thompson, Dorothy, *Let the Record Speak* (Cambridge, Mass., 1939)

Thompson, Neville, *The Anti-Appeasers. Conservative Opposition to Appeasement in the 1930s* (Oxford, 1971)

Thorne, Christopher, *The Limits of Power* (London, 1972)

——, *The Approach of War 1938–1939* (London, 1968)

Toscano, Mario, *The Origins of the Pact of Steel* (Baltimore, Md., 1967)

Tuleja, Thaddius V., *Statesmen and Admirals: The Search for a Far Eastern Naval Policy* (New York, 1963)

Watt, Donald, *Personalities and Policies* (London, 1965)

Weinberg, Gerhardt L., *The Foreign Policy of Hitler's Germany* (Chicago, Ill., 1970)

Wendt, Berndt Jürgen, *Appeasement 1938: Wirtschaftliche Rezession und Mitteleuropa* (Hamburg, 1968)

——, *Economic Appeasement: Handel und Finanz in der Britischen Deutschland Politik 1933–1939* (Düsseldorf, 1971)

Whalen, Richard J., *The Founding Father* (New York, 1968)

Wheeler-Bennett, Sir John W., *Munich: Prologue to Tragedy* (London, 1948)

——, *The Nemesis of Power: The German Army in Politics 1918–1945* (New York, 1967)

Williams, Francis, *A Pattern of Rulers* (London, 1965)

Williams, William Appleman, *The Tragedy of American Diplomacy* (New York, 1972)

Wiskemann, Elizabeth, *The Rome–Berlin Axis* (London, 1966)

Wrench, John Evelyn, *Geoffrey Dawson and Our Times* (London, 1955)

Articles

Barraclough, Geoffrey, 'Hitler and Hirohito', *The New York Review of Books*, vol. 20, no. 9 (May 1973).

——, 'Watch Out for Japan', *The New York Review of Books*, vol. 20, no. 10 (June 1973).

Beals, Carleton, 'Totalitarian Inroads in Latin-America', *Foreign Affairs*, vol. 17, no. 1 (October 1938).

Haight, John McVickar, Jnr, 'France, the United States, and the Munich Crisis', *The Journal of Modern History*, vol. 32, no. 4 (December 1960).

Henson, Edward L., 'Britain, America and the Month of Munich', *International Relations*, vol. 11, no. 5 (April 1962).

Herwig, Holger H., 'Prelude to Weltblitzkreig: Germany's Naval Policy toward the United States of America, 1939–1941', *The Journal of Modern History*, vol. 43, no. 4 (December 1971).

MacDonald, Callum A., 'Britain, France and the April Crisis of 1939', *European Studies Review*, no. 2 (April 1972).

——, 'Economic Appeasement and the German "Moderates": An Introductory Essay', *Past and Present*, no. 56 (August 1972).

May, Ernest R., 'Nazi Germany and the United States: A Review Essay', *The Journal of Modern History*, vol. 41, no. 2 (June 1969).

Metzmacher, Helmut, 'Deutsch-Englische Ausgleichsbemühungen in Sommer 1939', *Viertelsjahre Hefte für Zeitgeschichte*, vol. 14 (October 1966).

Nerval, Gaston, 'Europe versus the United States in Latin-America', *Foreign Affairs*, vol. 15, no. 4 (July 1937).

Remak, Joachim, 'Friends of the New Germany: The Bund and German–American Relations', *The Journal of Modern History*, vol. 29, no. 1 (March 1957).

Sayre, Francis B., 'America Must Act', *World Affairs Pamphlets*, no. 13 (New York 1936).

Schacht, Hjalmar G., 'Germany's Colonial Demands', *Foreign Affairs*, vol. 15, no. 2 (January 1937).

V., 'The Destruction of Capitalism in Germany', *Foreign Affairs*, vol. 15, no. 4 (July 1937).

Watt, Donald C., 'United States Resources for the Study of British Foreign Policy, 1919–1939', *International Affairs*, vol. 38, no. 1 (January 1962).

Weinberg, Gerhardt L., 'The May Crisis, 1938', *The Journal of Modern History*, vol. 29, no. 3 (September 1957).

Index

Anglo-American trade treaty, 12–13, 24–5, 30, 50, 51, 85, 110–11, 114, 115, 118

Anglo-German payments agreement, 16, 80, 81, 86, 115, 118, 165

Anglo-Italian agreement, 77, 90, 119, 148

Anschluss, 75, 76, 77, 78, 79, 81, 82, 84, 85, 87, 88, 91, 104,105, 131

Anti-Comintern Pact, 4, 34, 36, 44, 47, 48, 50–1, 52, 60, 111, 119, 132, 144, 153, 163, 168, 179

Argentina, 126–7

Ashton-Gwatkin, Frank, Economic Councellor, Foreign Office, 22, 80, 130, 131

Australia, 148

Austria, 6, 28, 50, 71, 72, 73, 74, 75

Autarky, German, 3, 5, 10, 17, 27, 36, 63, 79, 83, 85, 107, 115, 131, 173

Baldwin, Stanley, British Prime Minister 1935–7, 17, 20, 22

Benes, Edouard, Czechoslovak President, 75, 82, 89, 94

Berle, Adolf A., US Assistant Secretary of State, 64–5, 76, 87–8, 95–6, 107, 159, 160, 175

Biddle, Anthony J. Drexel, US ambassador to Warsaw, 146, 165, 166

Bingham, Robert W., US ambassador to London, 3, 18, 19, 30

Bloom, Sol, US Congressman, 156, 159, 160

Bonnet, Georges, French Foreign Minister, 86, 145, 159, 176

Bowers, Claude, US ambassador to Madrid, 94

Brazil, 84, 85, 110

Britain, foreign policy of,
American role in, 16–33, 35–6, 42–9, 55, 56–7, 59, 67–71, 74, 77, 82, 90, 109–11, 114–15, 126, 134–5, 141, 142–3, 147, 151–2, 157, 161, 169–70, 173, 179, 180–1, 182

and appeasement, 13, 16–18, 25–6, 29, 32–3, 34, 42–4, 46–7, 53, 66–72, 74, 75, 77, 78–82, 88–90, 92–4, 100–2, 108–11, 114–16, 117–18, 126, 128–31, 134, 137, 140–3, 165, 174–5, 180

economic influences on, 16, 32, 42, 66–7, 79–81, 100, 101, 109–11, 115–16, 118, 129–31

and German 'moderates', 17, 81, 89, 90, 94, 116, 126–9, 157–8, 165, 172–3

and Italy, 32, 42, 46, 53, 66–9, 70–1, 72, 74, 77, 102, 115, 119, 131, 134, 144, 147–8, 158, 168–9, 177

and January crisis of 1939, 124–39

and Japan, 20–1, 34–5, 42–3, 45–7, 53, 55–7, 59, 61, 67, 77, 159, 161, 164

and *Kristallnacht*, 117–18

and Munich, 93–4, 100–2

and guarantee to Poland, 146–7

and Polish crisis of 1939, 168–74

and Sudeten problem, 81–2, 88–91, 92–3

and USSR, 79, 83, 102, 110, 143, 146, 155, 157, 160, 162

Brüning Heinrich, German emigré, 71, 81, 153

Bullitt, William C., US ambassador to Paris, 7, 8, 13, 27, 54, 86, 87, 91, 95, 97, 98, 102, 113, 132, 145, 148, 149, 152, 159, 166, 175

Cadogan, Sir Alexander, Permanent Under-Secretary of State for Foreign Affairs, 21, 55, 66, 67, 73, 166
Chamberlain, Neville, British Prime Minister
American view of, x, 24, 73–5, 76, 82, 88, 110, 165–6, 174
and Anglo-American naval cooperation, 53, 57, 59, 61
and Anglo-American trade agreement, 24–5, 51, 114
and Anglo-Soviet negotiations of 1939, 157
and appeasement, 16–18, 23–6, 29–30, 32–3, 42–3, 46–7, 53, 66–7, 78–9, 81, 88–90, 92–4, 100–2, 109–11, 114–16, 117–18, 126, 129–31, 134, 137, 140–2, 158, 174–5, 177
and conscription, 145, 152
differs with Eden, 23, 32–3, 44–5, 46–7, 48–9, 59, 62, 67–72
and the Far East, 20–1, 35–6, 42–3, 53, 56–9, 129, 148, 159
and imperial preference, 21–2, 181
and Italy, 66–7, 69, 70–1, 72, 77, 102, 119, 128, 131, 144, 148, 158,
and January crisis of 1939, 124–39
and Munich, 92–4, 100–2
and *Panay* crisis, 56–9
and Polish crisis of September 1939, 169–74
and Polish guarantee, 146–7
and rearmament, 17, 23–4, 26, 44, 53–4
and Roosevelt's conference proposal, 66–71, 179
speeches
at Birmingham, 28 January 1939, 126
at Birmingham, 17 March 1939, 141–2
at Blackburn, 22 February 1939, 130
at Foreign Press Association, 13 December 1938, 114
at the Guildhall, 3 November 1937, 44
and the United States, 21, 22–3, 25–6, 29–31, 34–6, 42–3, 48–9, 53–4, 66–71, 74, 77, 82, 114–16, 125–6, 129, 141–2, 151–2, 180–1
China, 34, 35, 36, 37, 40, 41, 42, 43, 48, 57, 59, 60, 61, 62, 63, 70, 78, 110, 115, 117, 118, 119, 129, 148, 159, 160, 164, 165
Churchill, Winston S., 78–9, 83
Ciano, Count Galeazzo, Italian Foreign Minister, 50
Colvin, Ian, British journalist, 146
Cooper, Duff, First Lord of the Admiralty, 95
Cudahy, John,
US ambassador to Warsaw, 1–2, 4, 8, 15
US ambassador to Dublin, 166
Czechoslovakia, 28, 36, 50, 73, 75, 76, 78, 79, 81, 82, 83, 84, 85, 86, 87, 88, 89, 90, 91, 92, 93, 94, 95, 96, 98, 100, 101, 102, 103, 104, 105, 137, 138, 140

Dahlerus, Birger, Swedish industrialist, 171, 172
Daladier, Edouard, French Prime Minister, 82, 94, 145, 149, 153
Davies, Joseph E.,
US ambassador to Moscow, 8–9, 12, 14, 27, 36, 61, 83
US ambassador to Brussels, 55, 133, 135, 162
Davis, Norman, US ambassador 'at large', 13–14, 25–6, 38, 45–8
Dieckhoff, Dr Hans Heinrich, German ambassador to Washington, 5, 54, 85, 86, 113
Dirksen, Herbert von, German ambassador to London, 87, 109, 110, 114, 125, 129, 141, 142
Dodd, William E., US ambassador to Berlin, 2, 3–4, 6–7, 12, 26–7, 55

Eden, Anthony, British Foreign Secretary 1935–8
and Anglo-American naval cooperation, 47, 53, 56–7, 59, 61, 69
and Anglo-American trade agreement, 24–5, 51
and Anglo-Italian negotiations, 70–2
at Brussels conference, 45–9
differs with Chamberlain, 32, 44, 46–7, 48–9, 59, 62, 69–72
and *Panay* crisis, 55–9
and rearmament, 19, 25, 32, 44, 53–4
and Roosevelt's conference proposal, 18–19, 68–9, 70–2
and the United States, 18, 24–5, 30, 35, 43–4, 48–9, 55, 56–7, 59, 61, 69–70

Fisher, Sir Warren, Permanent Under-Secretary of the Treasury, 20
France, 1, 6, 8, 9, 11, 13, 26–8, 53–4, 58, 66, 68, 76, 78–9, 81–3, 86–8, 92, 94–5, 97–102, 108, 122, 125, 127–8, 131–2, 134–6, 143, 145–6, 148–9, 152–6, 158, 164, 176–8
Fritsch, General Baron von, 5, 36, 71

Germany, ix, 1, 3–20, 23, 26, 32, 34, 36–40, 42–4, 47, 48, 50–5, 60–8, 70–95, 97–103, 105–39, 141–51, 153, 155–60, 162–3, 165, 166, 169, 170–82
Goebbels, Joseph, German Propaganda Minister, 5, 150, 158
Goerdeler, Carl, German opposition leader, 81, 93, 125, 128, 131, 150, 151
Göring, Reichsmarschall Herman, 36, 64, 81, 89, 117, 124, 165, 171, 172, 173, 181
Grange, Baron Amery de la, head of French air mission to US, 86, 98
Great Britain, *see* Britain
Greece, 140, 148, 155
Grew, Joseph C., US ambassador to Tokyo, 35, 55, 57, 60, 110, 138, 149

Halifax, Lord, Lord President of the Council (1937), Foreign Secretary (1938–40), 44–5, 47, 53, 66, 74, 77, 89, 90, 91, 95, 96, 100, 102, 110–11, 113, 119, 125, 126, 129, 130, 134, 141, 142, 143, 145, 147, 148, 149, 157, 158, 161, 168, 169, 173, 174
Harvey, Oliver, Private Secretary to Eden and Halifax, 68–9, 134, 147, 165, 169
Henderson, Sir Nevile, British ambassador to Berlin, 81, 82, 130, 171, 173, 174, 175
Hitler, Adolf, German Chancellor and Führer,
and *Anschluss*, 71–2, 75
and axis, 39, 128, 132, 135, 155, 171
and colonies, 7, 9, 11, 17, 26, 75
and January crisis of 1939, 125–9
and 'moderates', ix–x, 5, 15, 17, 26, 40, 64, 71, 81, 89–90, 157–8, 181
and Munich, 92–4, 100–5
and Nazi–Soviet Pact, 166–7, 168
and Polish crisis of September 1939, 168, 171–6
and Sudeten problem, 78–9, 91
and the United States, 124, 129, 150–3, 181
Hoare, Sir Samuel, British Home Secretary, 20–1, 114, 137
Holland, 58, 124–7
Honolulu, USS, 97
Hopkins, Harry, US Secretary of Commerce, x, 98
Hore-Belisha, Leslie, British Secretary of War, 152
Hornbeck, Stanley K., Head of Far Eastern Division, US State Department, 37
Hudson, Robert H., Secretary, Department of Overseas Trade, 80, 135, 165, 166
Hull, Cordell, US Secretary of State
and Anglo-American naval cooperation, 52–3, 54, 60–1
and Anglo-American trade treaty, 12–13, 21–22, 85

Hull, Cordell, (*contd.*)
   and Anglo-German economic talks
      of 1939, 133, 144
   and Anglo-Italian agreement, 70,
      77–8
   and appeasement, 3, 9–10, 37, 38, 40,
      48, 55, 60, 65, 66, 77–8, 84, 85,
      87, 90, 94, 95, 103, 104
   and Congress, 86, 97, 117, 156, 161
   and neutrality repeal, 86, 156

Ickes, Harold L., US Secretary of the
   Interior, 52, 78, 126, 127, 151,
   177
Imperial preference, 12–13, 21–2, 30,
   80, 85, 181
Ingersoll, Captain, USN, 61, 143
Italy, 1, 28, 32, 36–8, 40, 42–4, 46–8,
   50–3, 60, 62, 63, 66–72, 74, 77–
   8, 84, 102, 115, 119, 120, 128,
   131–8, 144, 147–9, 155, 158,
   168–9, 171, 177–8

Japan, x, 20–1, 32–5, 37–48, 50–3, 55–
   63, 65, 67, 70, 78, 84–5, 94, 110–
   11, 113, 115, 118–20, 122, 129,
   132–4, 137–8, 141, 143–4, 149,
   153, 158–60, 163–5, 168, 176
Johnson, Nelson T., US ambassador to
   Nanking, 60

Kennedy, Joseph P., US ambassador to
   London, 74, 77, 79, 84, 87, 90,
   95, 102, 107, 113, 131, 132, 133,
   135, 142, 143, 158, 169, 170, 174
Kristallnacht pogrom, 106, 113, 114,
   115, 117, 119, 120, 122, 124,
   136, 140, 180
Krock, Arthur, US journalist, 2–3, 14

Ladybird, HMS, 55
Latin America, German threat to, x,
   84, 99, 107, 108, 111–12, 126–7,
   180
Leahy, Admiral William, US Chief of
   Naval Operations, 52, 56, 149
Léger, Alexis, Secretary-General of
   French Foreign Office, 146,
   149, 175

Leith-Ross, Sir Frederick, Chief Economic Adviser to the government, 17, 21, 109
Lindsay, Sir Ronald, British ambassador to Washington, 1932–9,
   20, 24, 51, 54, 55, 56, 57, 66, 71,
   74, 75, 82, 95, 99, 132, 133, 134,
   143, 144, 157, 163, 164, 176
Lothian, Lord, British ambassador to
   Washington, 1939–40, 126–7,
   176
Ludlow amendment, 60

Messersmith, George, US Assistant
   Secretary of State, 6, 14, 60, 65,
   73, 83, 84, 87, 107, 116, 131,
   144, 151
Moffat, J. Pierrepont, Chief of the
   Division of European Affairs,
   US State Department, 37, 38,
   45, 73, 77, 82, 83, 132, 135, 145,
   158, 166, 170, 175
Molotov, Vyacheslav, Soviet Foreign
   Minister, 62, 162, 163
Morgenthau, Henry, US Secretary of
   the Treasury, 9, 56, 58, 95, 107–
   8, 116–17, 136, 138, 151, 165
Murray, Colonel Arthur, 112–13, 114
Mussolini, Benito, Italian Prime
   Minister
   and Albanian coup, 147–8
   and American appeasement, 11, 119
   and Anglo-Italian agreement, 66–7,
      72, 74, 77, 148
   and axis, 36, 119, 131–2, 134–5, 144,
      148, 155
   and Munich, 102, 104, 119
   and Polish crisis of September 1939,
      168–9, 171, 176

Nashville, USS, 97
Nazi–Soviet Pact, 155, 160, 163, 164,
   166, 167, 168, 169, 171, 176, 178
Neurath, Count Constantin von,
   German Foreign Minister, 5,
   18, 29, 32, 71, 89
Neutrality Act, 2, 7, 18, 39, 84, 86, 99,
   121, 122, 128, 137, 138, 139,
   143, 154, 155, 158, 181

New Zealand, 148

Panay, USS, 50, 55, 56, 57, 58, 60
Pearl Harbor, 182
Phillips, William, US ambassador to
   Rome, 28, 50, 51, 77, 119, 132,
   155, 158
Phipps, Sir Eric, British ambassador to
   Paris, 152, 153
Pittman, Key, US Senator, 143, 156
Poland, 140, 142, 143, 145, 146, 155,
   158, 166, 167, 168, 170, 172,
   173, 174, 175

Ribbentrop, Joachim von, German
   Foreign Minister, 4, 5, 6, 32, 51,
   81, 89, 106, 119, 160, 163, 168,
   174, 179, 181
Roosevelt, Franklin Delano, US
   President
   and aid to the democracies, 86, 95,
   98, 99, 105, 108, 112–13, 120–2,
   136, 178
   and Anglo-American naval cooperation, 58–9, 60–1, 143, 149
   and Anglo-Italian agreement, 70–1,
   78, 104, 144
   and Anglo-Soviet negotiations, 155,
   160–1, 162, 163
   and Anti-Comintern Pact, 50–1, 55,
   111–12
   and British conscription, 145, 152
   and British policy, 73–5, 76, 88, 94–
   5, 96, 99, 104–5, 108, 113, 115–
   16, 119, 127–8, 137, 139, 145,
   147, 148, 149, 153–4, 164–5,
   176, 182
   and countervailing duties on
   German goods, 107–8, 116–17,
   136, 138, 139
   and fleet movements, 85, 95, 136,
   140, 148–9
   and guarantee system, 140–54
   invites Chamberlain to visit US, 28–
   30
   and January crisis of 1939, 124–39
   and Japan, 55–62, 159–60, 164–5,
   176
   and *Kristallnacht* pogrom, 113–14

   and Munich, 77, 94–105
   and neutrality revision, 86, 88, 89,
   99, 117, 120, 122, 123, 128, 137,
   138, 143, 144, 145, 151, 154,
   155, 156, 158, 160, 161, 163,
   164, 171, 177, 181
   and *Panay* crisis, 55–62
   peace plan of 1939, 140, 150–1
   plans world peace conference, 2–3, 9,
   13–15, 27, 40–1, 47–8, 63–6,
   179
   and Polish crisis of September 1939,
   168–71, 174–7
   and rearmament, 50, 52, 65, 108,
   112, 117, 120–2
   speeches
   at Chautauqua, 14 August 1936, 2
   at Key West, 18 February 1939,
   136
   at Kingston, Canada, 18 August
   1938, 94
   message to Congress, 4 January
   1939, 122–3
   'quarantine' speech, 5 October
   1937, 38–9, 181
   radio address, 26 October 1938,
   112
   at Treasure island, 14 July 1938,
   85
   and USSR, 61–2, 155, 160–1,
   162–3
Rothschild, Baron, 137
Rumania, 140, 142, 145, 146, 148, 155
Runciman, Walter, President of the
   British Board of Trade, 21–2,
   24
   heads Runciman mission, 88, 89, 90,
   93
Russia, *see* USSR

Sayre, Francis, US Assistant Secretary
   of State, 51–2, 85
Schacht, Hjalmar G., German Minis-
   ter of Economics and head of
   Reichsbank, 5–6, 10–11, 13, 14,
   26–7, 36, 81, 125, 181
Schulenburg, Count Friedrich von der,
   German ambassador to
   Moscow, 162, 163

Schuschnigg, Dr Kurt von, Austrian
    Chancellor, 71, 176
Simon, Sir John, British Chancellor of
    the Exchequer, 20, 58, 92, 110,
    166, 175
Spain, 1, 5, 72, 131, 178
Stalin, Joseph, Soviet leader, 8, 62,
    157, 162, 168
Stanley, Oliver, President of the British
    Board of Trade, 21, 110, 130,
    133
Steinhardt, Laurence, US ambassador
    to Moscow, 163

USSR, 1, 8, 36, 61, 62, 78, 79, 83, 95,
    96, 102, 110, 138, 140, 143, 146,
    155, 157, 160, 162, 163, 164,
    165, 175
United States, foreign policy of
    appeasement, aims and objectives,
        1–15
    'appeasers' and 'anti-appeasers' di-
        vided over, 6–9, 37–8, 48, 60–2,
        64, 65, 77–8, 83–8, 91, 94–6,
        99–100, 102–4, 106–8, 113,
    and Britain, 12–14, 16, 29, 41–2, 65–
        6, 76–7, 109–11, 125, 127–28,
        133–6, 140, 142–3, 147, 149,
        153–4, 160, 164–5, 165–6, 168,
        169–70, 174–7, 180, 182
    economic factors in, x, 10, 32, 34, 40–
        1, 63–4, 103
    and German economic problems, 4,
        9–10, 40–1, 64
    and German 'moderates', 14–15, 32,
        38, 40, 65, 71, 179, 181
    and guarantee system, 140–54
    and Japan, 34–42, 45–6, 48, 50–2,
        54, 55–62, 63, 78, 84, 85, 94,
        113, 115, 118–19, 127, 132–3,

137, 138, 143–4, 149, 159–60,
    163, 164–5, 176, 178
    and *Kristallnacht* pogrom, 113–17

Vansittart, Sir Robert, Chief Diplo-
    matic Adviser to the
    government, 29, 93, 125,
    173

Welles, Sumner, US Under-Secretary
    of State
    and Anglo-German economic talks,
        74–5, 133–4, 135–6
    and Anglo-Italian negotiations, 70,
        71, 77–8
    appeasement plans, x, 1, 31, 38, 40–
        1, 47–8, 54–5, 63–6, 74–5,
        76, 87–8, 96, 102–3, 106–7,
        112
    and German danger, 112, 113, 132–
        3, 135–6, 138, 164–5
    and Japan, x, 38, 40–1, 63–4, 70, 77–
        8, 132–3, 158, 164–5
    mission to Europe in 1940, 177–8
Wiedemann, Captain Fritz, Hitler's
    aide-de-camp, 89–90
Willert, Sir Arthur, 145
Wilson, Sir Horace, Chief Industrial
    Adviser to British government,
    101, 103, 152, 165–6, 170,
    175
Wilson, Hugh S., US ambassador to
    Berlin, 81, 84, 90, 113
Wilson, Woodrow, US President, 2, 32,
    153, 179
Wohltat, Helmut, economic adviser to
    German Four-Year Plan, 165–6

Young, Arthur P., British industrialist,
    93, 150